Interactive Governance

Interactive Governance

Advancing the Paradigm

Jacob Torfing, B. Guy Peters, Jon Pierre, and Eva Sørensen

OXFORD
UNIVERSITY PRESS

OXFORD
UNIVERSITY PRESS

Great Clarendon Street, Oxford OX2 6DP
United Kingdom

Oxford University Press is a department of the University of Oxford.
It furthers the University's objective of excellence in research, scholarship,
and education by publishing worldwide.

Oxford is a registered trade mark of Oxford University Press in the UK
and in certain other countries

British Library Cataloguing in Publication Data
Data available

Library of Congress Cataloging in Publication Data
Data available

ISBN 978-0-19-959675-1

Foreword

Governance has become one of the most commonly used concepts in contemporary political science. Although commonly used, this concept remains in many ways under-specified and inadequately understood within the discipline. This book is an attempt to understand governance in general, and more particularly to understand interactive styles of governance. Although we place the interactive form of governance at the center of the analysis, we examine it carefully and critically, and we attempt to understand the strengths and weaknesses of the approach. The four of us began this collaboration with differing levels of commitment to the interactive form of governance, but the analysis is an attempt to be as fair as possible in analyzing this approach to governance.

This book is the product of several years of discussions and friendly debates among the four of us. We have met in several places in Scandinavia, in England, and in the United States. During this time, we have been through numerous iterations of each chapter. We each had responsibility for the first draft of several chapters and these drafts were subject to numerous discussions and revisions. The penultimate drafts of the chapters were then reviewed by experts in the field before the final draft of the manuscript was submitted. This was a rather protracted process, but in the end has produced a manuscript that reflects very careful deliberation about governance.

In addition to thanking one another for intellectual companionship and honesty in the process of writing this book, we are also indebted to colleagues who have provided their advice. These colleagues include Matthew Flinders, Erik-Hans Klijn, Jan Koppenjan, Daniel Kübler, David Levi-Faur, Felicity Matthews, Johan P. Olsen, Bert Rockman, Chris Skelcher, Martin Smith, and Kai Wegrich. We should also thank Dominic Byatt for his support and his patience in the rather long process that produced this manuscript.

JT, BGP, JP, ES

Contents

List of Figures

List of Tables

Introduction

All societies encounter fundamental challenges in governing themselves. Those challenges are even more severe when a society attempts to govern itself in a democratic manner, and to provide the public substantial control over the decisions being made in its name. Effective governing cannot be assumed, as the numerous cases of "failed states" around the world make clear. Even in less extreme cases, governments of affluent and seemingly successful countries have demonstrated numerous times that managing their economies and societies cannot be taken for granted. The economic crisis of 2008, and what followed from it, is but one obvious example. These seemingly more successful countries also encounter difficulties in ensuring popular control over policy decisions. Public policymaking is often driven by a combination of mass media, technocratic elites, and pressures from the global economy, which limits popular control over public policy.

The necessity of thinking about how to govern ourselves, and doing so democratically, has been emphasized by a number of transformations in contemporary societies. One major change has been the increasing complexity of policy problems and the increasing interdependency of policy areas, policy levels, and policy actors. Making appropriate public policy has never been easy, but it has become all the more difficult. Further, globalization has meant that the actions of any one society, and its government, must be considered in light of the actions of others, further complicating governing. Actors in civil society have themselves in many cases become more directly engaged with the processes of governing so that the opinions and actions of stakeholders may now affect policy choices. The numerous reforms in the public sector, each seeking to address some of the underlying problems in governance, also have raised additional questions about how best to organize governing. Each reform may solve some problems, but in turn raises additional problems. Finally, and somewhat paradoxically, those same citizens who may be engaged in some aspects of governing themselves are also

1

skeptical about governments and the public sector and may seek alternatives to traditional forms of governing.

Responding in part to the numerous challenges appearing in the real world of governing, "governance" has become one of the most commonly used terms in the social sciences. In this academic literature on governance, the spate of concern about governance, including a number of alternative definitions and conceptions, is the product of several forces. The interest in governance reflects general concerns about how to understand the changing role of public leadership in a variety of institutional settings and policy fields, and how to understand changing institutional and social patterns in society. The interest in governance also reflects a return to interest in organizations and institutions in political science, in contrast to the methodological individualism of behavioralism and rational choice theories that have dominated social and political science.

The interest in governance has been manifested in a number of different disciplines that are aiming to account for new societal phenomena or deal with new challenges. However, many of the issues being raised are similar or at least analogous across the disciplines. For example, in economics there has been a return to institutional economics and with that greater concern about how to organize public sector organizations as well as markets. Further, in sociology, network analysis and institutionalism have contributed to the study of governance. Likewise, in international relations, thinking about international and global governance adds additional dimensions to the analysis.

But what do we mean by the term governance? At its most general, governance in the public sector is about steering and control of society and the economy through collective action that aims to achieve common goals. In most traditional writing about steering and control, the dominant assumption has been that such steering would occur through formal state actors and governmental procedures. That type of formal, legal steering continues to be important and in many settings it is the dominant manner of governing. For example, policy areas such as foreign affairs, defense, and revenue collection are dominated by state actors and formal legal procedures. Likewise, some countries continue, for example those of Southern Europe, to rely heavily upon formal government decision-making and the bureaucracy for governance, although this reliance is sometimes jeopardized by the presence of "dark networks" based on illegal activities.

This book, however, is about another style of governance, one which we will discuss as "interactive governance." By interactive governance we mean *the complex process through which a plurality of social and political actors with diverging interests interact in order to formulate, promote, and achieve common objectives by means of mobilizing, exchanging, and deploying a range of ideas, rules, and resources*. This conception of governance still has the basic concern about steering the economy and society but approaches this problem through a very different route than that associated with traditional forms of governing. In particular, in this book we are interested in the manner in which organizations and individuals work together to govern, regardless of their official position and the consequences of that manner of governance.

At the extreme, the interactive style of governance has commonly been referred to as "governance without government," meaning that some advocates of this approach to governance argue that it is possible to provide steering and control to societies with little or no direct involvement of the public sector. This conception of governance without government does stand at the extreme if for no other reason than that in interactive forms of governance state actors are conceptualized as being one among several actors who are involved in making decisions. Hence, government is involved in governing even though it may not be employing command and control. Further, as we will explicate in more detail below, public actors generally remain important for defining and shaping the arenas within which interactions may be occurring.

Even in less extreme versions, interactive governance implies a very different style of governing than that associated with more traditional, state-centric forms of governance. While traditional forms of governance rely on top-down imposition of authority, interactive governance assumes that decisions will be made either from the bottom-up or through interactive processes, and empowered participation is orchestrated, and even sometimes initiated, by government agencies. This form of governance is argued by its advocates to provide both a more effective and a more democratic form of governing. It is thought to be more effective because it involves individuals and groups who are knowledgeable about the policies in question and are capable of finding among themselves good means of solving policy problems. Apart from this general consideration, other scholars have considered the importance of altering the instruments used to govern and implement public policy. The traditional instruments of governance depended heavily on command and control, and tended to permit little interaction with the "targets" of the policy. The instruments of "New Governance" depend more on bargaining and negotiation to achieve their policy goals than on authority so that interaction shapes these more proximate connections to the delivery of public services and may make them more effective.

Interactive governance is thought by its advocates to be more democratic for some of the same reasons that it is considered more effective. Rather than depending upon periodic elections and representative democracy, the interactive mode of governance involves affected interests in society more directly and continuously. We will point out in some detail that these assumptions must be considered with a number of *caveats*, and most importantly that those groups involved in governance may not be representative of the general public. There are, however, important democratic arguments that can be addressed by considering interactive forms of governance and the possibilities of more continuous formats for public involvement.

Although a good deal of the actual decision-making associated with interactive governance involves relatively autonomous actions by social actors, these apparently autonomous actions can be framed and influenced by official actors in the public sector. We will be discussing the role of the public sector in this process as "metagovernance," which we will define as the governance of governance. This management and indirect control of interactive governance processes may occur through the use of formal authority and the manipulation of resources, or it may come through more interactive means, but the fundamental point is that interactive governance may always be conducted within a "shadow of hierarchy" (Scharpf, 1994) that can in the end shape and legitimate the outcomes.

It is crucial to remember in reading this book that the discussion of interactive governance must always be considered within the framework of broader concerns about governing and governance. The interactive format for governing is an important case of governance, but is *not* all of governance. This style of governance has become more important in many industrial democracies, especially those in Northern Europe, but is not feasible for many if not most countries of the world. Likewise, this form of governance may not be appropriate for all policy areas, especially those that involve what Richard Rose (1974) has referred to as the "defining functions" of the State, for example, law, defense, and taxation.

The linkage between traditional state-centric governance and the interactive forms of governance discussed in this volume can be seen clearly in Figure I.1. The governance model outlined below shows the coexistence of tendentially unicentric forms of traditional governance through *government* and more pluricentric forms of *interactive governance*. Both government and interactive governance may contribute to the *governing* of society and the economy in the broad sense of identifying problems and challenges and formulating and achieving common objectives. When not acting in a strictly state-centric manner, government plays a crucial role in *metagoverning* interactive governance by means of shaping its structural and institutional conditions and by designing, managing, and directing the interactive governance arenas. The proliferation of interactive governance arenas also affects government; not by creating a hollow State, but by *transforming* the overall role and functioning of the State in the face of the growing recognition of the limits of unilateral state action and the need for participating in and regulating interactive governance arenas.

This volume therefore will move beyond a number of by now standard discussions of changes in the State and policymaking, especially for the

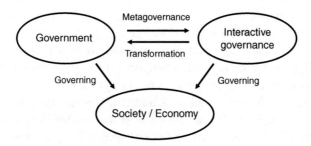

Figure I.1. Linkages among forms of governance

advanced democracies. Much of that discussion has been dominated by the New Public Management (NPM) and its assumptions that governance can best be accomplished through market mechanisms. Likewise, our approach will avoid the Scylla of the hollowing out of the State and the Charybdis of a neostatist reduction of interactive governance to merely a new tool of government. We attempt to understand a variety of different approaches to governing while not making any exclusive commitment to any one of them.

It is crucial to recognize that the arguments presented here are neither neoliberal nor neostatist. We are not rejecting the State in favor of the dominance of the market. On the other hand, while we recognize the continuing importance of government in public governance, we are arguing neither that the State can be seen as the sole actor involved nor that the State is necessarily the most fundamental actor in governance. The basic point is that no single actor can alone account for contemporary governance. Depending on the problem or task at hand, government, markets, interactive forms of governance, or some mixture of the three will offer the "right" governance solution.

The fact that interactive governance is a particular form of governance does not, however, diminish its importance. A good deal of governing, and perhaps an increasing amount, is done through interactive means and we need to understand how these processes function, and how they differ from the traditional modes of governing. Further, elaborating this model of governance enables us to use it for comparative purposes, both across countries and across policy areas. Finally, the detailed examination of interactive governance enables us to evaluate the claims and counterclaims concerning the efficacy and democracy of interactive governance.

The contents of the book

With these basic points about governance, and especially interactive governance, in mind, we will proceed to develop the argument and to examine the nature of interactive governance. In so doing, we will attempt to fill some of the gaps that are still to be found in the growing research on interactive governance. It is our hope that the attention we pay to some of the less developed themes in the current debate on interactive governance will help to consolidate and advance this particular paradigm. When we seek to advance the interactive governance paradigm, it is not because we consider it as the "right" paradigm, but simply because it needs much more elaboration in order to match the competing paradigms emphasizing the rule of representative governments or the allocation of goods and services through competitive markets.

Chapter 1 presents a thorough examination of the contemporary debates surrounding governance in the social sciences and particularly in political science. This chapter provides a strong justification of the use of governance and interactive forms of governance as an approach for political inquiry.

Chapter 2 extends the discussion of governance to consider its use in other social science disciplines. Ranging from development studies to decision sciences, this chapter considers how governance is considered in other academic disciplines and what these other versions of governance have to offer for our approach to governance. While governance studies have been centered in political science, it is clear that the other strands of the social sciences do have a great deal to contribute to this inquiry.

Power is a fundamental concept in political science, and *Chapter 3* explores ways in which the study of power can inform the study of governance. Many approaches to governance have tended to ignore the central role of power and politics, but we point out how crucial it is for understanding interactive governance and explore the different ways that power is exerted and manipulated in attempts to provide collective directions to a society.

In the contemporary social sciences, for any concept to be of any substantial utility there must be some means of measuring it. Governance is no different, so we have in *Chapter 4* considered the ways in which this concept can be measured. While there appear to be few opportunities for measuring governance in a quantitative manner, there are a number of ways in which we can develop instruments that can be used in a variety of settings to understand the extent to which governance goals are being achieved though unilateral and multilateral action.

Governance cannot be provided to society through any single government or any singular government organization. Thus, in *Chapter 5* we consider the horizontal and vertical dimensions of governance. There are multiple actors and organizations involved in governance, and these are found at all levels of government. The complex interactions involved in governance can therefore be considered in terms of intergovernmental as well as interorganizational relations.

To be effective, the structures and procedures involved in any system of governance must be institutionalized. That is, those structures and procedures need to develop some capacity to persist in the face of challenges, and further they will function better if it is possible to develop common values, symbols, and routines that support governance. The danger, however, is that the procedures will become overly institutionalized with rigidities that prevent adaptation to changing environmental conditions. *Chapter 6* discusses these factors in institutionalization of governance, and the special issues that arise relative to interactive forms of governance.

Interactive governance involves a variety of processes that permit the social actors and public sector actors some latitude to make decisions on their own. However, since interactive governance might not emerge spontaneously and is prone to failure, there is a need for authoritative decision-makers in the public sector to "metagovern" interactive governance arenas by imposing some more or less subtle forms of control over the devolved decision-making. This process may involve using a range of instruments that attempt to steer the interactive governance process, albeit steer it through rather indirect and "soft" means that maintain at least some of the autonomy of the actors involved. *Chapter 7* defines and discusses the notion of metagovernance and provides an overview of its different objectives, means, and forms.

Chapter 8 discusses the roles that social and political actors play in interactive governance. Roles are a means of linking individual behaviors and the structures involved in governing. These roles are defined by the expectations of the actors involved in the process, and by the ways in which actors involved perceive what they are expected to do. The roles played by governance actors in interactive policymaking tend to be significantly different from those played in more conventional forms of governing, and this chapter explores those differences and their implications for governance.

Governance involves fundamental issues of producing societal regulation and delivering public services. Interactive governance also involves the production and delivery of public regulation and services, albeit through more complex formats such as partnerships and networks. We therefore need to understand how effective interactive governance is, and further how to make that kind of governance even more effective. These management issues for interactive governance will be to some extent more difficult than might be less complex means of service delivery, although the options for "co-opting" social actors into the process may enhance effectiveness. *Chapter 9* discusses how effective interactive governance can be measured and how it can be improved through metagovernance.

The final two substantive chapters discuss issues of democracy and accountability in interactive governance. *Chapter 10* discusses the relationship of democratic participation and control to interactive governance. In addition to the familiar mechanisms of representative democracy, interactive governance also involves a number of other opportunities for participation, although these methods also involve some risks to effective democracy. Further, *Chapter 11* discusses the role of transparency, which is a fundamental condition for holding governance actors accountable. Although the conventional wisdom argues that transparency is crucial for accountability, there are also some virtues in maintaining discretion and privacy in governing. This chapter discusses the trade-offs involved in governing by means of traditional forms of government and more interactive forms of governance.

The book ends with a conclusion that summarizes the findings of the research and offers a program for additional research on interactive governance. This form of governance is almost certain to continue as a major alternative to traditional hierarchical governing, Therefore, although this book has made a major contribution to understanding interactive governance, there are a number of questions that remain and we identify those and provide some guides for continuing research.

1

The governance debate and the rise of interactive governance

The current popularity that the notion of *governance* enjoys among both practitioners and academics can be explained only by the great promises that people ascribe to governance. As such, governance is associated with enhanced interaction between public policymakers and relevant stakeholders, competent and knowledge-based decision-making, innovative policy solutions, flexible and coordinated policy implementation, and democratic ideals about inclusion, empowerment, and ownership. Actual governance arrangements often fail to deliver on these promises, but that does not seem to ruin the attractiveness of what is commonly referred to as "new forms of governance." People appear to have made a Faustian bargain, where they only see the positive aspects of the deal and ignore the darker consequences in terms of the risk of governance failure and the lack of democratic accountability (Peters and Pierre, 2004: 76).

The promises ascribed to governance are a simple inversion of the problems associated with traditional forms of hierarchical government, which are often accused of being too closed, formalistic, narrow-minded, conservative, rigid, uncoordinated, and exclusive. The declining confidence that citizens have been expressing in their governments is indicative of some recognition of these perceived government failures, but most people continue to demand and expect services from the public sector and its allies. This dilemma has forced central decision-makers to search for alternatives to the classical forms of governmental rule and, since the early 1990s, the new forms of governance have been celebrated as a key part of the solution that also includes an increased reliance on competitive forms of market regulation. The lack of a precise definition of governance has made it easy for people to attach all kinds of positive meanings and expectations to governance.

The embrace of governance is founded on a critique of the *modus operandi* of traditional forms of government. The current discourse on governance is also

9

conceived as a response to a more fundamental *problematization of the role of the State*. Hence, as Bob Jessop (2002) succinctly puts it, we are currently witnessing a threefold development involving the denationalization of statehood, the de-statification of politics, and the internationalization of policymaking. The link between the State and its national territory is weakened as old and new state powers are displaced upwards to international and transnational organizations; downwards to local governments, public service institutions, and user boards; and outwards to emerging cross-border regions and global city networks. The result is that state power is exercised at different and interconnected sites and scales. At the same time, the State is gradually losing its alleged monopoly on public policymaking as an increasing number of private actors such as expert communities, interest organizations, NGOs, citizen groups, consultancy firms, and private businesses become involved in the formulation and implementation of public policy. Last but not least, the national space for making and amending public policy is transgressed as policies are increasingly being uploaded to and downloaded from international policy arenas through policy diffusion and policy transfer.

The threefold problematization of the nation state as the central locus for governing society and the economy has further stimulated the search for an alternative to government that was triggered by the critique of the traditional forms of bureaucratic rule. The result of this search has been the rise of the widespread, but strongly contested, assertion that we are witnessing *"a shift from government to governance."* Numerous books and articles are making this claim, which has a strong appeal as it urges us to focus on the more or less informal processes of public governance rather than the formal institutions of government. However, there are also some implicit dangers of the assertion of a transition from government to governance. First, it creates a far too simplistic image of a unified past and future: before government was omnipotent and now it has suddenly lost its momentum and is stripped of its former powers. Second, it builds on a highly problematic assumption of a zero-sum game, according to which governance can only expand at the expense of government. Third, it seems to deny government any role in public governance, or at least obfuscates what this role might be. In order to avoid these pitfalls, we will in this volume perceive governance as a *"new perspective on an emerging reality."* The balance between different ways of governing society and the economy is shifting and this transforms the role of the State and prompts us to amend our views and theories about how collective goals are formulated and achieved.

Hence, unilateral top-down steering is increasingly supplemented and partially supplanted by multilateral action based on negotiated interaction among a host of different actors, and both hierarchical government and the interactive forms of governance are transformed by their mutual interplay. The result is an uneven and combined development of traditional forms of government and new forms of governance that varies from country to country, from policy area to policy area, and between different scales. The new and emerging reality tends to render the traditional pluralist model obsolete. Pluralist theory is by no means blind to the active role of private organizations and lobbyists in shaping public policies. However, pluralism tends to view nongovernmental actors as independent pressure groups competing over political influence on public policy and it portrays government as a neutral and relatively insulated mechanism for aggregating the plurality of demands and translating them into legitimate policy outputs and effective policy outcomes. The implicit idea of a strict separation of the public and private realms fails to capture the mutual dependency and institutional intertwinement of public and private organizations, and the explicit view that policy interaction involves a mixture of open competition and aggregation of interests fails to capture the negotiated interaction among public and private actors that gives some private actors a privileged access to the central policy arenas and tends to foster a high degree of policy integration.

The notion of governance is offering a way out of this impasse by providing a fresh perspective on the public policymaking process that emphasizes the plurality of interconnected policy arenas, the mutual exchange of knowledge, resources, and ideas through negotiated interaction, and the blurring of the lines of demarcation between the public and the private realm. However, we are convinced that governments at different levels will continue to play a crucial role in governance, both as a central and resourceful participant and as a metagovernor that facilitates, manages, and directs the various governance arenas. As such, governance is offering a new perspective on an emerging reality that recognizes the central influence of government in and over governance. Governments are gradually transformed by their participation in and metagovernance of governance as they must learn to participate in complex policy interaction, develop their reflexive and monitoring capacities, and find ways of governing governance that do not rely on brute force and imperative command.

In this chapter, we take a closer look at the rise of governance and the critical objections that have been raised by people who believe that governance has little or nothing to offer when it comes to understanding the governing of society and the economy. We begin with a brief discussion of how we define the notoriously slippery notion of *governance*. In generic terms, governance can be defined as the process of steering society and the economy through collective action. However, in this volume we will focus on *interactive forms of governance* in terms of quasi-markets, partnerships, and governance networks that are a prominent part of the new and emerging reality and seem to both challenge and transform the role of government in governing society and the economy. In the second section, we argue that the interactive forms of governance add a new layer on top of the old layer of hierarchical government and the recently added layer of competition-based market regulation and managerialism associated with New Public Management reforms. In the third section, we explore the theoretical roots of interactive governance in order to show how the notion of interactive governance emerges as a common solution to problems, puzzles, and challenges emerging in different subdisciplines within what we can broadly define as political science. After the genealogical account of interactive governance, we move forward in time in order to consider, first, the current debates on governance, and second, the many objections of the new research governance that we will summarize in terms of "three stages of denial." After having provided a critical response to the three standard objections to interactive governance, the chapter is concluded with a defense of the bold claim that governance is producing a significant and irreversible change in the governing of society and the economy.

Defining governance and interactive governance

An initial look at the etymology reveals that governance has its distant roots in the Latin word "gubernare" that means "to direct, rule, guide" and the Greek word "kybernan" that means to "steer or pilot a ship" and forms the basis of the notion of cybernetics. From the sixteenth century onwards, the notion of "government" becomes a frequently used term in the English-speaking world when referring either to the "actions of governing" or "the system for governing." Interestingly, government is derived from the French "gouvernement," which in turn comes from the medieval French notion of "gouvernance" that referred to the art of governing. Hence, we might conclude that "governance" is an old term for providing direction to society that went out of fashion a long time ago and only recently rose to its current fame.

Today, the notion of governance is used in many different contexts and often in conjunction with a particular prefix. As such, there are recurrent references to global governance, corporate governance, good governance, multilevel governance, project governance, IT governance, etc. Although the addition of a prefix to governance aims to establish a more precise concept by linking governance to a particular context, it does not help us capture the meaning of governance itself. Hence, in his seminal work, *Understanding Governance*, Rod Rhodes (1997a) identifies six different meanings of governance but fails to provide a concise definition of governance. Kees van Kersbergen and Franz van Warden (2004) draw up an even larger inventory consisting of nine different meanings of governance, and the seemingly endless lists of governance concepts lead Claus Offe (2008) to conclude that governance is an "empty signifier," that is, an expression without any precise content. To escape this conceptual morass, we must establish a generic definition of governance that we can then branch out into a number of radial definitions of particular forms of governance.

Contemporary political science commentators tend to define "governance" either as the formation of a collective will out of a diversity of interests (politics), a system of rules and norms shaping the actions of social and political actors (polity), or a political steering of social and economic relations based on soft, cooperative policy instruments such as best practices, standards, certifications, and benchmarks (policy) (see Treib et al., 2005). However, these different definitions do not really capture the distinctiveness of governance, because they fail to show what governance adds to the traditional and well-established notions of politics, polity, or policy.

Therefore, let us briefly consider some of the alternative definitional strategies that are found in the field of governance studies. First, the World Bank (2007) defines governance as the process of selecting those in authority, the capacity of the government to effectively manage its resources and implement sound policies, and the respect of citizens and governments for the institutions governing the interactions between them. The obvious problem with this definitional strategy is that it betrays the fundamental idea that governance implies a problematization of the role and nature of unicentric forms of government. Although it does make a reference to institutionalized forms of interaction, the World Bank definition of governance is primarily focused on the institutions and procedures of government.

Second, Jessop (1998, 2002) defines governance as "the heterarchy of reflexive self-organisation." This definition tends to associate governance with civil society. The problem with this definitional strategy is that it gives rise to an unwarranted normativism as it is implicitly assumed that governance is more consensual, egalitarian, trust-based, and deliberative than hierarchies and markets because it reproduces the intrinsic values of civil society.

Third, Kooiman (1993a), Mayntz (1993a, 1993b), Scharpf (1994), and Klijn (2008) tend to equate governance with network forms of governance that are either defined as a hybrid of hierarchy and market or as a distinctive mode of governing supplementing hierarchies and markets. Although networks are clearly an integral part of governance, the conflation of governance and networks creates a far too narrow definition of governance that excludes those forms of steering, control, and coordination that are not provided by stable, horizontal networks.

Finally, Bevir and Rhodes (2003) tend to see governance as a new neoliberal language game that leads to different interpretations and institutionalizations in different political and cultural contexts. The problem with this postfoundationalist view is that it becomes difficult to put bounds on governance. Governance becomes everything and, thus, nothing.

The available definitional strategies either define governance too narrowly or leave the definition open for an endless number of contextual interpretations. To avoid these twin problems, we shall here define *governance* as *the process of steering society and the economy through collective action and in accordance with some common objectives*. Although governance in this generic sense of the term can take many different forms, it is not tied to any particular institutional form of governance be it state, market, civil society, or networks. However, while evidently moving beyond the narrow definitions of governance, our generic definition clearly puts bounds on the notion of governance and, thus, rescues it from unwarranted concept stretching. As such, the generic definition of governance insists that governance is the process of managing and regulation society and the economy and that the process is based on collective action and aims to achieve some commonly accepted goals.

In the field of public policymaking, governance has typically been associated with a formal and legal steering provided by governments at different levels, but in the new and emerging reality unilateral action is increasingly supplemented and supplanted by "interactive forms of governance" where steering, control, and coordination are results of many hands rather than the iron fist of government. As the role of government in public governance has received a lot of attention in public policy research, we shall devote this volume to the study of the role and impact of *interactive forms of governance*, which we shall define as *the complex process through which a plurality of social and political actors with diverging interests interact in order to formulate, promote, and achieve common objectives by means of mobilizing, exchanging, and deploying a range of ideas, rules, and resources*.

This definition emphasizes three important features of interactive governance. First, interactive governance refers to a *complex process* rather than a more or less unified set of formal structures and institutions connected in a linear fashion. The initial studies of government were constitutional and legalistic and aimed to map out the formal structures of government and describe the different competences of public authorities. Subsequently, the behavioral revolution has drawn attention to the actions and inactions of politicians, public managers, and voters (Dahl, 1961, 1963), and the study of bureaucratic politics has highlighted the dynamic interplay between the political struggles inside government and the institutional framework of rules and norms (Peters, 1978; Dunleavy, 1991). However, the notion of governance takes a further step in focusing on the complex processes linking governmental and nongovernmental actors in different institutional arenas that facilitate interorganizational and intersystemic policymaking based on dynamic exchange and feedback loops.

Second, the process is driven by a collective ambition to define and pursue *common objectives* in the face of the presence of divergent interests and preferences. In private markets, the economic actors aim to produce value for themselves, whereas in governance the social and political actors aim to define and achieve common objectives and to produce public value, despite the fact that they may have different and often conflicting interests, wants, and beliefs. Interdependency forces the public and private actors to interact in order to find joint solutions that solve emerging problems and exploit new opportunities and thus somehow contribute to the advancement of the interests of the different actors.

Third, the process is *decentered* in the sense that common objectives are formulated and achieved in and through negotiated interaction among a plurality of actors from the State, the economy, and civil society. Hence, although governments often play a crucial role as facilitator and manager of policy interaction, there is no privileged center in public policymaking, but a number of competing actors and arenas, each of which contributes important resources, experiences, and ideas. In this perspective, civil society and the market do not merely constitute an external environment for the operation of government, but are societal subsystems populated with groups, associations, and organizations that are actively engaged in the formulation and achievement of common objectives.

Forms of interactive governance

Our definition of interactive governance captures an array of interactive governance arrangements that play an increasing role in the formulation and implementation of public policy. We shall here pay special attention to typical forms of interactive governance arrangements such as quasi-markets, partnerships, and governance networks.

Quasi-markets are a child of NPM and the implicit idea that it is possible to reap the supposed efficiency gains of private markets without losing the equity gain associated with traditional forms of public steering and funding. Public authorities are cast as purchasers of public services that are produced and delivered by private providers who are bound by a contract aiming to specify the price and quality of the relatively standardized services provisions that are delivered to the customers (Bartlett and Le Grand, 1993). The recent experience with the purchaser–provider model shows that it is extremely difficult and time consuming to make contracts that are capable of regulating the complex and conflict-ridden interaction between the public purchaser and the private providers. In addition, it proves to be difficult to ensure a trust-based exchange of innovative methods and creative solutions in the competitive environment

15

created by quasi-markets. In response to these problems, a new type of relational contract has been developed and new arenas for exchange of ideas and experience have been created. Relational contracts specify the procedures for sustained negotiation and interactive dispute settlement between public purchasers and private providers, and the new interactive arenas aim to bring purchasers and providers within a certain policy field together in order to build trust and forge more cooperative relations.

Partnerships between public and private actors come in many shapes and colors (Rosenau, 2000). Some are based on informal agreements between public and private partners aiming to reap some mutual benefits from cooperation about concrete problem-solving, policy innovation, or strategic planning. Other partnerships are based on formal contracts that specify the terms of cooperation and how benefits are split between the partners. Public–private partnerships (PPPs) are a well-known example of the latter type of partnership (Hodge and Greve, 2005). PPPs are defined as a "structured cooperation between public and private parties in the planning, construction and/or exploitation of infrastructural facilities in which they share or allocate risks, costs, benefits, resources and responsibilities" (Koppenjan, 2005: 137). The constitutive feature of PPPs is the presence of some kind of risk sharing and financial contribution of the private partners (Walker and Smith, 1995; Whettenhall, 2003). Without this feature, we might still have a partnership in the sense of a "structured cooperation," but it will not qualify as a PPP. There are two types of PPPs. The first type is the concession model in which a private partner designs, finances, and constructs a public sector project. The second type is the alliance or consortium model in which public and private parties cooperate to develop, construct, maintain, and operate a public facility (Koppenjan, 2005).

Governance networks can be defined as a horizontal articulation of interdependent but operationally autonomous actors who interact through negotiations that take place within a relatively institutionalized framework and facilitate self-regulated policymaking in the shadow of hierarchy (Sørensen and Torfing, 2007). There are different types of governance networks. Some networks aim to facilitate cooperation in terms of knowledge sharing. Other networks aim to enhance coordination in order to maximize joint efforts. Finally, some networks aim to facilitate collaboration through the joint definition and solution of emerging problems and challenges. Governance networks may also take different forms. Some are mandated from above while others are self-grown from below. Some are formal and relatively close while others are informal and relatively open. Last but not least, some networks are formed within public organizations (intra-organizational networks), between public organizations (joined-up government), or between public and private actors (policy networks).

Quasi-markets, partnerships, and governance networks are typical examples of interactive governance in the field of public policymaking. As such, negotiated interaction is a common feature of all three governance arrangements. The differences between the three governance arrangements become clear when we consider the problems they are supposed to address and the solutions they are supposed to provide. Hence, in the case of quasi-markets, the problem is inefficient public monopolies and the solution is state sponsored competition. In the case of partnerships, the problem is the lack of creative ideas and public resources and the solution is joint venture projects with or without risk sharing. Finally, in the case of governance networks the problem is complexity and fragmentation and the solution is crosscutting exchange and negotiation.

Empirically, the three typical forms of interactive governance are combined in various ways in different countries and at different levels. The conditions of emergence of interactive governance include the presence of capable and resourceful actors, a high degree of trust among public and private actors, and the possibility of ensuring voluntary compliance. Political factors such as political cultures and traditions, the need to enhance input and output legitimacy, and the capacity to metagovern interactive governance will also influence the spread interactive governance. When first the interactive governance mechanisms are in place, positive and negative feedbacks will generate virtuous and vicious circles leading to the institutionalization or deinstitutionalization of interactive governance (see Chapter 6).

The rise of interactive governance

After the Second World War, a government-based combination of democratic steering and bureaucratic control was seen as the primary tool for realizing the objectives of the modern welfare states that were developed in most of the Western societies. Accordingly, the public sector expanded in order to meet the needs of the citizens and regulate private markets. Public service and regulation were not only to have a firm legal foundation but should also be rational, cost efficient, and effective. Moreover, with the persistent growth of the public sector there has been an increasing emphasis on coordination and comprehensive planning. In most of the advanced industrial societies, the result was the development of a large, public planning machine that aimed to provide a detailed regulation of society and the economy through hierarchical steering.

The rise of interactive governance, both as a discourse and a recommended practice, can be traced back to the Trilateral Commission (Crozier et al., 1975), which in the mid-1970s gave rise to a heated discussion about the "overload of government," allegedly resulting from the mounting expectations of the citizens and the limited capacities of public bureaucracies. The overload thesis was advanced in conjunction with an equally alarming thesis about "the ungovernability of society" that was supposed to arise from the growing fragmentation of social and political life and the decline of public-spirited values. This bleak diagnosis was particularly troublesome for the Western European welfare states that relied heavily on the governing capacity of the State and had high ambitions with regard to the possibility of governing society and the economy. The problems were aggravated by the economic crisis in the 1970s and 1980s that contributed to what was generally known as the legitimacy crisis of the modern welfare state.

The economic and political crisis paved the way for neoliberal governments and policies that aimed to solve the problem of government overload by means of privatizing public enterprises, contracting out public services, and commercializing the remaining public sector through the introduction of corporate management techniques from the private sector. If the State was overburdened and no longer could do the job, the market should take over and alleviate the burden of the State by providing a growing number of public services. Hence, NPM reforms sought to limit the role of elected politicians to the formulation of overall policy objectives, leaving the responsibility for the production and delivery of public policy in the hands of quasi-autonomous public agencies and a host of private providers operating on the basis of contracts and agreements with central government agencies. In response to the increasing ungovernability of society, NPM aimed to mobilize the resources and commitment of private organizations and firms in public governance through the formation of partnerships and strategic alliances and sought to stimulate the active engagement of the citizens in the production and delivery of public policy through increasing consumer choice and the creation of user boards.

With Finland, New Zealand, and the United Kingdom as the epicenters, NPM reforms spread throughout the world and soon became a dominant fad in the established Western democracies, the transitional democracies in Eastern and Central Europe, the newly industrialized countries in South-East Asia, and developing countries confronted with Western demands to adopt the principles of good governance. In the countries where NPM caught on, it led to an increasing fragmentation of the public sector as services and regulation were delivered by an increasing number of special purpose agencies and private service providers. This growing fragmentation of the public sector stimulated the need for institutional mechanisms that could provide horizontal coordination in order to avoid duplication of efforts and create synergies.

At the same time, an increasing number of traditional policy problems such as physical planning, regional development, and environmental protection were redescribed as "wicked problems" (see Rittel and Webber, 1973), and a series of new crosscutting policy areas such as preventive health care, public safety, and job creation came to the fore. This development further strengthened the call for horizontal coordination through institutionalized interaction among relevant public and private actors.

Finally, there has been a growing emphasis on civic engagement in the public sector. This participation was fostered for clients, users, and citizens in general as for the lower echelon employees of public organizations. The clearest examples of participatory governance are found in North America with initiatives such as the National Performance Review (the Gore Commission) in the United States and PS2000 in Canada. Another crucial example is the participatory budgeting in Porto Alegre and other cities in Brazil. A final example is the many European attempts to establish user boards in public institutions and to involve users and street-level bureaucrats in public innovation projects. These participatory governance reforms sought to empower various groups in society to have greater influence over policy and over the manner in which policies were delivered (see Peters, 2001). They assumed that government could not govern alone as effectively as it could in concert with citizens and previously disempowered employees.

New forms of joined-up government, relational contracts between public purchasers and private providers, PPPs, and governance networks are typical responses to the rising demand for empowered participation and crosscutting coordination at the local, regional, and national level (Rhodes, 2000a). In federal political systems and in multilevel systems such as the European Union (EU), where authority is shared by a number of states and across multiple levels, interactive forms of governance have been introduced in order to provide a flexible vertical coordination and to integrate private stakeholders in policy formulation and policy implementation, thereby enhancing input and output legitimacy (Scharpf, 1999; EU Commission, 2001; Marks and Hooghe, 2004). Finally, in the absence of an overarching political authority in terms of a world government, global regulation and policymaking increasingly takes place in transnational networks and international regimes in which not only nation states but also a growing number of private enterprises, NGOs, and experts communities that are often spanning different countries and scales interact on the basis of a mutual recognition of interdependency (Betsill and Bulkeley, 2004; Djelic and Sahlin-Andersson, 2006).

Although it is tempting to construct a simplistic narrative about a transition from hierarchical government via market-based NPM to interactive forms of governance, such a narrative fails to understand the dynamic coexistence of the different ways of governing society and the economy. Inspired by historical institutionalism (Thelen and Steinmo, 1992; Thelen, 2003), we should rather see the institutional forms for governing modern society as an evolving path consisting of several layers that are added on top of one another. The new top layers in terms of the different forms of interactive governance are highly visible when seen from above, but if we cut a slice of the evolving path, we can clearly see how the different layers of government, market regulation, and interactive governance support and build upon as well as interact and merge with one another.

The theoretical roots of interactive governance

There are many different strands in the research on interactive governance, especially in the studies of public policymaking. In a North American context, Hugh Heclo (1978) has observed that policy decisions are sometimes moved from macro-level policy systems involving the presidency, congressional leaders, the Supreme Court, mass media, and the general public to policy subsystems in which issue-specific actors from the public and private sector interact on the basis of interdependency. In Germany, researchers at the Max Planck Institute in Cologne (Marin and Mayntz, 1991; Mayntz, 1993*a*, 1993*b*) and at the Center for Interdisciplinary Research in Bielefeld (Héritier et al., 1996) have explored the systemic limitations of both hierarchies and markets that call for the development of new modes of governance based on negotiated interaction. A number of British scholars have replaced the corporatist notion of Iron Triangles with a broader notion of policy networks that includes both relatively tight and exclusive policy communities and relatively loose and inclusive issue networks (Marsh and Rhodes, 1992; Rhodes, 1997*a*; Marsh, 1998). Their Dutch colleagues have been focusing on the growing societal and political complexity and the surge of wicked problems and tend to view complex networks and PPPs as a response to this development (Kickert et al., 1997; Kooiman, 2003; Koppenjan and Klijn, 2004). Finally, the Roskilde school in Denmark has aimed to distinguish between different theoretical approaches to democratic network governance and applied these approaches in empirical studies (Bogason and Zølner, 2007; Sørensen and Torfing, 2007).

Interactive governance has also been the center of attention in adjacent fields of study. A cross-national school of collaborative planning has emerged that sees planning as a result of interactive governance based on power sharing, relation building, mobilization of local knowledge, and mutual learning supported by sustainable institutional designs (Healey, 1997, 2007; Innes and Booher, 2010). The new and growing literature on innovation systems emphasizes the complex interrelations between economic and political actors that are engaged in the creation of local, regional, and national capacities for learning and innovation (Lundvall, 1992; Edquist and Hommen, 1999). The long-standing research on science and society interaction emphasizes the role of networks, partnerships, and deliberative experiments in bringing together government, industry, universities, and civil society actors (Andersen and Jæger, 1999; Callon et al., 2001; Banthien et al., 2003). The recent studies of multilevel governance aim to capture the vertical and horizontal interaction in federalist and quasi-federalist systems (Scharpf, 2001; Bache and Flinders, 2004). Last but not least, International Relations (IR) theorists have problematized the realist paradigm that emphasizes the privileged role of national states in international politics and explored the advocacy coalitions, epistemic communities, international regimes, and transnational networks that bring together a host of governmental and nongovernmental actors (Krasner, 1983; Haas, 1992; Sabatier and Jenkins-Smith, 1993; Djelic and Sahlin-Andersson, 2006).

The multifaceted research on interactive governance seems to revolve around Jan Kooiman's famous assertion that, today, no single actor, public or private, has the knowledge and capacity to solve complex, dynamic, and diversified problems (Kooiman, 1993a: 4). This assertion is implicit to all the above-mentioned strands of research and is echoed by local and regional policymakers engaged in strategic planning, national government officials aiming to respond to acute needs for policy reform, the official governing strategies of the EU, and other emerging regional powers, and, most recently, by President Obama's international partnership strategy that got him an early Nobel Prize in 2009.

The wide-ranging theoretical and practical resonance of the assertion of the limits of unilateral steering and problem-solving reflects the new and emerging reality described above. However, the surge of interactive governance research has been prompted by new societal and political developments. The new governance paradigm is also rooted in a number of analytical puzzles and theoretical developments that tend to converge in the appraisal of the analytical value of the notion of interactive governance. Let us take a closer look at some of the theoretical trajectories that have spurred the interest in studying pluricentric forms of interaction.

The first trajectory brings us from pluralism via corporatism and neo-corporatism to policy networks and governance. In the European context, corporatism seems to offer a more accurate description of state–society interaction than the pluralist model, which in its initial, American formulation claims that all preferences and interests would be spontaneously articulated by interest organizations that are engaged in an open and equal competition over political influence on government policy (Truman, 1951; Dahl, 1956). Hence, corporatism and neo-corporatism captured the privileged access of, and close bonds among, functional defined peak organizations that participate in institutionalized and issue-specific policy arenas engaged in the formulation and implementation of public policy (Schmitter, 1974; Lehmbruch, 1984; Cawson,

1985). However, the growing recognition of policy arenas with a more open access and participation, loose couplings among actors with varying resources bases, and a more sporadic interaction with the character of consultation led to the development of the more encompassing notion of policy networks that empirically could vary from tightly organized policy communities to loosely connected issue networks (Marsh and Rhodes, 1992; Rhodes, 1997a; Marsh, 1998). More recently, a gradual shift from the question of how interest groups can use different kinds of networks to further their interests to the question of how public value can be produced through public–private interaction has complemented the research on policy networks with a study of governance networks and other interactive forms of governance (Koppenjan and Klijn, 2004; Sørensen and Torfing, 2007).

The second trajectory leads us from behavioralism via systems theory and cybernetics to policy subsystems. The behavioral revolution in political sciences exploded the constitutional, legalistic, and highly normative approach to the study of politics (Dahl, 1961; Eulau, 1961; Almond and Verba, 1963; see also Rhodes, 1995), but it left us with a rather descriptive account of the patterns of individual behavior with little attempt to provide an overall understanding of political processes, institutions, and functions. Such an understanding was provided by the system theoretical approach to the study of politics advanced by Talcott Parsons (1951) and David Easton (1965a). The tendency in Easton's political systems analysis to portray the political system as a black box translating political inputs into policy outputs was compensated by the integration of insights from cybernetics that helped to understand organizational communication and coordination through notions of feedback, information flows, and social learning (Deutsch, 1963). However, the system theoretical approach tends to lose sight of the political actors. As such, there has been a growing need to refocus the analysis by looking at how different social and political actors interact in institutionalized contexts that condition and shape their actions and inactions (Peters, 1999). The new research on governance provides a promising starting point for such an analysis as it aims to balance the focus on patterns of interaction with the study of the emerging institutional frameworks that structure and are structured by social and political interaction (March and Olsen, 1995; Scharpf, 1997).

The third trajectory takes us from society-centered theory via state-centered theory to a focus on interactive governance arenas. Both liberalism and Marxism are society-centered theories that conceive the State as a resultant of political forces and pressures rooted in civil society and the economy (Dahl, 1963; Poulantzas, 1978; Miliband, 1983). Theda Skocpol and her colleagues have opposed this view of the State arguing that it fails to recognize the relative autonomy and political capacities of the State, which in many cases is capable of withstanding societal and economic pressures and initiate and drive policymaking (Evans et al., 1985). The discussions following in the wake of the attempt to bring the State back in tend to result in an unproductive oscillation between the emphasis on the power of social and economic actors and the capacities of the State (Jessop, 1990). What we need is rather a balanced account of the interaction between governmental and nongovernmental actors emphasizing the political capacities and liabilities of both parties. The interactive governance paradigm provides such an account as it emphasizes the horizontal interaction of public and private actors, each with their own rule and resource base, and pays attention to both the interdependency and the operational autonomy of the actors (Kooiman, 2003).

The fourth trajectory brings us from the mechanical conception of organizations via the understanding of organizations as open systems to an interorganizational view of governance theory. Originally, organizations were conceived as integrated and rationally organized machines with clearly defined boundaries, precisely defined tasks, and hierarchically defined lines of communication and command (see Morgan, 1986). In the 1950s and 1960s, sociological organization theorists began to pay more attention to the environment of organizations. As such, organizations were increasingly conceived as open systems adapting to changes in their environment (Mintzberg, 1979). Later on, the recognition that this environment consists of other organizations fostered a new focus on the interorganizational exchange of information and resources taking place through relatively stable networks (Benson, 1978; Aldrich, 1979). The notion of "organizational fields" advanced by Walter Powell and Paul DiMaggio (1983) paves the way for the development of the interactive governance paradigm.

The fifth trajectory leads us from top-down implementation theory via bottom-up approaches to backward mapping of the multiple actors engaged in policymaking. At first, top-down implementation theorists aimed to explain the gulf between desired and actual policy outcomes by looking at the problems and barriers that emerge as policies are making their way down from the executive level to the frontline delivery systems (Pressman and Wildawsky, 1973). Vague program theories, goal displacements, bad communication, and the lack of control and resources impede the realization of the centrally defined policy objectives. By contrast, bottom-up implementation theory claims that implementation problems cannot be explained solely by distorted communication and the absence of coordination and control, and sets out to analyze the strategies of street-level bureaucrats who are aiming to cope with cross-pressures in the local service delivery (Lipsky, 1980). While top-down and bottom-up theories focus on specific actors in terms of central government and street-level bureaucrats, respectively, other implementation researchers have taken a further step arguing that implementation studies should begin with the identification of a certain policy output and then undertake a backward mapping of the complex networks and processes that led to the production of the specific policy output (Hjern and Porter, 1981; Hjern and Hull, 1984; Elmore, 1985). This clearly takes us far into the land of interactive governance research.

A sixth trajectory, associated with the implementation literature, can be found in the literature on policy instruments that has moved from a focus on regulatory tools based on coercion via an emphasis on procurement and service contracts toward more voluntary forms of compliance and self-regulation. Lester Salamon (2002), for example, has argued that governments are increasingly moving away from command and control instruments toward softer instruments that involve interactions with the groups and individuals affected – something he refers to as the "New Governance." This follows on from the continuing interest in the Canadian tools literature that policy instruments should be minimally invasive into the lives of citizens (see Howlett, 2000). Likewise, the "soft law" literature in the EU and elsewhere represents attempts to make policy instruments more interactive (Mörth, 2004).

The seventh trajectory guides us from intergovernmentalism via supranationalism to multilevel governance. In the burgeoning number of EU studies, there has been a growing recognition of the *sui generis* character of the EU, which defies both the characterization as an international organization based on sovereign member states (Moravcsik, 1998) and the description as a supranational political system (Hix, 1994). The EU seems to be more than an international organization and less than a federalist system as political powers are distributed across a number of different levels, institutions, and actors that are connected through tangled networks. The result is the formation of a "networked polity" (Kohler-Koch and Eising, 1999) and a "multi-level governance system" (Scharpf, 2001) in which governmental and nongovernmental actors interact in multiple, but well-connected, arenas.

The final trajectory steers us from realist IR theories via liberal IR theories to theories of global governance. Classical and neoclassical realism characterizes IR as an anarchy in which sovereign states use their power to pursue their national interests (Morgenthau, 1954). Liberal IR theories and the neorealism of Kenneth Waltz (1979) have argued that nation states are not the sole actors in international politics and emphasized the role of international rules, norms, and ideas founded on universal values such as peace and democracy. Nation states interact with multinational corporations and international advocacy coalitions and their actions are constrained by regulatory and normative standards advanced by large international organizations (Keohane and Nye, 1977). The result is the creation of a tentative international order that tends to reduce anarchy to a default option that emerges when particular international regimes malfunction or break down (Wendt, 1992). Theories of global governance radicalize the liberal theories of IR by expanding the range of participating actors and insisting that the rules, norms, and ideas on which the tentative international order is built are socially constructed through hegemonic struggles taking place in multiple arenas. Governments are disaggregated into a range of public authorities (municipalities, regions, and ministries) and they are flanked by multinational corporations, NGOs, experts communities, etc. The public and private actors interact in competing and overlapping governance arenas because they are dependent on each other's resources, ideas, and energies.

Our bold claim is that the rising focus on interactive governance is a response to theoretical puzzles and debates in a variety of disciplines that have come to recognize the limits of unicentric forms of governing. Neither large government institutions, clusters of sovereign states, nor the more or less government-controlled Iron Triangles can govern alone. The governing of society and the economy is a result of negotiated interaction involving a plethora of public and private actors.

The current debate on interactive governance

Today governance and interactive governance are debated all around the world. The *European governance debate* is particularly strong and reflects the surge of interactive forms of governance at all levels and in most policy areas. In Western Europe, there have been favorable conditions for collaboration between public and private actors in terms of the rule of law, stable institutional rules, a high level of mutual trust, a unique combination of strong states and strong civil societies, and a growing need to mobilize experts, lay citizens, and third sector actors as partners in the reinvigoration of the public sector and the modern welfare state. Networks have facilitated empowered participation and policy innovation. Partnerships have facilitated resource exchange and created synergies between the public and private sector. Last but not least, quasi-markets have been created in order to curtail the growth of public expenditures and enhance flexibility in service delivery. Interactive forms of governance have been studied intensely by political scientists, public administration researchers, and planning theorists. Whereas the first generation of governance studies documented, defined, and explored how new forms of interactive governance contributed to the governing of society and the economy, the second generation of studies has aimed to assess the performance and impact of governance and analyze how it can be improved through metagovernance (Kickert et al., 1997; Benz and Papadopoulos, 2006; Sørensen and Torfing, 2007). In Central and Eastern Europe where political trust is considerably lower and civil society less developed, the debate on interactive

25

governance is less pronounced and partnerships, networks, and informal forms of governance are often associated with the old regime and seen as antithetical to the attempt to secure the rule of law. However, the paradox is that input and output legitimacy would be greatly improved if public and private actors worked more closely together to find pragmatic and sustainable solutions to public problems and challenges.

In the study of the EU, governance through institutionalized collaboration has become an organizing concept for understanding European policymaking. The scholarly focus on policy interaction at the national level coincided with a significant increase in European level policymaking, which has been analyzed in terms of "EU governance" by large-scale research programs such as CONNEX and NEWGOV (Kohler-Koch and Rittberger, 2009). Economic globalization and societal de-nationalization have created an urgent need for new forms of collaboration either on the basis of the community method, characterized by a strong role for the European Commission and Parliament, or on the basis of nonhierarchical forms of public–private interaction in relation to the EU Committees or the structural and regional funds. According to Beate Kohler-Koch and Fabrice Larat (2009: 169–84), the number of research projects on EU governance increased dramatically toward the end of the 1990s. More than 30% of the projects were located in the United Kingdom, Germany, and at the European University Institute, but the intensity of governance research has also been high in France, the Netherlands, Austria, and Scandinavia. As for the content of the research projects, the study of European policymaking, the analysis of the role of various EU institutions, and attempts to conceptualize European governance clearly outnumber the studies of political participation and the normative dimensions of governance. More than half of the studies are anchored in political science.

The *North American debate* on interactive governance has focused on how networks, partnerships, and quasi-markets can enhance the role of private actors in the production and delivery of public service and how they can facilitate service integration and coordination of public and private efforts (Provan and Milward, 1995; Meier and O'Toole, 2003; Provan et al., 2004). The strong anti-state discourse in the United States means that the involvement of nongovernmental actors is crucial if governments want to achieve their purposes. However, there is also an important strand of governance studies that conceive interactive governance as a means to involve local citizens and private stakeholders in a multicultural society (Fung and Wright, 2003; Fung, 2004; Musso et al., 2006), and more recently a new strand of research has recommended interactive governance as a tool for cutting red tape and enhancing innovation in the public sector (Goldsmith and Eggers, 2004; Nambisan, 2008; Eggers and Singh, 2009). At a more general level, Donald Kettl (2002) has identified the roots of different forms of governance in American political thought and predicted that interactive forms of governance will play a crucial role in the twenty-first century. Globalization, devolution, and new government responsibilities mean that North American governments at all levels will become increasingly interconnected with private corporations and nongovernmental organizations. This raises the question of how governments can manage and direct networks, partnerships, and quasi-markets by exercising a practical and contextualized sovereignty. Indeed, exploration of the governmental strategies toward interactive governance is another important strand of the North American governance debate (Agranoff, 2003; Milward and Provan, 2006).

In *South America* there has been a neoliberal governance debate advanced by international organizations aligned in the Washington consensus. At the beginning the focus of the debate was on the introduction of new forms of governance such as privatization, contracting out, PPPs, and economic deregulation. Later, the poor performance of the Latin American economies prompted a rethinking of the role of the State and its connection with the private sector. As such, the new development model combined neoliberal reforms aiming to stimulate market-led growth with the enhancement of state capacities and NPM reforms. However, the various governance reforms have had a limited impact due to the persistent predominance of corporatism, clientelism, and informal systems of authority (Zurbriggen, 2011). Alongside the neoliberal debate on market-friendly governance, an alternative governance debate has emerged among progressive scholars, policymakers, and social movements. The alternative governance debate has focused on the strengthening of the relations between the State and the citizens in the face of the democratic deficit created by the long-lasting presence of authoritarian regimes. Governance is about improving state–citizen relations in order to enhance the legitimacy of state institutions and build a new kind of participatory citizenship that can contribute to the augmentation of civic participation and the democratic accountability of public authorities (Alvarez et al., 1998). The creation of new forms of empowered participatory governance is mostly found at the local and regional level and the experiment with participatory budgeting in Porto Alegre in Brazil is a case in point (Koonings, 2004). Participatory governance through sustained interaction between public authorities and individual and organized citizens has spread throughout South America and is widely debated as a way of reconnecting governments and citizens.

The *African governance debate* was triggered by a World Bank report *Sub-Saharan Africa: From Crisis to Sustainable Growth* (World Bank, 1989). In the 1970s and 1980s, the World Bank had aimed to spur economic development by calling for economic policy reforms emphasizing the need for economic discipline, privatizations, and deregulation. However, the continued lack of growth and development forced the World Bank to adopt a new strategy. The

African crisis was increasingly seen as a crisis of governance that was caused by the incapacity of the State to formulate and implement much needed policy programs and blatantly visible in a number of "failed States" that cannot even provide security for their citizens. In the light of this the World Bank called for institutional reforms for better governance. Economic development was seen to require an enhancement of the institutional capacity of public organizations to produce public value in an effective, transparent, impartial, and accountable manner (World Bank, 2000). In contrast to Europe, governance reforms in the African countries were supposed to strengthen government and its effectiveness and accountability, rather than to create networks and partnerships (Kjær, 2011a). However, empirical analysis shows that African governments are overly centralized and captured by particular elites (Mwenda and Tangri, 2005). Their ability to steer society and the economy is limited and accountability is prevented by the weakness of civil society and the presence of affective networks in which public officials are held to account by persons who are of the same kin or otherwise related, rather than by their superiors and the voters (Evans, 1995; Hyden et al., 2004; De Grassi, 2008). The neo-patrimonial state structures seem to prevent good governance reforms, and the World Bank (2007) now admits that the results of the campaign for institutional reform are at best mixed. The discourse on good governance is not only problematized by ingrained domestic governance structures. Its normative foundations in Western values and the idea that economic development is conditioned by good governance have also been questioned (Bratton and Hyden, 1992; Khan, 2004). In the wake of these criticisms, the African governance debate has focused on the question of whether to continue the attempts to adapt African governance structures to Western-style government, or whether to build upon and try to reform the neo-patrimonial state structures and the interactive governance arenas that in many countries fill the void of a well-functioning government at the local level (Grindle, 2004; Lund, 2008; Kjær, 2011).

In *North and East Asia*, the good governance discourse has been shattered by the fact that the countries with the highest growth rates (China, Vietnam, and the Four Tigers) are not characterized by good governance (Kang, 2002; Rock and Bonnett, 2004). From the point of view of the good governance debate, it is quite a paradox that a number of countries have seen a rapid economic development despite considerable corruption. The governance debate in Asia has focused on the emergence and role of "transitional institutions" that are different from the standard institutions in the Anglo-Saxon package (Qian, 2003). As such, there is a large debate on what is known as inclusive institutionalism. The focus is here on the development of State–Business Relations (SBRs) and the role of consultation, credible commitment, and monitoring/reciprocity (Doner, 1992; Ritchie, 2005). Attention has also been drawn to the relation between the rather technocratic SBRs and the political alliances and settlements behind these (Haggard 1998, 2004). As such, there has been a growing interest in the role and function of formal and informal interaction between private and public elites. In relation to Japan, some scholars have even talked about the rise of a network state (Okimoto, 1989), and in relation to China, Hong Kong, and other countries influenced by Chinese cultural legacies, the affinity between interactive forms of governance and Confucian values of harmony and reciprocity has been discussed (Tao et al., 2010).

The three stages of denial: A critical assessment

Despite the worldwide debates on governance and interactive forms of governance, there are still a large number of skeptics who believe that the new governance paradigm has little if anything to offer. The scholarly objections to the growing interest in interactive forms of governance seem to follow the three stages of denial in claiming: first, that interactive governance is a marginal empirical phenomenon that deserves little scholarly attention; second, that it might play a considerable role but is hardly a new phenomenon and covered by well-established theories; and, finally, that it is a new but regrettable development that should be countered by all means as it gives rise to huge problems in terms of the lack of transparency and accountability.

The *first denial* is an outright rejection of the claim that traditional forms of governance through government are challenged by the surge of new forms of interactive governance. For example, in an executive summary of the Danish studies of power and democracy, Peter Munk Christiansen and Lise Togeby (2006) assess the social and political challenges to the "parliamentary chain of government," according to which the sovereign people elect the national parliament, which in turn controls the government that governs the public administration through bureaucratic control. On the basis of a highly selective review of the literature, they contend that: "Looking back over the past 30–40 years, we cannot find evidence to conclude that the parliamentary chain of government has suffered severe damage" (Christiansen and Togeby, 2006: 22). They admit that citizens have become more actively involved in the implementation of public policy through user boards and free consumer choice, but they contend that this does not challenge the parliamentary chain of governance. It is merely an instance of individualized participation at the output side of the political system.

It is rare to find such a hard-headed denial of the significance of interactive forms of governance, which disregards the role of nongovernmental actors, the blurring of roles and responsibilities, and the negotiated character of public governance. Today, many scholars seem prepared to accept that interactive forms of governance probably play a crucial role in most Western countries. Still, many of them will deny that interactive governance is prevalent in their own country. This is often explained by the fact that the analytical approach adopted by many public policy analysts focuses on policy programs and the role of formal government institutions rather than on the interrelation between the governmental and nongovernmental actors that come into view when conducting a backward mapping of policy outputs in relation to particular policy problems.

The *second denial* claims that interactive governance is an important feature of most political systems, but that is not a new phenomenon and is well accounted for by pluralist theories of democracy (Marinetto, 2003; Colebatch, 2009). It is true that as an empirical phenomenon, policy interaction is hardly new. What is new is rather that interactive forms of governance are increasingly endorsed by central decision-makers in governments at various levels. If, previously, interactive governance was viewed with great suspicion because it introduces some kind of "private interest government," it is now more often viewed as an effective and legitimate way of governing our increasingly complex and fragmented societies and economies. Pluralism has addressed the question of policy interaction many years ago and looked at how different interest groups aim to capture the arenas for public policymaking and how they put pressure on elected governments. However, as mentioned above, pluralism has been unable to grasp the persistent blurring of the public–private divide that follows from the growing recognition of interdependency between governmental and nongovernmental actors in public governance. It has also failed to understand the transformation of the role of the State in relation to interactive policy arenas.

Finally, a number of scholars readily accept that public bureaucracies increasingly are supplemented and supplanted by quasi-markets, PPPs, and governance networks but tend to regard these new forms of interactive governance as an aberration that should be abandoned because it makes public governance less efficient and undermines cherished democratic principles such as transparency and accountability. The belief that interactive governance is new and significant, but essentially bad, constitutes the *third denial*. While the premise of this denial is correct, we believe that the conclusion is wrong. Interactive governance may lead to all kinds of coordination problems and make long-term planning more difficult. It may also take place in secluded arenas and involve constellations of actors that are difficult to hold to account for their actions and inactions. However, interactive governance has become a part of the standard repertoire of public governance mechanisms and carries a great potential for enhancing effective and democratic governance. Hence, the main challenge consists in finding ways of democratizing interactive governance and enhancing its efficiency through the exercise of metagovernance (see Chapters 9 and 10).

Conclusion

The proliferation of interactive forms of governance is a result of strategic and ad hoc decisions on the part of public decision-makers who realize that the scope for unilateral action is shrinking and respond to pressures from increasingly competent and demanding private actors who want to take an active part in public decision-making (Warren, 2002, 2009). It is a daily experience among public decision-makers at various levels that the governing of society and the economy through top-down steering is becoming increasingly difficult because of growing complexity of policy problems, the functional differentiation of society, the increasing interdependence among social and political actors, and the strategic uncertainties caused by globalization and conflicting rising public demands (Kooiman, 2003; Koppenjan and Klijn, 2004). It is also widely recognized that interactive forms of governance are facilitated by new information and communication technologies and a growing level of popular education and professionalization of organized stakeholders (Goldsmith and Eggers, 2004). Finally, there seems to be little doubt that interactive governance can enhance ownership to public policy initiatives and help to produce democratic legitimacy (Skelcher and Torfing, 2010). As the underlying social, economic, and political trends are likely to continue in the future, we can conclude that interactive governance is here to stay and likely to play an increasing role in the future.

More importantly, the rise of interactive governance seems to have produced a number of *irreversible changes*. First, the expectations of individual and collectively organized stakeholders to become actively involved in interactive policymaking have increased and are accelerated by the political empowerment of the stakeholders, which is an effect of their participation in collaborative governance arenas. Economic recession might augment the role of governments aiming to ensure fiscal discipline, but the expectations of relevant and affected actors to be involved in the attempts to solve the growing number of wicked problems will endure.

Second, public agencies have become transformed from relatively insulated bureaucracies to relatively open organizations that are engaged in negotiated interaction, joint problem-solving, and collaborative service delivery. Interactive governance has become a systematic and well-integrated activity that takes place on the basis of institutionalized rules of the game and requires constant monitoring and management through various forms of metagovernance (see Chapter 7). The institutional transformation of public bureaucracy has changed the logic of appropriate action so that many public administrators perceive the design, management, and direction of collaborative arenas as a necessary and legitimate task. Participation in interactive governance arrangements also seems to affect the organization of public bureaucracies

31

that tend to break down the silos and devolve power and competence to middle managers and street level bureaucrats. However, the pendulum might swing back toward a reappraisal of the classical bureaucratic ethos in terms of professionalism, impartiality, transparency, and accountability (Du Gay, 2000; Olsen, 2002), but a return to self-sufficient bureaucratic organizations that are merely interacting with an external environment as a bounded actor is unlikely in the face of the public sector's need for mobilizing knowledge, ideas, and resource of a host of stakeholders.

Third, the perception of interactive governance as a legitimate alternative to hierarchy and markets means that governance has become a more reflexive enterprise that is based on a context-dependent and issue-specific choice of a particular combination of governance mechanisms. There might be situations in which hierarchical control or market competition seems to be the obvious choice, but interactive forms of governance will be a strong candidate in policy areas characterized by uncertainty, conflicts, and the need to pool or exchange resources. Ideological bias may influence the political decision-makers' choice of governance mechanisms as strong defenders of the welfare state will tend to have strong preferences for hierarchical governance and liberal critics of the welfare state will tend to have strong preferences for market governance. However, in situations in which either hierarchies or markets fail, interactive governance will be the default option that might yield unexpected solutions.

These seemingly irreversible changes make the study of interactive governance a central task for political scientists and public policy researchers all over the world. We already know a great deal about the functioning of government and market forms of governance have been carefully scrutinized. By comparison, there are many unexplored research avenues within the new interactive governance paradigm. Therefore, it is our modest hope that this book will help to further advance the new paradigm by shedding light on some of the key questions about the study, functioning, and impact of inter-active governance.

2

Governance in other disciplines: One approach or many?

The majority of the literature about governance has come from political science and public administration research, and has been concerned primarily with governance at the national level. This literature has become extensive and is extremely rich, but it does not by any means cover the full range of writing about governance. The term has appeared in a number of other disciplines in the social sciences and has become a part of a general discussion about steering, control, and management. While to some extent the diffusion of the idea of governance represents concept stretching (see Sartori, 1970; Goertz, 2004; Offe, 2008), in some cases beyond all recognition, it also points to the generality of the need to reconsider steering and brings to our attention the contributions that alternative conceptions of steering can make to understanding governance.

As has to some extent been the case in political science, the growing interest in governance is a reflection of the institutional incapacity to govern. Even in academic disciplines where collective action, and political steering, is not a prime interest, governance as a theory has been employed to help explain how actors can coordinate their behavior toward joint objectives. Political institutions may or may not be part of this analysis, owing to the orientation of the discipline. Creating or strengthening governance could be seen as a strategy for resource mobilization and concerted action while, at the same time, resolving collective action problems. Thus, analyses of how actors and institutions create and reproduce governance are prefaced on the assumption that this is something desired by all or most of the key players. This is the case in the political arena, but less so in markets or in other types of social settings.

As with so many other instances of concepts and theories (e.g., institutionalism), which have become stretched and are subject to substantial internal division and variation, we need to consider whether there is sufficient agreement in theory and method among the approaches to say that there is one governance literature with numerous branches. The alternative would be to conceptualize governance as essentially a number of different concepts, albeit using the same word to describe them. While having the different conceptions of governance may enrich the literature in some ways, they may also create confusion and misunderstanding across and within the various disciplines that employ these concepts.

While it is apparent that the concept of governance has been stretched, it may be equally important to ask why all these various disciplines are concerned with governance. Perhaps the most relevant answer to that question is that the need to govern, and the manifest failures of governance in a number of areas of our collective lives, has raised the issue to a central position. This can be seen in the very obvious concern of development organizations with the failures of their client states. It can also be seen in the concerns of analysts of the international system who search for means of global governance, or at least regional governance. In short, governance has become important in a number of disciplines in large part because it has become challenged in a number of areas of the real world.

This chapter will therefore attempt to identify how the term governance has been used in various disciplines and subdisciplines (see also Kersbergen and Waarden, 2004). After enumerating these various approaches to governance, we will proceed to identify the extent to which there is any common ground among the approaches and further what dimensions of variation may separate the approaches. The identified similarities and differences will provide a useful intellectual map of governance to inform how we utilize the concept within political science and public administration. Further, in terms of the general purpose of this book, the examination of these alternatives enables us to understand more completely the nature of governance, and particularly the interactive nature of governing in the contemporary world.

Our examination of the use of governance in other disciplines has two purposes. The first is to demonstrate the linkages among the disciplines and the manner in which similar ideas and concerns arise in these disparate approaches to governance. It is important to recognize that the concern with governance, and especially interactive governance, is not just found in political science and public administration but rather reflects some common concerns within the social sciences. The second and related purpose is to identify what we, approaching governance from the perspectives of political science and public administration, can learn from these allied disciplines to strengthen our own arguments about the importance of interactive governance.

Governance in International Relations

The study of International Relations (IR) tends to be treated differently on the two sides of the Atlantic Ocean. In the United States, the study of IR tends to be considered a subdiscipline of political science, while in Europe it tends to be treated more as an independent discipline and frequently is organized as a separate department. On both sides of the Atlantic, however, the field of IR has its own research profile, its own journals, and a rather different conception of politics from that used by scholars more concerned with national or sub-national politics. Governance has become a part of the profile of IR although the term may be used somewhat differently.

Attempting to study governance in IR confronts a fundamental paradox. On the one hand, it has been clear in much of the IR literature that in the global system there is limited capacity to govern in the manner in which we usually think of governing. That is, there are few if any sources of legitimate authority that can make binding decisions and laws, or which can enforce sanctions on sovereign countries that transgress international agreements. Thus, to some extent, the conception of governance applied in IR has been analogous to the "governance without government" approaches that have become popular for some scholars in political science and public administration. This general approach to governance in the international system (Rosenau and Czempiel, 1992) has been described as "fragmented" as it assumes that there are contra-dictory pressures for collective steering along with continuing processes of differentiation and globalization.

Although there is no hegemonic source of governance in the international system, there are some approaches that argue for the presence of at least some forms of control. Perhaps more notably, there are international regimes that control action within some policy areas, with varying levels of control (Ronit and Schneider, 2004). Some of these regimes are associated with international organizations and treaties that do provide some realistic capacity for enforce-ment, for example the World Trade Organization (WTO). The European Union (EU) may be the limiting case of this form of international governance with clearly defined mechanisms for implementation and enforcement (Köhler-Koch and Rittberger, 2006). Other regimes are more informal and based on loose arrangements among states and nongovernmental actors (Rittberger and Mayer, 1995), and may be based on common ideas rather than coercive capacity.

The importance of ideas in defining regimes points to the crucial role of common ideas and normative standards for governance at the international level. Some of these ideas and standards have had a pervasive impact on governance, and have been diffused over much of the world. The obvious case of this type of governance through ideas has been the neoliberal project.

These ideas have been propagated in part through international organizations such as the World Bank and the International Monetary Fund, but have also had an independent impact simply through their widespread political acceptance and seeming appropriateness for controlling policy choices in the face of the problems of "government overload" and "societal ungovernability." Thus, if there are no means of enforcing laws or treaties, then the second best solution may be to gain acceptance of common ideas and standards as means of guidance.

These various strands of governance in IR have merged into the literature on "global governance." Under this banner the emergence of policy problems, which are universal in scope and impossible to solve other than through global action, has fostered growing concerns about the capacity to supply truly global governance. Interactive forms of governance may in some cases offer a way out of this impasse. Hence, global environmental issues such as climate change, issues about the respect for human rights, and criminal issues such as trafficking in drugs and people are increasingly addressed through international action that tends to involve civil society actors (Scholte, 2002). Also the dispute-settlement mechanisms within the WTO have to an increasing extent involved transnational advocacy and NGOs. Finally, a large number of public and private actors work together at the intersection between the national and international level to combat global health problems such as AIDS. As is true for the national level, this kind of interactive governance at the international level can provide some level of steering even in the absence of effective government. As such, interaction between governmental and nongovernmental actors can help to mobilize specialized knowledge, pool and exchange resources, and generate joint solutions, responsibilities, and understandings.

In sum, the literature on IR has several points of connection with the arguments we have made concerning interactive governance. Given the absence of any dominant source of authority in the international system, interaction between state and non-state actors is crucial for governing global issues.

Developmental studies

Just as the study of IR is closely related to political science, developmental studies have a strong basis in political science, although they also involve contributions from a number of other disciplines such as economics, sociology, and anthropology. These various disciplines are united in their common concern with changes in less developed countries with unstable and fragmented political systems. At the extreme, developmental studies must cope with the problem of governing in failed states and developing capacities for steering even when there are few existing political or social institutions that are capable of supplying effective guidance for the economy and society.

One standard issue in developmental studies is coping with informal patterns of governance that complement, or perhaps even undermine, more formal mechanisms for governing (Helmke and Levitsky, 2004). These methods of governing are interactive, in the definitions we are using here, but do not necessarily produce the positive outcomes assumed in much of the literature on quasi-markets, partnerships, and governance networks. Thus, in developmental studies, much of the emphasis is on finding means to overcome patrimonial and clientelistic structures that are common forms of social and political organization in these countries (Piattoni, 2001a; Roniger, 2004). Although these arrangements have provided some stability within less developed countries, they have also tended to undermine the capacity of governments in those societies to make coherent decisions about steering. To the extent that governance occurs in these systems, it is a highly disaggregated, almost personalistic form of governing rather than making and implementing more universalistic and accountable forms of steering. Further, these institutionalized relationships between particular political and administrative elites and particular ethnic or socioeconomic groups may block the political and social change necessary for further development. Somewhat paradoxically, some theorists of development have stressed the need to institutionalize political structures, but in this case the level of institutionalization may be an impediment to development.

The problem of governing in less developed countries has been addressed in the international aid community through the concept of "good governance." The World Bank in particular has reversed its one-sided market economic approach to development, assuming that to produce economic growth countries would be well advised to focus first on the capacity to govern effectively. Rather than democracy and good governance following from developing effective market economies, the World Bank began to argue that for markets to function adequately, they require effective systems of governance. In particular, markets require the capacity of some external actor (usually government) to enforce contracts as well as some legal and governmental stability that will create enough predictability for the economy to function and for economic actors to make rational investment decisions.

Despite their increasing importance in allocating assistance to less developed countries, the measures of good governance are extremely suspect (Pollitt, 2010). There has been a special emphasis on the reduction of corruption in governments in the less developed countries as a means of improving their governance capacity. This emphasis may over time improve the legitimacy of governments, and thereby their effectiveness, but it is not clear that the virtues of greater probity are more important for effective steer-ing than are other elements such as fair elections, administrative and fiscal capacity, or rule of law.

At the extreme, studies of governance carried out within developmental studies have to consider the nature of "failed states" (Rotberg, 2004) and the possibilities of governing in the almost total absence of effective authority. This is a situation very different from the "governance without government" discussed with respect to the more affluent countries of Europe, North America, and the Antipodes. In the failed states, there is a genuine absence of authority, not just delegation of that authority, and governance is either impossible and absent, or provided by more or less informal negotiations among powerful civil society groups or more formal partnerships between aid organizations, local businesses, and community associations. This type of governance might take the form of interactive governance, but in contrast to the arenas of interactive governance in the affluent Western societies there is little or no public metagovernance.

As with the study of governance in IR, governance in developmental studies is often conducted in situations with limited hierarchical control. Develop-mental studies point to the capacity to provide some steering in these difficult situations. Further, this research helps to illuminate some of the limits of interactive governance and the desirability in many situations of having the capacity to produce "good governance" through more direct and formal means.

Urban politics

Urban politics is a research area, which features a distinct institutional system that almost regardless of national context or political economy seems to struggle to maintain its capacity to govern. The urban governance literature typically focuses on three features of governance. One is the political and institutional constraints imposed on cities; with massive cross-national varia-tion, cities have a limited autonomy in relationship to higher levels of gov-ernment, be it national, state, or federal government. Scandinavian cities are among the most autonomous while cities in the United Kingdom are highly constrained in terms of what they can do. This means that urban governance tends to include a dialogue with higher institutional levels in order to extract financial resources or to gain effective autonomy on some specific set of issues. This dialogue or bargaining with higher institutional levels nowadays also includes transnational institutions like the EU, and various models of multilevel governance have been outlined to capture these increasingly complex institutional relationships. Indeed, the large literature on multilevel governance that has arisen largely in relationship to the EU might well have been written concerning the role of urban areas within complex national systems of governance.

The second feature of urban governance is the predominance of private capital and corporate resources. The key forerunner to the focus on urban governance in the urban politics field in the United States was urban regime theory, which departed from the limited capacity of the city to act. In order to enhance that capacity, the urban political leadership forges coalitions with the corporate leadership. While such arrangements significantly boost the city's governing capacity, it also puts it in a complex dependency toward the corporate sector; governing capacity is purchased at the expense of political democracy and the democratic process.

The third feature of urban governance that should be mentioned here is the relationship between the city and civil society. The local level in most countries has a long tradition of territorially defined mobilization of resources, which includes not only the city proper but also, as has been noted in a number of studies, the local business community, NGOs, and the plethora of local community associations. When New Public Management (NPM) emerged as a model of public service delivery, its ideas fitted well into this tradition of cooperation across the public–private border, and it has to an extent emphasized the interactive nature of governance at the urban level. The involvement of civil society actors in urban governance is promoted by local governments aiming to mobilize resources. In the United Kingdom, the national government recently launched a nationwide campaign for the development of *Flourishing Neighborhoods* that involves the creation of local platforms for empowered participation and interactive governance.

The inclusion of civil society actors in interactive governance of local planning and development issues is highlighted by the literature on collaborative planning that departs from the recognition of the limitation of the rational and linear planning models based on quantitative extrapolations and expert judgments (Healey, 2007; Booher and Innes, 2010). As such, there was a growing recognition during the 1970s and 1980s that the comprehensive planning systems failed to cater for local needs and often created fierce opposition against new infrastructure projects. In order to create more well-informed planning and overcome policy deadlocks, the local planning practices have changed and now tend to involve a large number of local stakeholders in policy deliberation at various stages of the planning process. That said, these interactive arrangements also slow the planning process and may produce suboptimal results because of the extensive negotiations involved.

Urban governance thus looks at the role of local political institutions in facilitating governance and their particular roles in that process. In addition, there are urban governance analyses that take a broader societal view of how localities are coordinated and planned through decentered forms of interactive governance that are results of the need of local governments to mobilize private resources and secure consent. Thus, some aspects of urban governance may resemble the "governance without government" ideas that have emerged in other areas of the governance debate, although, as noted, the majority of the research has emphasized interdependencies among public and private actors. Perhaps most importantly, the research on urban politics points to the importance of vertical interaction through some form of multilevel governance.

Economics

Economics comes into play in the study of governance in several ways. Even early liberal economists such as Adam Smith argued that the rule of law and other aspects of governance were necessary for markets to perform adequately. As mentioned above, this same logic has been adopted by contemporary donor organizations and private firms that argue that "good governance" is crucial for effective socioeconomic development. These scholars may assume that constitutions, courts, and other mechanisms for governance can best be understood through economic principles (see Buchanan and Tullock, 1962). Nevertheless, they provide some place for governance in their understandings of the market.

In addition to the requirement for governance to manage the economy, the management of economic actors is also described as a form of governance. For example, the concept of corporate governance, which has often been described as one of the several alternative definitions of governance (see Demirag, 1998), has emerged in the field of business economics and is today commonly employed. Although the notion of corporate governance refers to a rather basic conception of the responsibility of business managers vis-à-vis the shareholders and to some extent also the local stakeholders, it has become more important in an era in which there is increasing discontent among the public about perceived excesses by corporations and a growing recognition of the impact of corporate governance on the performance of the economy as a whole. Thus, corporate governance has become the analog of "good governance" in developmental studies.

For the study of public governance, economics and political science have become somewhat more allied, at least among those scholars who have adopted some version of the rational choice approach to political analysis. This use of microeconomic reasoning within political science has become sufficiently pervasive that it may be difficult to isolate the two disciplines

(Lichbach, 2003). That having been said, there are two particular aspects of the economics contribution to political science and the understanding of public governance, which need to considered more carefully as we assess these multiple disciplinary perspectives.

Perhaps the most important of these contributions is the work that Elinor Ostrom and others have done on managing common pool resources such as oil, joint grazing areas, and water for irrigation that are limited and easily exhausted if all the individual actors pursue their short-term interest in maximizing their share (Ostrom, 1990; Ostrom et al., 1992). Again, this work has some elements of discussing "governance without government," as it examines the way in which these difficult resource allocation problems can be addressed without the resort to formal rules and institutional structures. In this conception of governing, rules and procedures for managing the scarce resources are argued to emerge from voluntary cooperation without the use of formal governmental interventions from the public sector.

Ostrom claims that almost all of the solutions for solving the problem of the commons involve the creation of formal rules and means of enforcement that reside outside the individuals involved in exploiting the resources. She argues that the individuals involved may, however, be able to resolve their own problems by making voluntary contracts or other binding agreements. These may also be enforced by the parties to the contract, whether directly or through hiring an agent who can monitor compliance and enforce the contracts. Her later work also points to the ways in which the participants learn to make and enforce these arrangements rather than face long-term losses from the exhaustion of the resources in question.

The other major contribution of economics to the understanding of governance is the use of the principal–agent logic to understand the management of delegated and devolved processes of governing. One of the most common features of contemporary reforms of governing has been to delegate responsibility for public functions and services to agencies within government, market organizations through relational contracts, or nonmarket organizations through partnerships agreements (Huber and McCarty, 2004). Whether through contracts, partnerships, or networks the private actors can be used to implement services and perhaps even be involved in shaping policies. This emphasis on delegation has been found in the NPM as well as a variety of "governance" approaches to public administration.

The "governance without government" literature, and a good deal of the less extreme versions of the network governance literature, has argued that the involvement of the nongovernmental actors is largely self-organizing. By contrast, the principal–agent approach assumes that there is active delegation from the public sector and that a crucial part of the task of government is to control the actions of the agents so that they conform to the wishes of the principal. Thus, as Fritz Scharpf (1997) has argued, the agents are operating in the "shadow of hierarchy" so that the principal can always retract the delegation that has been made. The economics assumptions are that agents will have incentives to pursue their own goals and that information asymmetries prevent the principal from establishing the degree to which the agents are shirking. However, if the overall result is really poor, the principal might impose sanctions or centralize service production.

In all of these versions of economic analysis in governance, the rationality assumptions of neoclassical economics are utilized to understand how collective institutions develop and how hierarchical relationships among actors function to control actions of the participants in the process. Interestingly, however, these conceptions also to some extent attempt to find means of circumventing strict rationality assumptions in order to govern, rather than merely pursuing individual interests. Thus, the economics approach to governance may be better at identifying the sources of governance problems than it is at designing mechanisms for resolving those problems (but see Calvert, 1995). That said, the emphasis on the market does demonstrate another form of interaction to that found in networks of social actors.

In summary, economics provides several alternative approaches to understanding governance, some based on institutional analysis and some more on the logic of principals and agents. Economics also emphasizes the importance of the interactions of economic actors in other forms of governance, including corporate governance and the use of market mechanisms in governing.

Sociology

The discipline of sociology does not appear to have as much to say about governance as the other disciplines being discussed in this chapter, but it certainly does have some relevance. There are at least four aspects of sociological theory that speak to the capacity to govern. The first and perhaps most obvious is social network theory. We have been discussing networks as they have appeared in political science and public administration, but much of the root of that literature can be found in sociology (see Wasserman and Faust, 1994).

The sociological literature on networks differs from that found in political science in several important ways. First, the sociological literature is less directly concerned with policy and managing public programs than it is with patterns of interaction among individuals. A second and associated difference is that the sociological literature has been more quantitative, and has developed a number of quantitative measures of the structure of interaction of networks. Some of this type of analysis has been used in political science, especially in areas such as community power studies (see Laumann and Knoke, 1987). The mapping of patterns of interaction has been used less in the study of policy networks, but it could be extremely useful in identifying how power is exercised within networks and between social networks and the public sector (see Chapter 3). All that said, the absence of content within those networks does not help to understand how the networks may actually influence policy choices and governance.

A second contribution of sociology to the study of governance has been made through its various contributions to organization theory and the new institutionalism (see March and Olsen, 1984; DiMaggio and Powell, 1991). The study of rules, norms, values, and cognitive schemes that structure organizations and their interrelations is crucial for understanding how organizations function and how they can contribute to processes of steering and control for societies. Most public sector functions are conducted through formal organizations, and indeed the private sector partners are themselves formal organizations that function as any other formal organization. Likewise, the interactions between public and private organizations also have structural features that can be understood through organization theory.

Several organization theorists have considered the impact of their approaches on governance and public policy. Indeed, the foundation of institutionalism in organization theory provides a clear linkage of organization theory to the governance of states. Further, organizational theories that focus on internal control in public or private organizations, or the management of organizational fields, have clear relevance for the analysis of governance (DiMaggio and Powell, 1991). For example, Scott (1995) among others has developed a thorough conceptualization of the nature of organizations and how they may be able to govern themselves and society.

A third contribution of sociology comes from its strong interest in the development of the welfare state and its role in legitimating contemporary governments (Esping-Andersen, 1990). Creating, maintaining, and transforming the programs of the welfare state has been a major activity for governing in most industrialized democracies, but it has also been crucial for the governance capacity of these states more generally. Further, the pressures for reforming social programs and for reducing the financial commitments of governments to social policies has provided a major governance challenge to these states (Pierson, 2000a).

Finally, the governmentality literature in sociology also has relevance for the study of governance (see Dean, 1999; Sørensen and Torfing, 2007). This literature has linked the question of governing policy and public concerns with much broader questions about how society as a whole is controlled and how power is being exercised. The question then is how to create some form of organization in societies that appear increasingly self-organizing and/or disorganized. Social networks comprise part of this answer, but the govern-mentality approach is broader, and also more diffuse, than simply social networks, as it tends to focus on the role of discourses and governance technologies for governing society and the economy. These discourses and technologies are also broader than just those in the public sector so that general social values and structures are seen as a condition for governance.

In sum, we can say that although sociology does not address the issue of public governance head on, there are several relevant strands of sociology that either provide helpful tools for studying interactive governance or help us to understand the institutional, political, and discursive conditions for governance.

Decision theory

Decision theory is less developed as a discipline than some of the others mentioned here, but it still has relevance for the questions of governance that we are discussing in this chapter. Calling this a discipline may be some-what inappropriate, given that the study of decision-making combines a number of elements of economics, psychology, statistics, and perhaps other more conventionally defined disciplines. That having been said, decision sciences do provide an important perspective on governance by asking how decisions are made and what elements are brought together to make decisions that have a reasonable probability of resolving an issue in ways that corre-spond to the demands of the participants in the process. Further, decision theory has itself been evolving to consider less well-defined problems that confront decision-makers in the public and private sectors (Ney, 2007).

The study of policymaking in relation to wicked and complex problems represents a particularly important direction of research that is relevant for the study of governance. Governance of even simple policy issues can be difficult enough (see Bovens et al., 2001), but policy issues with high levels of technical difficulty and with several feedback mechanisms are even more difficult to manage. That said, however, these problems are becoming more prevalent, as evidenced by the importance of issues such as global warming and other aspects of environmental protection.

Rather as Ostrom has argued for economics and the management of com-mon pool resources, complexity theorists concerned with governance have argued for alternative and more interactive mechanisms for exerting control. Klijn and Snellen (2009), for example, point to the possibilities of direct control and trust as alternative means of coping with the problems arising from complexity (as perhaps would be true for all governance issues). They also consider the possibilities of coevolution of the problem and the organizational solution to the problem so that a certain isomorphism between the two elements of governance emerges. However, although complexity does present a number of substantive challenges to public administration and to policymaking, much of the logic for coping with those challenges is analogous to the logic for coping with other types of issues.

The interactive forms of governance that we discuss in this book pose perhaps even greater problems for making decisions than would the risk and adversity characteristics associated with much of decision theory (see Dror, 1986; Miller and Page, 2007). Not only are the substantive policy problems being addressed complex but so too are the processes by which the decisions are being made. While one response from decision theorists might be to reduce that complexity, the political and administrative logics associated with interactive governance might make that choice less palatable. As such, decision theory may be very important for outlining the challenges to policy-making but tends to be less successful in finding solutions and in including the crucial political and participatory questions in the analysis.

Legal theory

Even in interactive governance, there is often a legal basis for the delegation of authority to the interactive arena. In the chapters that follow, the constitutional and legal basis of governance appears in a number of settings. For example, much of the regulatory approach to governing involves the use of law as the principal instrument for achieving the policy goals. Further, policy instruments such as taxation depend heavily upon the ability to create compliance with public law.

Public law is central to any understanding of government. In any effective system of governing, the rule of law is an important element in producing stability and predictability in the decisions made by governments. To some extent, however, that logic of law is associated more with the logic of formal governance institutions (see Scott and Trubek, 2002) than with the interactive approach to governance being discussed in this volume.

Law tends to establish clear hierarchical parameters for action, with some actions being legal and others illegal. While no system of law can maintain perfect controls over action, this instrument provides a basis for assessing behavior. Indeed, especially in the international arena, there appears to be a conflict between those who look to international law to establish effective regimes for governing issues such as the environment and others who consider standards and commitments produced by governance interaction among both official and less official actors to be a more effective means. For example, Bodansky (1999) sees a rather sharp conflict between the two approaches, with interactive governance undermining attempts to create the rule of law. Subsequent scholars (D'Aspremont, 2006) do not consider the incompatibility of the approaches to be so sharp, yet they do recognize the different approaches.

Although interactive governance may not appear to be the logical locus for an interest in public law, there have been developments within legal theory that do contribute to our understanding of interactive forms of governance. One of the most important contributions has been the work of Günther Teubner and his conception of "reflexive law" (Teubner, 1983). The idea of reflexive law is that rather than imposing formal standards for all aspects of social behavior, the law should be used only to establish broad frameworks within which social processes, and especially democratic processes, are allowed to flourish.

The general tenor of reflexive law can be found in other formats involving law and governance that have been developed over the past several decades. For example, the general emphasis on "soft law" as a replacement for black letter law has been found in a number of national systems as well as in the EU. At the national level, the use of instruments such as negotiated rule-making in the United States has opened up the formal legal processes of regulation to greater interaction with social actors (Freeman, 1999). Further, the use of instruments such as benchmarks and voluntary agreements in the place of command and control regulations also has made the law more interactive, procedural, and "reflexive."

At the level of the EU there have been perhaps even greater developments in the use of soft law (Mörth, 2004). These instruments have been developed in part around the Open Method of Coordination, and the concomitant involvement of the EU in policy areas over which it has rather little formal authority. The use of the soft instruments has meant that the national actors can agree to policy goals at the EU level through the voluntary agreements and then use more substantive instruments at the national level to achieve the goals. Even at the national level, however, there tends to be significant involvement of social actors in the policy implementation process.

In both reflexive law and in the discussions of soft law, the State can be seen as using its legal powers to establish a framework within which other actors will operate. There will still be legal parameters in place, but these constitute a relatively broad space within which social actors and public actors can all interact in order to govern. As already noted in several places, this may constitute governance in the shadow of hierarchy given that the State may at some point wish to withdraw its grants of power to the social actors, and also may wish to curtail the autonomy of some public sector actors. Still, until those types of decisions are made, the law can be used for enabling rather than constraining action.

The interest in softer legal mechanisms should not be taken to imply that the use of hard law is totally passé. There are still a number of elements of a hard regulatory State in place (Moran, 2002) and the public sector continues to employ its legal powers to control. Indeed, after the economic crisis beginning in 2008, the State may wish to use those powers even more frequently to control economic actors who have demonstrated their need for greater control. The monopoly of legal power continues to be a major force in governance, but one which is tempered by a number of developments within the academic study of law as well as within the law itself.

Conclusion

This chapter has considered how scholars other than those working in political science and public administration have considered the concept of governance. Although each discipline brings its own concerns and its own analytic recipes to the table, many of the issues raised and many of the answers offered are similar. Perhaps the most notable commonality is that all of the approaches being discussed raise questions about the capacity of governance to be created without the active involvement of a government, however amorphous that government may be (as in international relations). The solutions offered to how governance may be created without some effective form of governance external to the actors vary, but the concern is rather pervasive.

There was also an alternative perspective that emerged in these literatures, which was to some extent the opposite of the first. This alternative was the question of how to organize governance, and what instrumentalities might be available for steering society, the economy, and even the organizations involved in governance themselves. Thus, even the literature that has stressed trust also had some sense of organization and control (Edelenbos and Eshuis, 2009). Thus, the governance question in many settings appears to be how to balance formal and informal mechanisms for control.

Still bearing those points of commonality in mind, it is also remarkable the extent to which the different approaches arrive at some of the same questions through very different means. Those different avenues arise in part from the disciplinary blinders that we all wear, and they arise also from confronting a range of different substantive problems. Economics probably is the best example of the former source of difference among the approaches, while urban studies and international relations clearly face rather different substantive problems from the other approaches discussed.

3

Power and politics in interactive governance

If we define *power* as the ability to shape and secure particular outcomes and *politics* as the conflict-ridden decisions that are structuring and shaping social and economic relations, it seems to be clear that *interactive governance is intrinsically linked to power and politics*. First, interactive governance is about collective decision-making in institutionalized settings in which a plurality of actors with different resources and strategies are continuously engaged in political conflicts and power struggles. Second, the political struggles eventually produce policy outputs that directly or indirectly influence the governing of society and the economy. Third, the growth and importance of interactive governance makes it an object of metagovernance as governments at different levels aim to influence the processes and outcomes of networks, partnerships, and quasi-markets. Finally, interactive governance may even be seen as a particular form of power that aims to shape and regulate free and autonomous actors' self-regulation.

Grasping the power-ridden character of interactive governance is crucial in order to understand what goes on in interactive policy arenas and to grasp the mutual impact of interactive governance arrangements and their social and political context including the traditional forms of government. Neither practitioners nor public policy researchers should fool themselves into believing that interactive governance involves an unpolitical exchange of resources through a rational, consensus-seeking deliberation among policy experts and relevant stakeholders who are merely aiming to make technical and consensual adjustments to public policy or secure a harmonious coordination of the manifold efforts to implement public policies. As Robert Agranoff observes, "despite the cooperative spirit and aura of accommodation in collaborative efforts, networks are not without conflicts and power issues" (Agranoff, 2006: 57). Interactive governance involves complex power games and those who fail to understand this will not be able to maneuver successfully in the emerging world of pluricentric governance. Nor will they be helpful in ensuring that the essentially political forms of interactive governance are subjected to democratic control and assessed in terms of their democratic quality and performance (Hirst, 2000: 33).

In order to advance a realistic, political account of governance, this chapter aims to explore *how interactive governance can be analyzed in terms of power*. The basic assumption underlying our exploration is that power is not only visible in the negotiated interaction among a plethora of public and private actors who aim to influence collective decisions. Henceforth, in order to grasp the intrinsic link between interactive governance and power, we must analyze not only "power *in* interactive governance" but also "power *of* interactive governance," "power *over* interactive governance," and "power *as* interactive governance." We need to consider all the different ways that interactive governance and power are related in order to fully understand the essentially political character of interactive governance. The multifaceted analysis of the interrelation between power and interactive governance will seek to demonstrate that although traditional concepts of power can help to shed light on how power is exercised in the context of interactive governance, the interactive forms of governance also affect and transform the ways that power is exercised. Hence, just as the emphasis on power and politics changes our perception of interactive governance, interactive governance also modifies our understanding of power.

The chapter proceeds in the following way. The first section documents and explains the neglect of power and politics in the study of interactive governance. The second section analyzes the exercise of power within interactive governance arenas. The third section looks at the power of interactive policy arenas as they are influencing wider society. The fourth section envisages the attempt to exercise power over interactive governance through various forms of metagovernance. The fifth section draws on poststructuralist theories of power in order to show how interactive governance can be analyzed as a new historical form of power. The conclusion summarizes the argument and reflects on the practical and political implications of different ways of relating power and interactive governance.

The neglect of power in the study of interactive governance

The study of power was originally linked to the study of the formal institutions of government and the behavior of the governmental actors. Governments, parliaments, political parties, and what was generally known as the "ruling elite" were either perceived to be exercising power single-handedly, depending on their various resources and capacities, or were seen as targets of societal actors aiming to influence public decision-making. The American community power debate in the 1960s excelled in this kind of power studies, but since then, the advance of methodological individualism and rational choice theory has diverted the interest of the global political science community away from the fundamental studies of who holds power and how power is exercised. Instead, political scientists have focused on the rational and incentive-driven actions of individual actors who are incurring individual gains and losses while producing more or less suboptimal collective outputs. If the study of power has survived, it has been in the form of either the analysis of the division of formal and real authority in complex political systems such as the European Union or the study of the relative influence of key actors in particular decision-making arenas.

The advent of new forms of interactive governance might trigger a new debate on power as policy outputs and policy outcomes become subject to political conflicts and power struggles. However, so far there is no evidence of a revival of the American community power debate, although government sponsored research programs in the Scandinavian countries have aimed to assess the impact of societal transformations on power and democracy (for a brief overview, see Sørensen and Torfing, 2001). Public decision-makers are not concerned with the power aspects of interactive governance. Hence, Chris Skelcher and his colleagues have shown that there is almost no place for power and politics in actual discourses of partnerships in the United Kingdom (Skelcher et al., 2005). It is even more alarming that power and politics are also frequently neglected in scholarly studies of interactive governance (see Walters, 2004; Goetz, 2008). This troubling neglect is found both in studies of those forms of interactive governance, such as quasi-markets, which bring together public authorities and private firms in negotiations based on relational contracts (Ferlie, 1992; Greve, 2007), and in studies of the different kinds of partnerships and networks that involve actors from state, market, and civil society (Kickert et al., 1997; Goldsmith and Eggers, 2004; Hodge and Greve, 2005). As such, interactive governance is often depicted as a pragmatic "problem-solving" process (Kohler-Koch and Eising, 1999: 5) devoid of politics and power. Interactive governance is allegedly "recognizing the capacity to get things done" (Stoker, 1998: 24); not through the use of state authority, but through consensual deliberation and exchange among the relevant actors who are holding important information, knowledge, and other key resources. Thus, interactive governance is seen as a *depoliticized process of collaboration* guided by common purposes and technical rationalities. Opinions might differ and collective action problems are frequent, but on the whole interactive governance arenas are not perceived as conflict-ridden battlegrounds where political actors struggle over the authoritative allocation of societal values. This is particularly evident in the good governance literature where prolific slogans about "partnership," "co-responsibility," and "mutual benefits" tend to gloss over conflicts and power struggles that only feature as a potential source of governance failure (Agere, 2000; IMF, 2005; UNESCAP, 2009).

A notable exception to this depoliticized view of interactive governance is found in the work on network types of governance by leading scholars such as Fritz Scharpf (1994) and Rod Rhodes (1997a) who clearly recognize the presence of political conflicts, resource asymmetries, and power games. However, especially Scharpf is relatively optimistic about the prospect for the creation of a smooth coordination among rational actors responding to incentives provided by the institutional framework, and neither Scharpf nor Rhodes attempts to theorize the link between governance networks and power. Another important exception is found in the recent work of Miles Kahler and colleagues who explore the link between power and transnational governance networks (Kahler, 2009), but do so in isolation from the political science and public administration discussions of power and policy. Finally, it should be mentioned that those parts of economic and sociological institutionalism that focus on networks and interactive governance also make occasional references to power. However, in this literature, power is often treated instrumentally as a means to enforce contracts, achieve economic goals, or build a strong organization (see Moulaert and Cabaret, 2006).

The widespread idea that interactive governance is a kind of technical, rational, and evidence-based way of solving problems and getting things done through consensus-seeking interaction among relevant and affected actors is part of a broader *post-political vision* of contemporary society (Mouffe, 2005). The post-political vision downplays the role of political conflict and power struggles that are perceived to belong to an antiquated "modernist" quest for emancipation through collective action. Alternatively, it highlights the importance of pragmatic, managerial attempts to fix policy problems and improve the daily living conditions of individual citizens through collaborative policy interaction and partnerships.

One explanation of the post-political vision of governance is the normative celebration of interactive governance as an alternative to hierarchy and market (Moulaert and Cabaret, 2006: 52–4). Both practitioners and academics tend to view interactive governance as an attractive ideal to pursue because of its flexibility, innovative capacity, low transaction costs, mobilization and empowerment of private actors, and ability to generate trust and ownership. The preoccupation with the normative promises of interactive governance hides the real-life experiences of conflict, disruptive power struggles, and governance failures, or reduces those experiences to undesirable exceptions to the rule. The result is a systematic overlooking of political conflicts and power relations.

Another, and more practical-political, explanation of the post-political vision of interactive governance is that the concept of governance has been appropriated by New Public Management, which tends to deploy interactive forms of governance in an instrumental manner to solve coordination problems. Some commentators view interactive forms of governance as a reaction to fragmentation caused by the first wave of NPM reforms (Rhodes, 1997b). Truly, the proliferation of semiautonomous public agencies and the increasing competition among public agencies and private contractors have created a strong need for crosscutting coordination and cooperation. This need has in some cases triggered a recentering of power (Dahlstrom et al., 2011), but it has also persuaded the protagonists of NPM to include interactive forms of governance as a part of their toolbox. Hence, a second wave of NPM reforms recommends enhanced knowledge sharing, joint policymaking, and coordinated implementation efforts as means of solving policy problems and improving public services in an increasingly differentiated polity (Bogdanor, 2005; Christensen and Lægreid, 2007). The problem is that NPM reduces interactive forms of governance to managerial tools for enhancing crosscutting coordination and cooperation in the face of fragmentation and competition. In order to achieve this objective, the participating actors are often selected on the basis of a strong interdependence or even shared objectives and preferences. This instrumental use of interactive governance as a tool for smooth coordination among like-minded actors prevents an understanding of the political and conflict-ridden character of interactive governance arrangements engaged in agenda setting, strategic policy development, and implementation of innovative policy proposals. In an equally instrumental manner, the EU applies interactive governance as a managerial tool for reducing the "overload" of bureaucratic, top-down government by means of mobilizing the resources and expertise of stakeholders in and through rational, goal-oriented, and evidence-based governing processes, which endorse what Offe and Preuss refer to as a "style of ruling without an opposition" (Offe and Preuss, 2006: 9).

A third, and more theoretical, explanation is that interactive forms of governance often, and quite wrongly, are associated with civil society (Esmark, 2009). Hierarchical steering is supposed to take place within the State; competition is thought to be intrinsic to more or less regulated markets; and governance through negotiated interaction is seen as a deliberative practice emanating from civil society. The problem with the apparent association of interactive governance with civil society is that it invokes the implicit normativism of civil society that tends to characterize social interaction as processes of mutual recognition, normative integration, and consensus formation. This leaves us with an unfortunate but typical image of interactive governance as a harmonious problem-solving process that provides a welcome alternative to the systemic power of states and markets.

A final explanation is that interactive governance is often defined in terms of a horizontal exchange between different public and private actors. The term "horizontal" refers to the fact that none of the participating governance actors has the authority to resolve conflicts and disputes that emerge through interaction. However, this "horizontal" feature of governance is often misconstrued by people who take it to mean that all the actors are completely equal in terms of resources and strategic capabilities and that, therefore, no actor can exercise power over other actors (Lake and Wong, 2009: 131). A related explanation is that some commentators tend to view governance not only as an egalitarian decision-making arena but also as an arena in which the presence of a large number of actors implies a diffusion of power that invokes a kind of "power neutrality" (Doyle and McEachern, 1998).

The depoliticization of interactive governance is clearly visible in the works of Anthony Giddens (1994, 1998) and Ulrich Beck (1994, 1997) who had a strong influence on the New Labour government in the United Kingdom. Although the academic advocates of a Third Way between neoliberal marketization and Social Democratic statism do not explicitly associate interactive governance with a nonadversarial politics, they clearly invoke the image of a new kind of consensual policymaking through networks, partnerships, and public–private interaction. The first evidence of the implicit nonadversarial view of politics is that both Giddens and Beck claim that politics is no longer based on political clashes between left and right but takes the form of post-ideological problem-solving and service improvement based on individual experiences, local knowledge, collaborative interaction, and everyday experiments. The second evidence is found in the idea that the new partnership strategy will not only empower civil society but also transform the State through increased devolution, greater transparency, and enhanced responsiveness to civil society actors. Giddens goes as far as to talk about the advent of a New Democratic State defined as "a State without enemies" (Giddens, 1998: 77). The final evidence is the argument that interactive forms of governance introduce a new type of "dialogical democracy" (Giddens, 1994: 112–15). Although Giddens admits that not all conflicts can be settled through dialogue, the durable conflicts are not seen to lead to antagonistic conflicts and clashes among political adversaries because people will learn to live "along with each other in a relation of mutual tolerance" (Giddens, 1994: 115).

The depoliticization of governance is also visible in the works of James G. March and Johan P. Olsen (1989, 1995) who are much more relevant for studying public governance than Giddens and Beck. In their seminal book *Democratic Governance*, we learn that interactive governance involves the actions of individuals and collectivities that occur within shared meanings and practices, which can be understood as institutions and identities (March and Olsen, 1995: 30). Through processes of political socialization and normative integration, social actors come to define themselves in terms of their identities and to accept the rules of appropriate actions associated with those identities. When the actors are interacting in institutional arenas of democratic governance, it is paramount to create a sense of solidarity that connects individuals to the political community, and to civilize conflicts by sustaining norms about empathy, generosity, and patience and securing political processes based on reflection and discourse (March and Olsen, 1995: 60). While March and Olsen's account of rule-governed action provides a sound alternative to rational choice theory, their persistent emphasis on shared meanings, solidarity, and the civilization of conflicts paints an overly harmonious picture of interactive forms of governance. Governance is about developing the identities and capacities of political actors. It involves developing joint accounts of political events and developing an adaptive political system by facilitating mutual learning (March and Olsen, 1995: 44–7). This normative institutionalist perspective on interactive governance clearly downplays the role and impact of power, which is a term that is seldom used in March and Olsen's manifesto on democratic governance.

The post-political vision of interactive governance is unfortunate as it prevents us from grasping its political and power-ridden character. Portraying interactive governance as a consensual and pragmatic tool for providing "motherhood and apple-pie" will surely create a lot of disappointment when people encounter the conflict- and power-ridden reality of interactive governance. It also makes it difficult to understand and manage the political conflicts and power games implicit to interactive governance. An even greater problem caused by the post-political vision of governance is that interactive forms of governance tend to be exempted from democratic demands. Hence, if interactive governance arrangements are considered to be unpolitical and devoid of power, there is no reason for making a fuss about their democratic performance and scrutinizing their democratic quality (Hirst, 2000: 33).

By contrast, we shall argue that interactive governance arenas are ridden with political conflicts and power struggles not only because of the lack of a joint utility function or different pay-offs among the actors involved in interactive governance (Scharpf, 1994), but also because social and political actors tend to create identity through opposition, that is, through the construction of friend–enemy divisions (Laclau and Mouffe, 1985; see also Coser, 1956). However, the recognition of the conflict- and power-ridden character of interactive governance does not necessarily mean that interactive governance arrangements are characterized by damaging antagonistic conflicts and bitter and irreconcilable struggles between enemies seeking to eliminate each other. There might be examples of antagonistic conflicts and destructive battles, but this will not be typical in the context of interactive governance as resource interdependencies and emerging institutional rules will tend to transform enemies into adversaries who are contesting each other's views and actions within a common frame of reference and on the basis of generally accepted rules of the game (Mouffe, 2005).

Our exploration of the intrinsic link between power and interactive governance is based on the analytical observation that the study of conflict and power within interactive governance arenas is important but does not exhaust the analysis of power in relation to interactive governance. Therefore, the analysis of the exercise of power *in* interactive governance will be supplemented by an analysis of the power *of* interactive governance, the power *over* interactive governance, and the historical articulation of power *as* interactive governance. As we shall see, power is conceptualized differently in the four different analytical approaches to analyzing the interrelation between power and interactive governance. Moreover, in each of the four approaches, the exercise of power is affected by the interactive governance mechanism on which it is brought to bear. As such, the different concepts of power not only prove to be relevant for studying interactive governance, but the study of interactive governance also suggests important modifications and developments in the study of power.

Power in interactive governance

Political science has developed a number of conceptual tools for analyzing the exercise of power in interactive forms of governance. Power is most often defined as "power over," referring to attempts to affect the actions of human agency in order to secure a certain outcome. Steven Lukes' seminal essay (1974) on the three faces of power is a clear example of this conception of power. In his account of the first face of power, Lukes invokes Robert A. Dahl's famous definition of power (1957) as the successful attempt of an individual or collective actor A to make another actor B do something that B would not otherwise have done. Here, power is conceived as an intentional behavior that makes it possible for A to prevail in open conflict with B (direct power). In his account of the second face of power, Lukes refers to Peter Bachrach and Morton Baratz's argument (1970) about how A can exercise power by regulating and controlling the political agenda in order to hide conflicts by suppressing proposals and decisions promoted by B (indirect power). Lukes himself adds a third face of power by showing that A can also exercise power over B by manipulating B's subjective perception of his or her interest in order to align B's perceived interests with A's objective interests, thereby avoiding conflicts altogether (ideological power).

Some scholars argue that Lukes' actor-centered conceptions of power need to be supplemented by a discourse-theoretical conception of power in order to capture the way that more or less institutionalized discourses shape the overall conditions of action of both A and B by forming their identities, interrelation-ship, vocabularies, rationalities, and world views (Foucault, 1990; Dyrberg, 1997; Torfing, 2009). Despite the ontological differences between Lukes' actor-centered concepts of power and the structure-centered discourse-theoretical notion of power, the four conceptions of power tend to complement one another. Whereas the first three faces of power capture the different ways actors exercise power over other actors, the "fourth face of power" captures the way that the actions of all these actors are structured and shaped by institutionalized meaning systems. Lukes flirted with the idea of introducing a more structural notion such as a fourth face of power but decided against it because of his strong adherence to a Kantian ethics. However, if we grant that institutional structures are ambiguous and unstable and never present social and political actors with a fait accompli, we can still retain the idea of human responsibility.

The exercise of *direct power* in open conflicts about concrete decisions is quite frequent in interactive governance arenas as many social and political actors will seek to influence collective decisions in order to pursue their interests. However, there are two important caveats that we should consider. The first caveat is that big, formal decision moments are relatively rare in interactive governance arenas as the actors seldom rely on voting but tend to continue their formal and informal negotiations until decisions appear to mobilize a general support despite minor dissents and grievances (Sørensen, 2007a). Of course, direct power can also be exercised in long-stretched and relatively informal processes of bargaining and deliberation, but in such processes the exercise of direct power becomes more difficult because the actors will not know when to mobilize their resources and authority in order to prevail in open conflicts. The decision-making process is blurred and consists of many small decision moments. In this situation, resilience, timing, and luck might prove to be just as important as the possession of resources and authority.

The second caveat is that the strong and resourceful actors are constrained in their exercise of direct power by the exit power of the weaker actors. Deploying all your strength and resources to put pressure on weaker actors will often appear to be counterproductive as participation in interactive gov-ernance is voluntary and the pressurized actors are free to leave the network (Lake and Wong, 2009: 130). The exit of some marginalized actors will prevent exchange and pooling of resources, ideas, and energies and may undermine the legitimacy of the networked policy solutions. Exiting an interactive gov-ernance arena will prevent the exiting actor from influencing the policy decisions, but if the actor is feeling marginalized, the loss is negligible and the exiting actor may still be able to enjoy the benefits of a negotiated solution. As such, the costs of marginalized actors leaving an interactive policy process will often be higher for the stronger than for the weaker and marginalized actors.

Indirect power aiming to control the political agenda as well as *ideological power* aiming to influence other actors' perception of their interests seems to be more important in interactive governance than the exercise of direct power. The agenda in interactive policy arenas is often quite open, and indirect power strategies seeking to control it therefore become crucial for securing particular outcomes. The exercise of indirect power is also encouraged by the fact that many interactive policy arenas are committed to preventing the eruption of open conflicts because the actors fear that open conflicts will prevent compromise formation and jeopardize the prospect of future cooperation. Likewise, the actors' interpretations of their interests are often ambiguous and malleable, and the attempt to influence the perception of other actors' interest through ideological power is, therefore, a decisive means for generating support for one's own ideas and proposals (Koppenjan and Klijn, 2004). The exercise of ideological power is also motivated by the actors' search for common ideas and reference points that can help to ensure that the centripetal forces balance out the centrifugal ones. The search for cognitive consonance tends to make the actors susceptible to the propagation of storylines aiming to provide a common and simplifying understanding of problems and solutions.

The actors engaged in interactive governance processes may try to influence each other and advance their interests through actions and inactions pertaining to the three faces of power described by Steven Lukes. However, the different power games among the actors are often framed and structured by more or less institutionalized discourses that define what is considered as valid knowledge, what can be talked about how, when, and by whom, what are the normative premises for formulating and selecting joint solutions, and what are the rules governing appropriate actions and exchanges in the interactive arena (Sabatier, 1988; Fisher and Forrester, 1993; Hajer, 1993, 1995). To illustrate, it has been shown how negotiation and compromise formation in a national policy network on employment policy were facilitated by a hegemonic storyline and some generally accepted decision-making premises that clearly marked out the terrain within which the policy solution was going to be found (Torfing, 2007a). Although the discursive structures framing policy interaction are both intentional and unintentional results of social and political agency, they are neither master-minded nor controlled by any privileged agency. The discursive framing of interactive governance processes emerges through a gradual codification and naturalization of ideas resulting from political battles for political and moral–intellectual leadership. Nevertheless, the discursive structures are often taken for granted by the policy actors who tend to become discourse takers rather than discourse makers. This does not mean that the actors are deprived of effective agency as the actors are capable of exploiting conflicts and ambiguities in discursive rules, norms, and vocabularies and selectively invoking some aspects of the available discourses rather than others. As such, even though the concept of *discursive power* has a structuralist origin, the actual effects of structural power are always mediated by social and political agency.

Accepting that social and political agency play a critical role in all four faces of power, although less so in the structural framing of policy interaction, it becomes paramount to assess the participating actors' ability to prevail in open conflicts, control the agenda, influence perceptions, and invoke different interpretations of discursive rules and norms. The standard political science approach to making such an assessment is to look at the actors' individual resources and capabilities and explain these in terms of the underlying socioeconomic structures and mechanisms that generate material inequalities and cultural disparities (Held and McGrew, 2002). Drawing up a structurally induced resource profile of individual or collective actors will help us to determine their strategic capacities and their ability to exercise power either through hard-nosed bargaining or through persuasion based on metaphorical redescriptions, manipulation, or personal charisma. However, when analyzing power in interactive governance arenas where the actors become nodes within a relational structure, this attributional approach to the study of power must give way to a more relational approach that relates the capacities and power of the actors to their position within a relation system (Kahler, 2009: 12). As such, the interactive governance paradigm calls for an expansion of the narrow dyadic view of power advanced by Lukes and an adoption of a multi-actor view of power.

Social network analysis highlights two forms of relational power that both emphasize the structural position of actors in wider networks of actors: bargaining power and social power (Kahler, 2009: 12–13). *Bargaining power* increases when an actor, or node, is well connected to other actors who are otherwise weakly connected. Such a relational position provides leverage through the threat to severe links and exclude actors from the interactive arena or the promise to consolidate or expand the network by strengthening particular links or forging new ones. It also permits an actor to control the flow of information, narratives, and discursive artifacts. A certain kind of bargaining power is achieved when a particular node provides the sole link between two or more clusters of well-connected nodes. Such a relational position turns an actor into a powerful broker who can steer and control interaction by shaping the form and content of negotiations.

Social power is another variant of relational power in interactive governance that derives from the centrality of particular actors or nodes. The underlying assumption is that social power is determined by the social capital of an actor.

The more links that an actor has, the more knowledge, experience, trust, and reach it will have, and thus the greater impact it will have on the policy interactions in the network as a whole. For example, the Danish government hosted the UN Climate Conference in Copenhagen in December 2009, and the many bi- and multilateral contacts to governments, experts, and NGOs prior to the conference gave the Danish government much more bargaining power than it would otherwise have had, being one of the smallest EU countries. As such, its social power was augmented, although not enough to control the complex negotiations and lead them to a successful result.

The relational view on social and political actors' ability to exercise power in interactive governance arenas is an important supplement to the traditional attributional view on agency power. The next step consists in analyzing how the various actors mobilize their differing capabilities in interactive processes of bargaining and deliberation, and exploring how the actual interaction is shaped by the political context (see Kriesi et al., 2006).

Power of interactive governance

When talking about the power of interactive governance, we treat the interactive policy arenas as more or less unified actors with access to particular resources and analyze their ability to govern society and the economy, influence their immediate social and political environment, and shape the decisions of governments at different levels (Stone, 1989; Kahler, 2009: 5). As such, the power of interactive governance involves both a "power to govern" through the capacity for joint action and societal regulation and a "power over government" through the capacity to affect governmental decisions and regulations. Hence, when studying the power of interactive governance we are interested in the way that negotiated interaction in quasi-markets, partnerships, and networks influences the formulation and implementation of policy. In other words, we should be focusing on the particular attributes of interactive governance arenas that seem to condition their political impact and power.

The societal and political impact of interactive forms of governance seems to depend on their life cycle (Lake and Wong, 2009: 133). In their embryonic phase, networks, partnerships, and other forms of interactive governance are very fragile as there is little reciprocity, high transaction costs, limited administrative support, unclear rules for interaction, and persistent conflicts about the scope and content of policy negotiations. Therefore, collective action is difficult and the overall impact of interactive governance is limited. By contrast, consolidated governance arenas with a stable regulative and normative foundation, strong administrative support, trust-based interactions, and a high degree of positive coordination are more likely to produce collective action that affects the governing of society and the political decisions of government. Later on, highly consolidated governance arenas may lose their momentum as they fulfill or outlive their original mission, fail to create new interdependencies, or no longer provide net benefits to the participants. In the following discussion of the power of interactive governance, we will focus on the factors determining the impact of relatively consolidated forms of interactive governance.

There are no general rules about which attributes of interactive governance are likely to produce a high impact on the external environment. Nevertheless, it is possible to identify a number of factors that under certain circumstances and in particular contexts are likely to enhance the political influence of interactive governance arenas.

The particular way that interactive governance arenas are *designed and institutionalized* plays a crucial role in determining their impact. This is well established in the literature on policy networks that distinguishes between loosely connected, unstable, relatively inclusive, and imbalanced *issue networks* and strongly integrated, stable, relatively exclusive, and well-balanced *policy communities* (Rhodes, 1997a). Although the distinction between issue networks and policy communities is mainly based on differences in terms of interdependencies and resource distributions, it is implicitly assumed that the distinction between the two kinds of policy networks also hinges on how they are institutionalized. In policy communities, interaction among the highly interdependent actors is supported by sedimented rules, norms, and values that tend to create a tight and unified structure, whereas in an issue network there is only a weak institutional underpinning of the interaction among the less interdependent actors and the result is a much more sporadic interaction and the persistence of diverging interests. The institutionally conditioned difference between issue networks and policy communities seems to have an important impact on their ability to shape policy outcomes. Hence, whereas the tightly knit policy communities are capable of blocking new public policy initiatives and ensuring policy continuity, the loosely integrated issue networks might facilitate consensus building between public and private actors and thus lead to policy change (Marsh, 1998; Thatcher, 1998). A good example of the former is the agricultural policy community in Britain that underpinned a policy of high production and high subsidies for more than fifty years (Marsh, 1998: 11). A good example of the latter is the issue network formed in relation to the need for deepening the Scheldt Estuary in the Netherlands. In a situation in which the Dutch and Flemish governments had failed to bring about a new solution, the issue network created a generally accepted plan for regulating the Scheldt Estuary (Buuren et al., 2007).

Scalability defined as the ability of interactive governance arenas to rapidly expand their membership at relatively low costs without fundamentally changing their organization is another crucial factor determining the power of governance (Kahler, 2009: 15). Transnational networks with a high degree of scalability will be powerful if their influence relies either on mass mobilization, as in case of the transnational Make Poverty History networks (Yanacopulos, 2009), or on the spread of particular normative, technical, or regulative standards, as in the case of European management education networks (Hedmo and Sahlin-Andersson, 2007).

Adaptability defined as the ability of governance arrangements to transform their institutional design and incorporate elements of hierarchy in response to shifting political demands or changing environments may also affect their capacity for effective collective action (Kahler, 2009: 15–16). For example, an interactive governance arena that needs to increase information exchange and facilitate mutual learning might want to adopt a highly decentered network model. By contrast, an interactive governance arena that aims to advance certain ideas or interests through negotiation with national governments in an international organization regulating global trade might want to strengthen its core nodes or introduce an element of hierarchical organization in order to enhance its operative capabilities and exercise of leadership. Shifting from one mode of interaction to another mode of interaction will enhance the interactive governance arena's capacity for goal attainment, but it requires a high degree of adaptability.

The *legitimacy* of the institutional forms of interactive governance is also likely to determine the power of interactive forms of governance. There are three important sources of legitimacy in interactive governance (Scharpf, 1999; Grote and Gbikpi, 2002). First of all, interactive governance arenas may derive *input legitimacy* from the composition of the participants. In some cases, the inclusion of all the relevant and affected actors will enhance legitimacy, whereas in other cases, the inclusion of what are considered as appropriate actors in terms of the social partners, private business, or scientific experts will do the trick. Second, interactive governance arenas can derive *throughput legitimacy* by showing that the internal policymaking processes have lived up to commonly accepted normative ideals about fairness, responsiveness, and transparency. Third, interactive governance arrangements can derive *output legitimacy* from providing desirable, useful, and promising policy solutions or from earning a reputation as a successful mechanism of governance or trouble-shooting. A high degree of output legitimacy can sometimes compensate for the lack of input and throughput legitimacy (Scharpf, 1999), but in the long run, interactive governance arenas require some degree of input legitimacy through inclusion and representation of relevant and affected actors.

Last but not least, *expediency* in terms of the inclination of governments to avoid large-scale conflicts and ensure program ownership enhances the ability of interactive governance arenas to put pressure on governments and force them to accept negotiated policy outputs. When presented with what appears as a carefully calibrated compromise aiming to solve a wicked policy problem, most governments will tend to succumb and accept the compromise without trying to open what might be a Pandora's box.

The listing of the different attributes that under certain circumstances will enhance the power of interactive governance should not hide the fact that this power also depends on the political environment and the form of government. As such, it seems clear that political systems with a strong tradition of participatory governance and corporatist involvement, a fragmented and devolved political system with many access points, and multiparty systems based on coalition governments will tend to enhance the impact of interactive forms of governance. In such systems, there are many points and instances where interactive governance arenas can emerge and gain access to government, and attempts to influence government will be considered as legitimate. Conversely, etatistic, unitary, and centralized political systems based on one-party majority governments will tend to mitigate the impact of governance. Bob Jessop refers to the effect that different state forms have on the formulation and realization of particular governance strategies in terms of the "strategic selectivity of the State" (Jessop, 2002).

Analyzing the power of interactive governance is an important complement to the analysis of power in interactive governance. Interactive governance arenas are often multitiered, unevenly developed, and heterogeneous, but in so far as they constitute a tendentially unified whole, we must analyze and assess their political impact on the governing of society and the economy as a form of power. Focusing on the power of interactive governance might give the impression that interactive governance produces a power effect on its external environment that mitigates the power of other key actors such as the elected government. However, we do not believe that the impact of interactive governance and traditional forms of government is a zero sum game. More often than not, governments will be able to do things that they cannot do alone by mobilizing, facilitating, and directing interactive forms of governance.

Power over interactive governance

Interactive governance is on the rise, but the processes of negotiated interaction are constantly shaped and regulated by governments at different levels that aim to exercise power over interactive governance. Governments increasingly rely on interactive forms of governance, although there is considerable variation between countries and policy areas. They initiate, facilitate, and manage interactive governance processes, but they also seek to influence what goes on in the interactive governance arenas and aim to lead the interactive policy processes in a certain direction. Governments, and other resourceful and legitimate actors, aim to exercise power over interactive governance. However, as they cannot do so through top-down commands, decrees, prohibitions, etc. that risk undermining the self-organizing aspirations of the interactive governance arenas in question and give rise to fierce resistance from the participating actors, they have to rely on different forms of *metagovernance* that aim to shape and influence governance arenas in subtle and indirect ways (see Chapter 7).

The power of governments to open up and close down interactive governance arenas in relation to different policy issues is significant. Governments have the power to convene public and private actors who are relevant for different policy concerns. These actors are willing, or even anxious, to participate given that governments have substantial resources. Furthermore, social actors are reluctant to be absent when important decisions are made in their specific area. Just as governments can initiate interactive governance, they can also terminate and close down interactive policy arenas, although not without resistance and political costs (Scharpf, 1994).

Regulating the access to interactive governance arenas is a crucial metagovernance tool for governments that seek to influence the process and outcome of interactive governance. Metagoverning the inclusion and exclusion of actors is paramount in strengthening and weakening particular interests and voices in quasi-markets, partnerships, and policy networks (Edelenbos and Klijn, 2006; Schaap, 2007). If governments cannot control the negotiated interaction in governance arenas, then at least they can secure certain majorities and prevent particular actors from participating and causing trouble. However, power over interactive governance through the metagovernance of access can only be gained when governments at different levels act as the initiator and convenor of the participants in governance. As soon as the interactive policy arena is established, the ability of governments to control inclusion and exclusion fades. Sometimes, this loss of control can be compensated by a selective empowerment of particular actors or by giving certain participants veto power in the negotiations.

Another way of exercising power over interactive governance through metagovernance is by *constructing the agency* of those participating in interactive governance arrangements (Triantafillou, 2007). In relation to traditional forms of government, the citizens are constructed as subjects, clients, or voters and private organizations and enterprises are depicted as pressure groups. When recruiting actors to interactive governance arenas, they must be

63

interpellated in a different way as they are expected to deploy their resources, energy, and free action in the production of public value within a framework. As such, the actors in interactive governance must on the one hand be hailed as resourceful, capable, and free and on the other hand be constructed as rational, interdependent, and responsible. This molding of the identity and logic of appropriateness of the actors in interactive forms of governance is surely an exercise of power as it tends to affect the way that the social and political actors interact. For example, hailing the central labor-market organizations as "social partners" might spur the development of cooperative rather than competitive games in national negotiations about labor-market reforms.

Governments can also exercise power over governance by *framing the negotiated interaction that takes place in various governance arenas*. Governments can construct or invoke a particular legal and normative framework. They can apply a particular funding scheme, provide administrative resources, and create economic incentives. They can formulate overall policy goals and tell stories about the role and mission of the interactive forms of governance (Sørensen and Torfing, 2009). Although such a framing of governance is a rather blunt instrument of power that does not permit any detailed steering of the interactive governance process, it provides a nonintrusive way of defining the parameters for negotiation and policy exchange. Governments frequently put pressure on governance arenas to adhere to overall policy goals and mission statements by threatening to use the government's power to veto solutions that are considered to be out of line. This can be done in very subtle ways, for example by letting the public know that the government is convinced that policy interaction will not produce outputs that divert from the remit and therefore have no political future. However, governments are here playing a dangerous game as there is no guarantee that the governance actors will follow the more or less subtle instructions.

Assessment of the performance of interactive governance arenas and the participating actors is a way of exercising power over interactive governance that reinforces the construction of free and responsible actors and reasserts the political and discursive framing of the interactive governance process (Damgaard and Torfing, 2010). By monitoring and assessing performance of the individual actors and the governance arrangement as a whole, everybody is reminded of what they are supposed to be doing. The interacting governance actors know that they are observed by government and that their performance will be scrutinized and either rewarded or penalized through "naming and shaming." As such, it is not important whether the performance assessment is completely accurate, as the governance actors will look at themselves through the eyes of the government, or some other metagovernor, and tend to shape, correct, and even censor their conduct so that it is more or less in accordance with the official norms, goals, and indicators.

Finally, it should be mentioned that governments can also exercise power over interactive governance by *changing the overall architecture of the interactive policy arenas* by creating new ones and closing down old ones; by energizing certain arenas while putting other arenas on hold; or by integrating or segmenting arenas in order to broaden their focus or prevent conflicts and obstacles caused by an overly broad and complex policy agenda (O'Toole, 2007). This kind of juggling around with interactive governance arenas can be very efficient from the point of view of governments, but this type of metagovernance will often be met by fierce resistance and strong criticism from the interactive governance arenas that are being marginalized.

The above listing of ways of exercising power over governance through metagovernance is by no means complete, but it well illustrates that governments are not rendered powerless in the face of the proliferation of interactive governance. Governments, as well as other would-be metagovernors, can influence the process and outcomes of governance in subtle ways that do not revert to statist forms of repression, although the power over governance often relies on a more or less explicit threat that government will take over if the interactive forms of governance fail to deliver (Scharpf, 1994). However, as pointed out in Chapter 7, the ability of governments and other actors to exercise power over interactive governance through different kinds of metagovernance is not only conditioned by their different attributes but also determined by their nodality, that is, their relational position vis-à-vis the actors participating in the governance arrangement in question. In order to gain centrality, the metagovernors will have to develop relatively close links with the various governance actors and offer information, knowledge, and other forms of relevant support. As such, metagovernance will use hands-on strategies as well as hands-off strategies in order to create and sustain a central position in relation to interactive governance arenas.

Power as interactive governance

Poststructuralist theories of discourse are not content merely to analyze the exercise of power "in," "of," and "over" interactive governance but go one step further in suggesting that, today, power is increasingly exercised in and through interactive forms of governance and that we should therefore analyze power *as* interactive governance. Interactive governance is conceived as a particular historical form of power that has become dominant in advanced liberal societies in which governments aim to "govern at a distance" through the mobilization and inclusion of free and autonomous actors in more or less self-regulating governance arenas (Rose and Miller, 1992).

The poststructuralist view of governance as a certain way of exercising power at a particular point in history is advanced by the French philosopher Michel Foucault (1991) and his followers. In his archaeology of knowledge, Foucault (1972) analyzed the discursive conditions for the production of statements. Later, with the development of his genealogical method, he began to study how discourses are shaped and transformed through a myriad of power struggles (Foucault, 1986a). The genealogical turn led Foucault to reject the classical association of power with repression (Foucault, 1990). Instead, he emphasized the productive aspects of ubiquitous power strategies. In response to his critics, who are claiming that the notion of power as a discursive production of identities, meanings, and relationships eliminates individual freedom, Foucault developed a theory of governmentality that claims that power presupposes freedom and increasingly aims to shape free actions (Foucault, 1986b, 1991; Rose, 1999). Power presupposes the capacity of social and political actors to act freely, but it aims to shape the way that this freedom is exercised in order to ensure conformity with a hegemonic set of goals and norms. By defining power as a "way in which certain actions may structure the field of other possible actions" (Foucault, 1986b: 222), Foucault aims to escape the choice between "power over" and "power to." Power is neither the capacity to do, consume, or destroy things nor simply a relation of domination (Foucault, 1986b: 217–19). For Foucault, power is first and foremost the structuring of a more or less institutionalized field of possible actions that subsequently may empower certain actors and create relations of domination and subjugation.

Foucault (1986b) equates power with "government," which he defines as the "conduct of conduct." Playing on the double meaning of the term "conduct" in both the French and English language, "the conduct of conduct" refers to practices through which the current and future actions of free and resourceful actors are mobilized and shaped in accordance with some overall goals and norms. As such, Foucault's notion of government as the "conduct of conduct" clearly transgresses the classical understanding of government as the sovereign power exercised by elected politicians and public administrators. Government is basically a process of "subjectivation" in the double sense of shaping identities and forms of subordination and control. The historical conditions of a particular form of government are captured by the notion of "governmentality" (Foucault, 1991). Governmentality is defined as the institutionalized mentalities, calculations, and technologies that circumscribe our collective understanding of how to govern and be governed. As such, governmentality is an "art of government" that conditions concrete "acts of government" (Dean, 1999).

Governmentalities are transformed through problematization of the existing governmentality. Such problematizations will trigger political struggles to form a new governmentality program. The liberal governmentality emerged in the eighteenth century as a part of a new kind of biopolitics that constructs the population as the primary object of regulation. Before that, the State had merely been preoccupied with defending its territory, collecting taxes, and building the infrastructure of society. New social statistics revealed a number of problematic tendencies and effects in the rapidly growing population that could not be adequately governed within the framework of the family. In response to this problematization of the regulatory capacity of the family, the regulation of the population was increasingly seen as a task for the State. The social welfare of the population should be enhanced through an elaborate system of state interventions based on statistical information and expert knowledge and carried out through a combination of bureaucratic rule, comprehensive planning, and a host of disciplinary and normalizing technologies targeting different sections of the population.

In the Western world, the welfare state was expanded throughout the nineteenth and twentieth centuries, until the deep economic recession in the early 1970s led to a fiscal crisis that threatened to bring the expansion of the welfare state to a halt. The crisis of economic stagflation paved the way for a neoliberal revolution in the 1980s. Neoliberal governments claimed that the welfare state was too big, rigid, and inefficient, and called for the expansion of the free market forces through privatization and contracting out of public services and commercialization of the remaining public sector. The consecutive, but uneven, waves of marketization in the 1990s reveal that "more market" does not necessarily lead to "less State." Private markets need to be governed and regulated in order to remove institutional and political barriers to market competition (see Vogel, 1996) and construct the individuals as rational, calculating, and risk-taking entrepreneurs (Rose and Miller, 1992). The failure of the neoliberal governmentality program to reduce public expenditure and alleviate the burden of the State has prompted the development of a new form of advanced liberal government.

Advanced liberal government introduces a more reflexive governing of society and the economy that carefully considers how different tasks can best be solved (Dean, 1999). Is it through the imperative command of public authorities, through an increasing reliance on the free market forces, or through the construction and regulation of free and responsible actions of self-regulating citizens, communities, firms, partnerships, and networks? The latter options point in the direction of a proliferation of interactive forms of governance where public and private actors have shared responsibility for governing social and economic relations on the basis of negotiations, contracts, standards, and performance management.

The governmentalization of the State through the gradual involvement of the State in the government of the population and its welfare resulted in a displacement of the dominant power strategy of the State (Foucault, 1991). Previously, the citizens of the feudal State were subjected to a *sovereign power* based on centralized authority, laws, prohibitions, and physical punishment. In the administrative State, which emerged in the transition to modern liberal society, power was increasingly exercised by the deployment of *disciplinary techniques* aiming to create docile bodies through institutional regulation of corporeal behavior in time and space and *normalizing practices* aiming to shape and regulate the soul by means of defining what is normal and what is pathological. Later, with the mounting emphasis on the government of the population by the State, power was increasingly exercised by subtle attempts to *mobilize and shape the freedom of individual actors and target groups* on the basis of institutionalized goals, standards, and norms specifying how this freedom should be exercised and what its exercise should accomplish.

In the field of active employment policy, we find many examples of this kind of interactive governance and power through the mobilization and shaping of freedom (in the research literature, this is often analyzed in terms of the deployment of "soft law"). Hence, the employment guidelines, which are formulated by the EU as a part of the open method of coordination (OMC), construct the member states as obliging policy entrepreneurs aiming to enhance the "employability" of the laborers, preferably in cooperation with the social partners. National campaigns for Social Corporate Responsibility hail private business firms as socially responsible benefactors aiming to combat exclusion from the labor market. Finally, local workfare policies interpellate the unemployed as subjects and objects of active offers of education, training, and therapeutic counseling aiming to enhance their motivation and ability to return to gainful employment.

Conclusion

In this chapter, we have aimed to counter the unfortunate tendency in much of the governance literature to assume that interactive governance arenas provide a power-free zone in which technical or consensual solutions are found through rational or deliberative processes that do not produce any notable dissent, opposition, or adversaries. Moreover, although it is tempting to focus merely on the obvious in terms of the exercise of power among the social and political actors involved in interactive forms of governance, we have insisted on taking a broad and multifaceted approach to the study of governance and power that not only endeavors to analyze power "in" governance but also analyzes power "of," "over," and "as" interactive governance. We believe that this broad approach to the study of power and politics in interactive governance captures many more aspects of power than are usually envisaged in the relatively few studies on governance and power. Indeed, by focusing on "power of" and "power over" interactive governance, we are able to connect interactive governance to traditional forms of government and to assess the governing capacity of interactive governance arenas. Furthermore, by focusing on interactive governance "as power," we open up for historicization of the exercise of power and the collective understanding of how to govern and be governed.

At the conceptual and analytical level, we have found that the different perspectives on power and interactive governance invoke different notions of power and that the analysis of interactive forms of governance challenges and changes our conception of how power is exercised. The analysis of "power in" interactive governance focuses on how certain actors exercise power over other actors and the analysis suggests that interactive forms of governance tend to prevent strong and resourceful actors from abusing the power that they possess because of the exit power of marginal actors who may decide to leave the governance arena. The analysis also urges us to transgress the dyadic view of power that is found in the seminal works of Steven Lukes and adopt a multi-actor view that emphasizes the relational positioning of actors in wider actor networks. The study of the "power of" interactive governance defines power both as the power to govern and as a power over government and lists different political and institutional attributes that help explain the power of interactive governance. This kind of analysis is important if we want to learn more about the factors that determine the political and societal impact of interactive governance. The examination of "power over" interactive governance aims to analyze power in terms of influence and domination, but recognizes the limitations that the self-regulatory aspirations of interactive governance arenas impose on the exercise of power through imperative command. Indeed, the analysis shows that power over interactive governance is best exercised through subtle and indirect attempts to structure and shape the interactive governance arenas. Finally, the analysis of "power as" interactive governance aims to escape the choice between "power to" and "power over" by defining power as the actions that structure other possible action through the construction of particular sets of rules, norms, identities, and calculations that shape the interactions of a plurality of social and political actors in advanced liberal societies. This analysis introduces a new decentered conception of power that conceives power as a complex strategic situation in which social action and inaction are shaped by institutional technologies that recently have tended to emphasize "the regulation of self-regulation."

The practical and political implications of a closer analysis of the different interrelations between interactive governance and power are clear. Understanding the exercise of power among a plurality of actors in particular governance arenas draws our attention to the repertoire of power strategies available to relationally positioned governance actors, and points out the limitations to the exercise of direct power in open conflicts. Grasping the various determinants of the power of interactive governance helps us to explain why some governance arenas are more influential than others. Appreciating how power over interactive governance can be exercised through the deployment of different forms of metagovernance enables governments and other would-be metagovernors to shape and influence the process and outcomes of interactive governance. Last but not least, the conception of power as interactive governance tends to historicize the exercise of power in liberal societies and highlights the subtle ways that power presupposes, crafts, and shapes the free actions of individual and collective actors.

The normative implication of the analysis of the many ways that interactive governance and power are interrelated is perhaps the most important. The recognition of the political and power-ridden character of interactive governance means that the analysis of the democratic implications and performance of interactive governance becomes an urgent task. Democracy is a normative standard that we apply to political arenas and situations in which society and the economy are regulated through the exercise of power. Perceiving interactive governance as a power-free realm of reasoned debate and technical and consensual decision-making would exempt it from democratic scrutiny. However, the intrinsic link between power and interactive governance urges us to assess and improve the democratic performance of interactive governance arrangements (see Chapter 10).

Whereas government and power are close companions, the study of the intrinsic link between power and interactive forms of governance has just begun. Future research must continue to explore the different ways that power and interactive governance are related and provide detailed empirical studies of how power is exercised in interactive governance arenas; how interactive governance arenas can influence government and contribute to the governing of society and the economy; how legitimate and resourceful (public) actors can exercise power over interactive governance through metagovernance; and how power is exercised in and through governance technologies that shape the way that we govern ourselves and others.

4

Measuring governance

As the term governance has become used more commonly in both the academic and practitioner communities, it is only natural that the individuals interested in the concept would attempt to find some ways of measuring the concept. There have been some notable attempts to develop indicator systems for governance (see Kaufman, 1999; Bertok et al., 2006). We will argue, however, that these existing indicator systems have substantially less utility for academics interested in governance as an intellectual concept than they have for international organizations, especially donor organizations attempting to facilitate political and socioeconomic development. As is often the case, the generality and the high levels of aggregation tend to disguise the underlying processes involved.

Some of the indicator systems being used by the World Bank and United Nations, among others, focus on the internal management of governments, as well as their accountability institutions. For example, the indicator system for governance advanced by the World Bank (Knack et al., 2003) has forty-five indicators that cover a range of public sector activities and some aspects of the performance of government (or of the political–economic system). These indicators all say something about the performance of the political system, and have the virtue of being aggregate indicators that are available from official or semiofficial sources.

Despite the virtues of the indicator systems that have been developed, they do not appear to capture the essence of governance. As we will discuss below, governance at its most basic level means the capacity of actors (both official institutions themselves and those operating in concert with social actors) to set and pursue collective goals, and secondarily to do so in a democratic manner. Therefore, these existing indicator systems, as important as they may be for assessing many aspects of development, do not assess effectively the goal-setting and process attributes that, we will argue (see below), are central to understanding governance.

In addition to the difficulties in measuring governance per se, there are perhaps greater problems involved in measuring interactive governance. In addition to the issues involved in the capacity to influence the economy and society, there is the need to understand how interactions with social actors are involved in these processes. This may therefore involve greater concern with processes as well as with the most basic issues of the consequences of governing.

Conceptualizing governance

Conceptualization must always precede measurement (Sartori, 1970), so before we begin to think about measuring governance we will need to be sure of the meaning of the concept itself. This sequence of intellectual activity is especially important for a complex concept such as governance, which involves multiple actors and multiple activities, and also has been subject to considerable intellectual debate (see Stoker, 1998; Pierre, 2000; Pettai and Illing, 2004). Indeed, there are a range of alternative definitions of governance that could have almost contradictory implications for understanding the process and therefore for measurement.

That having been said, if an approach to contemporary political science is to have any power, both in absolute terms and relative to contending approaches, it could be measured. Given the generality of governance approaches, there is the danger that they become like structural-functionalist or systems approaches that once dominated comparative politics. Governance theory is in essence a functional theory, arguing that the function of governing must be performed and then determining what structures perform this function, in what manner, and how well. These approaches, like governance, were sufficiently general to cover almost any type of political system but were also rather vague and proved to be impossible to measure in any meaningful way and likewise proved impossible to falsify.

We will be arguing that in its most fundamental conceptual sense, governance means steering the economy and society toward collective goals (Pierre and Peters, 2000). This social function has traditionally been allocated to the formal institutions of government, and although contemporary conceptions of governing tend to emphasize the importance of nongovernmental actors in governance, the public sector must remain a central element for steering. For purposes of measurement, the central role of formal public institutions may be in establishing the goals, or at least in validating collective goals established through other processes. Identifying collective goals is especially important for governance studies because they constitute the standards against which the outcomes of policymaking must be judged.

This book is focusing on the interactive aspects of governance; therefore, we must also be concerned with the extent to which these basic governance functions involve interactions with social actors. Further, we need to assess the extent to which aspects of governing are altered because of the involvement of the social actors. That in turn involves making choices about what the basic process of governance would be, and then what the independent impact of interactions would be.

From simplicity to complexity in conceptualization, and in measurement

In discussing the measurement of governance, we will begin with a very simple, indeed too simple, model of governance based on hierarchical government, and then muddy the waters substantially. The muddying will be the result of attempting to include a wider range of actors in the process as well as recognizing the dynamic and adaptive nature of any successful governance system. Finally, we will attempt to offer some thoughts about ways out of the extreme complexity that results from attempts to make the model of governance more or less isomorphic with the complexity of the process of governing itself.

The simple model

It would be easy to make an analogy between governance studies and implementation studies in that they both could take instances in which the actors involved did not reach goals, or did not implement policies, exactly as intended by the "formators" (Lane, 1983) to represent failures of the process. This case is somewhat easier to make for implementation, however, than for governance. If the implementors are conceived as the agents of the lawmakers, whether they be legislatures or bureaucracies or even the courts, then the failure to implement as intended represents some agency loss. Thus, Pressman and Wildavsky's seminal work on implementation (1973) assumed that the program needed to pass through each of the dozens of "clearance points" unscathed for good implementation to be occurring, and this model in essence was the basis for measuring implementation.

The simplest approach to measuring governance is to accept the analogy with implementation and to examine the extent to which the actions taken by the public sector, or its agents, conform to the goals that have been selectedthrough the political process. Such an approach to measuring governance does provide a relatively unambiguous conception of governance and therefore *perhaps* an equally unambiguous means for measuring governance.

This conception, and the associated measures, also can be associated with ideas about the success and failure of governance (Bovens et al., 2001).

We emphasized the word "perhaps" in the above paragraph because this seemingly simple and unambiguous means of understanding governance contains a number of important problems. The first of these arises from the ability, or inability, to define the goals being pursued in the process of governance. Goals rarely are defined in legislation or government statements in a way that would make them necessarily measurable. The stated goals of policy may be "motherhood and apple pie," stating very general, non-contentious, and pious hopes for the future without clear standards against which to measure the achievement of the goals. Virtually any outcome that is not totally negative can then be made to appear to be goal achievement, and hence successful governance.

Goals also occur at a number of levels. A government may state its goals for its term of office, and in many coalition systems may have to agree on those goals as a part of the negotiations to form a government. For example, a new Finnish coalition is mandated to produce a coalition statement with basic policy intentions as well as a program statement listing the major crosscutting priorities for the government. But beneath that level, individual ministries will have goals, generally now made more explicit in their own management documents and programs, and smaller organizations will also have their own goals. Which of these goals should we be concerned about for governance, and how should we manage the cascading of goals that occur (see below on performance management)?

The specification of goals does not end, however, with the official actors in the governance system because social actors involved may have their own goals that they are pursuing through their involvement with public programs. While the pursuit of those goals may be treated more appropriately in the following section of this chapter, they are relevant here in that they represent one more addition to the large and complex array of goals that may be pursued in any particular set of governance decisions.

Although the goals of policy are important, so too are the means through which the policy is to be achieved. Certainly, in a democratic system, citizens may want to have some influence over the instruments through which governments function, and (in a good garbage can manner) means may shape ends as well as ends may shape means. Further, the availability of means may influence the ability of any actor to have an issue placed on the active agenda of the governance system—if there is no feasible means of pursuing a goal that goal will be ignored. Finally, means may be crucial in defining the ability of the governance system to achieve its goals in an efficient manner, or perhaps achieve them at all.

The above having been said, the performance management movement in government has tended to make programs, and governments as a whole, specify more clearly their goals. The specifications tend to be related to measurements, and one of the standard critiques of performance management is that the indicators used do not capture adequately the complexity of the goals involved (see Bouckaert and Peters, 2002). Some performance management systems, such as those used in New Zealand and Canada (OECD, 2007), differentiate between broader strategic goals of the governance system as a whole and the lower-level, operational goals of the organizations.

In summary, governing is about the pursuit of goals. Therefore, to be able to measure governance we need to be able to specify the goals being pursued, and also understand that there are multiple goals being pursued by numerous actors within the public sector. The specification of goals becomes all the more complex once we take into account the actors involved in interactive forms of governance, for example, networks or partnerships, and attempt to integrate those goals with the already large range that may be operative in the public sector.

Increasing complexity: Accepting the multiplicity of goals and actors

Even for implementation, however, the sense of a top-down process was softened substantially by ideas such as "backward mapping" (Elmore, 1978)—meaning that it was desirable to identify what policy interventions were the most feasible and then design policies around that understanding. This rather formalistic conception of success and failure may not make a great deal of sense given that most legislation is written in the form of enabling laws rather than in terms of "tamper-proof legal instruments," with the expectation that a certain amount of discretion will be exercised as the framework for a program is fleshed out through implementation. Thus, the discretion granted to numerous employees in the public sector street-level bureaucrats as well as more senior officials (Meyer and Vorsanger, 2003; Page and Jenkins, 2004) often leads to the meaning of the program being defined as it is being implemented rather than by its formal goals.

For governance, the rather simplistic conception of defining success and failure through the achievement of clearly and precisely stated goals may not be appropriate. First, as already noted, modern governments do not tend to make highly specific legislation but rather tend to draft enabling legislation expecting the bureaucracy or other actors to fill in the details as needed, and to be flexible in response to changing circumstances. Further, the instruments that contemporary governments use are increasingly of the "New Governance" variety, relying more on negotiation than on command and control (Salamon, 2001). These "soft laws" do not require point compliance but rather tend to specify broad bands of acceptable outcomes, allowing the participants to develop their own means of achieving the ends.

Thus, a conceptualization of contemporary governance, and especially democratic governance, must reflect a balance between at least two concerns. The first of these concerns is some sense of the "primacy of the political" in governing. That is, the actions of representative democratic institutions have substantial legitimacy and citizens may expect that the policies adopted by those institutions will be put into effect as planned. As noted, these institutions may be considered especially important for defining the goals to be pursued, although in contemporary governance those goals may be somewhat loosely defined.

The second set of concerns about governance represents the changes in contemporary governance defined in part above. In democratic terms, these represent expansions of the conception of democracy to include an ongoing capacity for public involvement, whether phrased in network terms (Sørensen and Torfing, 2007) or in even more direct forms of democracy (Smith, 2009). In this conception of governing, democracy does not end when representative institutions complete their actions, and indeed in this conception of governing the bureaucracy may become a central feature in democracy. Thus, the goals that social actors bring to the process of negotiation have, if not the same level of legitimacy as those posited by the representative institutions involved, at least sufficient legitimacy that they cannot be dismissed a priori.

As well as reflecting democratic values (see below) and legitimation capacity in governance, this more complex conception of governance as involving adjustment to the actors involved also may serve efficiency values. As noted, the more traditional conception of governance tended to assume that changes in programs or policies inherently meant that the process had failed. Those conceptions of failure were to some extent defined by normative criteria, for example, conservatives concerned about "regulatory creep" or "bureaucratic creep," and the expansion of public action that is not authorized in legislative language (Hutter and Jones, 2007).

A further complicating factor for the simplistic model of governance presented above is that the multiple organizations involved have multiple and often conflicting goals and, therefore, some capacity for coordination or prioritization must be involved in governance. We must assume that the goals of all the actors involved in governance cannot be pursued simultaneously, but to be able to assess the success or failure of the processes we need to understand something about the priorities and the relative weighting of the goals. In the end, the choice of goals may depend strictly on political power, and that attribute must be factored into the understanding of how goals change and the legitimacy of the changes.

If we can accept that some deviations from initial goals and/or procedures are permissible or even desirable in governance, we must then ask if all deviations are equal. And rather obviously they are not. That is, some deviations from stated goals and procedures reflect the legitimate concerns of relevant actors, or reflect an understanding by the organizations charged with implementation concerning better ways of delivering the programs in question. On the other hand, however, movements away from the stated intentions may occur as the result of corruption, regulatory capture, or the domination of bureaucratic (reflexive) objectives over the "official" policy objectives.

Accepting the more complex assumptions about contemporary governance as involving multiple actors, multiple goals, and relaxed standards for defining goal achievement does reflect reality, but it also makes the measurement process more difficult. The identification of a goal and the comparison of the products of governance processes with that goal provide a clear, if only dichotomous, standard for governance, while accepting that goals are changed or even discovered during the process, and that some latitude that is required for the participants in the process to alter the goals makes governance virtually unfalsifiable.

The apparent need to discover the nature and sources of deviations from a presumed path set by goals in governance leads toward methodologies, such as process tracing (George and Bennett, 2005) and qualitative comparative analysis (Rihoux and Ragin, 2008), for being able to understand governance. As noted above, much of the effort at developing indicators for governance has concentrated on aggregate indicators that can be gathered readily for a wide range of countries. The methodology implied here, however, is more qualitative and more focused on individual decisions and understanding political interactions involved in pursuing the collective goals discussed above.

Governance as a continuous activity

Much of the above discussion of governance considers it as a discrete activity, with a goal selected through some political process and a set of outcomes that can be assessed by the extent to which they conform to the original goal. Even when the more complex version of governance is adopted, governance tends to be considered as a set of discrete actions. This model of governance is perhaps acceptable when considering just the implementation of a particular policy project, but it is inadequate for studying governance processes when conceptualized as a process of social steering. This legalistic conception is especially questionable given the argument above concerning the primacy of politics, and the importance of political criteria at all stages of the policy process.

Governance might therefore be better conceptualized as a continuous and adaptive process, with a strong element of feedback and learning involved. As has been noted earlier about public policy, most governance activities are not discrete but involve ongoing processes of bargaining, learning, and adjustment (Hogwood and Peters, 1982). This conception of governance is therefore, to some extent, in contrast to the path dependence logic of historical institutionalism that assumes the persistence of policy paths once established (Pierson, 2000*b*).

The adaptive conceptualization of governance is hardly a recent invention. Karl Deutsch's *Nerves of Government* (1963) was an elegant conceptualization of a cybernetic process in which governments would respond to their own actions and adjusted their policy choices to reflect what had happened in previous cycles of policymaking. Although not very clear about measurement, Deutsch used the concepts of lag, lead, and gain (derived from cybernetics) to describe the extent to which governments were able to respond to changes in their environments and to learn from their own actions (see also Vickers, 1965; Sabatier and Weible, 2007).

Unfortunately, while intellectually appealing, the Deutsch cybernetic model of governance is very difficult to operationalize. There may be ways to use aggregate data, for example public spending or revenue data, to examine attempts of governance systems to respond to their environments, but again qualitative methods may be more appropriate to trace the processes by which these systems respond to their environment and to their own previous actions. Further, we can assess the extent to which these systems have developed the institutional capacity to respond to their environment and to learn effectively.

The above discussion has emphasized that the measurement of governance, given the conception that we have adopted, will have to be more qualitative. Even if we could develop the nominal classifications "governance" and "non-governance," moving to ordinal or interval levels of measurement would be even more problematic. Despite those difficulties, thinking in those terms is important for making the governance literature more compatible with the large majority of the contemporary social sciences that emphasize quantitative methodologies and rigorous measurement of the key concepts. So long as discussions of governance remain almost entirely at the verbal level, they are not likely to become central to the social sciences, although certainly the capacity of a society to govern itself is a key concern for both the social sciences and for real societies.

First, catch the dependent variable, but then what?

The above discussion of governance and the pursuit of goals may help to clarify the measurement issues for governance (at least from our perspective), but it may appear to be a dead-end street for systematic research on governance. The emphasis on cases and process tracing does not yield the convenient interval level measures of our "dependent variable" that most of the discipline now deems necessary for acceptable political science. That having been said, however, the development of qualitative techniques for aggregating case study materials will enable testing hypotheses and making some generalizations.

Even if we do have a dependent variable, we have not yet done very much to specify the independent variables that may be important for understanding the capacity to govern (see Painter and Pierre, 2006). These variables may be institutional, political, or may reflect the governability of the society in question. Therefore, as the process tracing and other qualitative methods are applied to the cases, again assuming the definition posited above, some attention must be paid to the possible independent variables.

Types of governance and measurement

Measuring governance also becomes at once easier and more complex when we apply adjectives to the term, and seek to identify important aspects of the more general concept. For example, the World Bank and other international organizations have been concerned with developing "good governance" in developing and transitional governments (Kaufman, 1999). By this term they have meant primarily the reduction of corruption and to some extent the improvement of administrative efficiency. There are some reasonable measures of corruption available that do provide a picture of differences among systems and changes across time. Likewise, other scholars have been concerned with democratic governance (Sørensen, 2006), and are able to measure (albeit not without massive academic debates) the concept of democracy in governing. Another example of this tendency to qualify the term governance is the research on "informal governance" (Christensen and Piatonni, 2003), implying that governance is conducted through actors and processes outside formal government.

The more important question, however, is whether those terms used by the World Bank measure "good governance" or whether they better measure the less grandiose concepts such as reducing corruption. Both conceptually and operationally, it is also important to distinguish governance from other related concepts. For example, much of the discussion around this concept has implied that governance has numerous similarities with the usual conceptualizations of the policy process (Jones, 1984). Governance certainly does use policy as the principal mechanism for steering, but governance is a substantially broader concept and involves a wider range of action and actors.

Likewise, advocates of "good governance" (Kaufman, 1999) employ conceptualizations and measures that focus on political and administrative corruption. Minimizing corruption is certainly an important value, but it should be considered as a conceptual and measurement exercise in its own right, rather than as measuring governance per se.

Dimensions of interactive governance and measurement

As we move from the conceptual level to more operational levels, there are several dimensions of interactive governance that can be used to understand this general concept better. These dimensions represent moving from relatively simple process questions to more complex questions of actually delivering governance and being capable of steering the society. While examining the processes is important and does tell us a great deal about how governance occurs, in the end the real question is how well are those actors involved in governance—both public and private in most contemporary settings—capable of providing direction?

Processes

The easiest component of interactive governance to identify, although perhaps not to measure, is the processes that are associated with that style of governing. The measurement here involves not only the success and failure of the process but also identifying who the participants are and what difference the involvement of different actors may make. We have already argued that one of the most important aspects of governing is establishing goals for the society. Further, there is a sense that governing requires not only goals but also goals that are reasonably compatible and coherent so that there is an integrated vision of governing and some common direction. Richard Rose (1974) once described government as "directionless consensus," but the problem often is government by nonconsensual directions, and a failure to develop goals that cut across individual programs or organizations.

Thus, one indicator of governance is how readily identifiable are the goals of the political system. It may be easy to find political statements of goals that are intended largely for public consumption, but it may be substantially more difficult to find clear statements of intentions and goals for a government. As well as identifying goals, governance requires bringing information and expertise to bear on the problems that are being considered. While the public bureaucracy is often a major source of this expertise, this is also one part of the process in which nongovernmental actors may have a major role to play in providing alternative sources of evidence, and perhaps especially evidence that is less attainable for official actors, for example the reactions of the clients of programs.

Then, at a next stage of a process of governance, we must ask to what extent are the multiple goals that exist in the political system harmonized and integrated? Governments have any number of policy areas in which they must attempt to make policy, but it can be argued that governing requires some attempt to create coherence. Creating coherence becomes all the more difficult when stakeholders have different goals, and goals that cut across conventional organizational boundaries in government. Thus, processes of coordination may be crucial for creating not only unified policy responses but also efficient mechanisms for addressing the issues facing government.

Given the above, measuring interactive governance processes is extremely difficult (Tilly, 2001). It means identifying the internal mechanisms within government, and between government and the private sector, that can translate demands on the system into effective outcomes. As well the basic process of governing, implementation, or the translation of the programs of the public sector into action becomes crucial. Again, this may be complicated, and possibly facilitated, by the involvement of nongovernmental actors. There is already a substantial literature on implementation that does not require repeating here (see Winter, 2003). Implementation is important, however, not only for its obvious impact on the success or failure of public governance but also because this is the stage of the process in which the social partners tend to be involved most legitimately.

Outputs

At a second stage, we will want to ask about the extent to which the processes mentioned above produced the capacity to govern, or a set of intermediate outputs that could then be related to actual governance. One of these outputs may be the institutionalization of revenue collection and other intermediate capacities required for governance. Some political systems encounter significant difficulties in raising revenue from personal or corporate taxation, and therefore must rely on indirect taxes or fees for services.

In addition to the capacity to raise revenue, governance also requires building a substantial legal and regulatory capacity. If the actors responsible for governing have legal instruments at their disposal, they will be able to govern with greater ease than if they have to invest in other instruments that use money or organization to deliver. The importance of legal instruments, however, also points to the dynamic elements in governance. The capacity to govern with legal instruments to a great extent reflects the legitimacy of the governing arrangements within the society, but on the other hand that

81

legitimacy depends in part on how well and how efficiently governance has been conducted in the past.

Outcomes

At the final level we might want to measure the outcomes of the governance process. What has happened in society as a result of the interventions of government and the social actors involved with the efforts to govern? As noted, much of the activity of international donor organizations has been directed at this variety of measurement. Have the goals established through the processes established above been achieved in reality, or do social and economic forces dominate over the attempts of the nominal political authorities to create a collective vision on the society? These and related questions about the consequences of the formal and informal arrangements that exist for governance are central to the measurement of governance. The basic measurement question for governance, therefore, is whether governance has been successful, and indeed whether governance, in terms of steering, has actually occurred.

Intellectually, we might begin with entropy or anarchy as the antithesis of governance. The complete incapacity of a political system to govern would be associated with the type of chaos observed in some less developed countries, or periods following war, for example in Iraq in 2004. Even though such absolute levels of chaos may not be observed often in real life that is a standard against which to compare the levels of guidance for society observed. At the other end of this dimension, we might envisage some form of totalitarian society in which there is little or no autonomous choice, whether for individuals or for social groups, and there is an attempt on the part of a dominant State to control all aspects of life.

Some elements of the contemporary governance literature argue that governance of the type that we are using as the standard here is less and less possible, given the increasing mobilization and influence of social actors. Further, it is also argued that the (primarily) top-down version of governance we are discussing is also not desirable on normative grounds, given the (presumed) capacity of more open forms of governance to involve social actors and enhance the democratic nature of governance.

If we refer back to the process ideas about governance, we can begin to develop measures of outcomes based on those indicators of the processes through which governance occurs. One can then, for example, assess at the end of the mandate of a coalition government the extent to which the goals that were articulated by the coalition were achieved. Likewise, if achieving policy coherence is an important component of an adequate policy process, then some attempts at measuring coherence are important.

The potential danger in relying on measures of governance that are based on the process stages, however, is that reaching *any* decision may be considered to be sufficient to say that governance has occurred. We would, however, argue that governance has not occurred unless the decisions taken are clearly moving toward predetermined social targets and have some real chance of reaching those targets. Alternatively, we might want to establish several levels of governance, with decision-making that largely reflects and maintains existing relationships being ascribed a somewhat lower level in a hierarchy than governance decisions that do move the society toward articulated social goals.

As well as the achievement of substantive goals, such as fulfilling an agreement among network partners, there are also other, more transcendent, outcomes from governance processes. For example, more effective governance may imply the capacity to innovate and to introduce new forms of policy. Perhaps the most important of these outcomes is the creation and maintenance of legitimacy for the existing governance system. Legitimacy is usually discussed with reference to the government per se, but for governance the legitimacy question must also refer to the total set of governance arrangements designed to steer the society. Thus, although academic analysts, and many of the participants in these governance arrangements, may consider them appropriate and desirable, if they are not legitimate among the public as a whole, then it is difficult to argue that governance has been successful. This distinction also reflects the difference between substantive and political success in Bovens et al. (2001).

Normative criteria

Finally, in addition to the empirical questions about governance, we should advance some questions about normative criteria for assessing governance. In particular, while there is a normative element to governance, it is important to distinguish between the empirical and the normative in the analysis. The notion of "good governance" that has been advanced by international organizations has an empirical element. There is, however, also a strong normative element in the use of corruption as a negative indicator of governance. The use of democracy as a crucial attribute for governance also has a pronounced normative basis (Sørensen, 2006).

Democracy is a crucial value for the analysis of politics and government, but unfortunately may not be central to a concept of governance per se. We can conceptualize governance as occurring with or without democratic inputs into the process, and perhaps in efficiency terms governance occurring more effectively with one or the other. Still, in normative terms we should be concerned with the openness of the process to democratic inputs. The involvement of democratic input is especially interesting in the context of the conception of governance as a continuous process, with democratic institutions potentially providing more effective means of adjusting to change.

Further, while democracy is a crucial value in governing, there may be other equally important values that should be considered in governance. For example, fairness and equity in the outcomes of governance processes are important means of assessing the quality of governance processes. Governance, and perhaps interactive governance, therefore balances a number of important values and attempts to design processes that can produce the most desirable outcomes.

Conclusion

This chapter has explored the conceptualization of governance, and the consequences that alternative views of governance may have for measurement. If the conceptualization advanced in this chapter is accepted, then many of the indicator systems presently available are not very useful for measuring governance. Rather than developing aggregate indicator systems, if governance is conceptualized as pursuing goals through a political process, then measurement of necessity becomes process-tracing and the use of qualitative methodologies to determine how decisions are made as governance systems attempt to govern.

The complexity involved in governance is ramified when the continuous and repetitive nature of governance is considered. This conceptualization is realistic but makes tracking the process and understanding the involvement of multiple actors all the more difficult to identify in a definitive manner. Attempts to simplify governance by adding qualifying terms like "good" or "democratic" can ease one aspect of the tasks involved in studying governance but may, at the same time, limit the utility of the concept as a broad approach to political science.

5

Horizontal, vertical, and diagonal governance

State-centric models of governance tend to focus on the role of political and administrative institutions and interactions among those institutions. This is because institutions harbor political power and control. Although that governance perspective typically argues that the sources of political power, and indeed the power of the State, are changing, states still control considerable power and resources. In interactive governance, on the other hand, agency is not directly tied to institutions or institutional levels, but criss-crosses among levels. Participation is defined by stakes, interests, knowledge, resources, and networking capability. Agency takes place in contextually defined governance arenas like networks, partnerships, or quasi-markets. Thus, while all models of governance stipulate some form of interaction, the trademark of interactive governance is its contextualization and informality of those interactions.

Interactive governance must be understood in its institutional and dimensional context. As discussed in detail previously, interactive governance denotes a process of steering and coordination that involves a plurality of actors. That process features connections either among actors at the same institutional level, or among actors operating at different institutional levels. In more complex cases of interactive governance, the vertical and horizontal dimensions are both present and jointly shape the process and outcomes of governance.

Given the interactive nature of governance, institutions become less important as carriers of political authority and instead more important as arenas for interaction. Interaction is driven by a search for valuable resources and commonality in terms of interests and objectives. This search is not confined to official channels of communication. Just as is the case in contemporary public administration and public management, interactive governance is about results much more than upholding a process. Actors are not constrained by formal rules when they engage actors with whom they can develop networks. Thus, interorganizational relations, and also the relationship between politicians and bureaucrats in horizontal governance, are not primarily characterized by command and control, but rather by shared beliefs, inter-dependency, and cooperation.

In vertical governance, on the other hand, the political center may not necessarily command regions and cities, but rather may only define the rules of the governance process. Vertical governance in this perspective is thus basically metagovernance, regulating inter-local interactions. Alongside these institutional roles and relationships, issue-specific forms of vertical gover-nance are frequently conducted by networks of politicians, bureaucrats, and stakeholders at different institutional levels of the political system. The above having been said, however, interactive governance may also occur with subnational governments interacting with the central government. Further, social actors may use subnational government as the locus for their involvement with the state. Thus, the interactive element may involve a variety of different forms of interaction with multiple points of access to the governance process.

Moreover, in interactive governance the horizontal–vertical distinction loses some of its significance and meaning as interaction is not defined strictly by hierarchy or other formal competences. The two dimensions still clearly matter although not so much in terms of how they define principal–agent relations but rather because they accord actors different roles and resources. Instead of horizontal or vertical governance, it is common to see patterns of "diagonal" or "zigzagging" governance as is the case when subnational bu-reaucrats and central government politicians exchange authority, knowledge, and expertise on matters of policy design. A similar pattern is found when local elected officials engage civil servants in central government, for instance to lobby for particular policies or to mobilize resources or to convey informa-tion about policy outcomes at the local level (Gustafsson, 1987). Both of these types of "diagonal" or "zigzagging" interactions are common in contemporary governance, yet our thinking about governance is still to a large extent shaped by the traditional models of vertical and horizontal institutional relationships. We will return to this issue later in this chapter.

These discrepancies between map and reality are exacerbated by the growing tendency for cities and regions to escape domestic institutional constraints and forge transnational coalitions with other cities or regions (Hobbs, 1994; Beauregard, 1995; Betsill and Bulkeley, 2004; van der Heiden, 2010). Again, thinking of cities and regions not as subnational but as international actors involved in global governance calls much of our previous understanding about the significance of domestic institutional arrangements into question and is at the same time a valid reflection of actual processes (Dannestam, 2008). As governance becomes less contingent on the formal nature of exchanges and interactions among a wide variety of actors, previously important distinctions between central and local, between politician and bureaucrat, and between public and private lose some of their significance in terms of how they structure governance. Instead, governance becomes a matter of sustained exchanges and the regulation of those exchanges in a metagovernance perspective.

In all aspects of governing, there is a complex relationship between institutions and actors where institutions both constrain and facilitate agency, which in turn and over time drives institutional change. Both horizontal and vertical governance are characterized by a mixture of public and private actors involved in steering and coordination. The analytical focus in the interactive governance perspective is on the mobilization and coordination of actors with a stake in a particular issue or set of issues. This perspective has several important consequences for our understanding of governance. One such consequence is the aforementioned moderate interest in formal institutions; they matter but more in terms of the resources they possess than in terms of their formal authority.

Additionally, focusing on actors and the interactions among them increases the importance of time and context. While institutions are perennial features of governing, actors come and go depending on their assessment of, and interest in, specific issues. Thus, interactive governance departs from context to a much greater extent than most other analyses of governing and governance; context defines to a large extent which actors will be involved and the type of interactive governance arrangement that evolves. Also, both vertical and horizontal governance depart from a constitutional blueprint—a metagovernance model defining the formal relationships among the actors—and in both types of governance that blueprint provides only the official version of how governance is organized. In interactive governance, the constitutional roles for public actors become contextualized. Formal patterns of command and control have less leverage than those formal rules suggest. Instead, there is an emphasis on negotiation, bargaining, information, encouragement, and reciprocity in the pursuit of collective goals. Indeed, the definition of those collective goals changes, too, as the cast of actors in governance changes.

The chapter departs from analyses of vertical and horizontal governance. It then proceeds to show how interactive governance transcends these formal models, both in the multilevel governance perspective and also in the more complex diagonal governance model. Multilevel governance should be seen as the interactive version of vertical governance; in the multilevel governance model, agency is not derived from institutions at particular levels of the political system but is propelled by shared meanings and objectives across those levels. This means that agents form networks and partnerships across institutional levels. Similarly, in horizontal forms of governance, interactive governance suggests that the public–private distinction becomes less significant in designing governance whereas proximity, localization, and shared problems and resources define new casts of governance actors. As interactions become increasingly important in both vertical and horizontal governance, the structuring role of institutions is weakened and agency-driven forms of collaboration become alternative frameworks of governance.

The fundamental argument we develop in this chapter is that the interactive governance approach uncovers complex patterns of formal or informal interactions that are essential to governance but which we otherwise would not have observed. This applies to both vertical and horizontal governance. Most importantly, interactive governance helps us understand "diagonal" or "zigzagging" forms of governance integrating horizontal and vertical patterns and processes of governance. The chapter first discusses the conventional models of vertical and horizontal governance, then brings in the interactive governance to elaborate on these dimensions and ends by discussing diagonal forms of governance.

Vertical governance: From intergovernmental relationships to multilevel governance

The overall argument advanced in this book is that the interactive governance perspective offers a new and more encompassing paradigm to understand policy, political and social agency, and institutions compared to more traditional accounts of governance. Vertical governance is perhaps the best example of the potential of this new paradigm. Conventional analyses of the relationship between central, regional, and local government were to a large extent preoccupied with constitutional mandates and the formal aspects of those relationships. Policy studies were often fragmented and tied to a particular level and could not—with few exceptions (Hjern and Porter, 1981; Sabatier, 1986)—observe the flow of resources, authority, and agency among different institutional levels. Even so, however, these accounts of policymaking and implementation are typically cast in traditional, top-down models of unilateral interaction. For instance, it is intriguing to see how Pressman and Wildawsky (1973) in their seminal study on implementation uncover the pathologies in the process of transforming federal programs to local action, but they do so with a rather static conception of intergovernmental relationships as their benchmark.

Much of the governance literature defines vertical governance as those processes of steering and coordination that include central government's interactions either downward with regions and local authorities, or upwards with transnational institutions such as the European Union (EU) or the World Trade Organization (WTO). However, vertical governance can also refer to relationships between a city and neighborhood organizations or informal networks. More traditional analyses of vertical governance typically focus on the formal relationship between institutions at these levels. The interactive governance perspective suggests that these relationships are less ordered than constitutional rules dictate. Instead, policy ideas, resources, knowledge, and influence flow both upward and downward in the institutional system and sometime bypass particular levels.

This perspective is typical to multilevel governance, which offers a more challenging and complex account of vertical governance (Peters and Pierre, 2001, 2005; Hooghe and Marks, 2003; Bache and Flinders, 2004; Smullen, 2010). Multilevel governance is a more interactive way of looking at vertical governance as it opens up for nonhierarchical relations among institutions and the inclusion of a wider group of actors. For instance, while traditional analyses of intergovernmental relations assume, explicitly or implicitly, that subordinate institutions follow directives and decisions made higher up in the hierarchy, the multilevel governance perspective suggests that institutional relations are frequently negotiated and renegotiated and that indeed policy frequently evolves in a bottom-up fashion (Rhodes, 1986; Gustafsson, 1987).

In a similar vein, Meier and O'Toole (2006: 16), observing preference aggregation, decision-making, and implementation in a governance perspective argue that "the governance perspective treats these three functions not as a linear progression [...] but rather as a set of inter-related and temporally overlapping functions." This perspective on the relationship between formal institutions and procedures on the one hand and political agency on the other speaks very much to vertical governance as well. Thus, in the interactive governance perspective, the institutional and functional attributes of a political system are believed to be relevant to an understanding of how that system works, but real-world agency may frequently divert from those formal arrangements.

All developed states have some form of division of tasks or functions between the political and administrative center and subnational government. The more specific arrangements vary obviously as reflections of the unitary or federal nature of the state and the tasks of the public sector. From an interactive governance perspective, these arrangements define formal roles and competences and the relationships between those roles. We will now look at potential conflicts in those role definitions in terms of formal jurisdictions accorded by institutions at different levels. We will then discuss the internationalization of subnational government and, further along that perspective, the growing importance of multilevel governance, as examples of the decreasing role of institutions in structuring governance.

Overlapping jurisdictions

One important dimension of intergovernmental relationships is the degree of jurisdictional overlap between different institutional levels. Different countries and even different policy sectors in the same national context display substantive variation with regard to the degree of overlap in terms of tasks and jurisdiction between different institutional levels. If there is significant overlap between the central and local government jurisdictions in a particular policy area, there will not be very much discretion for local government and that, in turn, constrains their ability to become engaged in governance. That having been said, however, overlapping jurisdictions also open up pathways for local government to shape the policies they are to implement. Thus, in the language of urbanists, a high degree of overlapping jurisdiction reduces the horizontal autonomy of cities, but may serve to increase their vertical influence (see for instance Gurr and King, 1987; Pierre, 1994). By the same token, when there is little overlap in the jurisdiction, cities have very limited means of shaping policy, but on the other hand they are less constrained in developing horizontal governance.

Almost regardless of how much we relax the notion of formal political and administrative control, autonomy remains an important precondition for the exercise of interactive governance. Local authorities in national contexts where local autonomy is limited, like the United Kingdom or the United States (see Gurr and King, 1987), have substantive problems in finding the discretion necessary for interactive governance. In the United Kingdom, local governance has typically been described as "messy" (Leach and Percy-Smith, 2001); cities have a very limited autonomy, which makes it difficult to forge coalitions with potential governance partners, yet this is precisely what central government expects them to do in order to enhance efficiency in service delivery. The 2000 Local Government Act places a statutory duty on local authorities to develop "community strategies" describing how the authority will engage NGOs, civil society, and other societal actors in the process of governance and public service delivery. Given the strong impetus from central government to local authorities to use these "community strategies" as instruments of governance, maybe it is not very surprising that there are now accounts suggesting that there are now too many interactive governance instruments in play (see Burns, 2000).

In countries where local autonomy is stronger, on the other hand, local authorities are less constrained by state rules and can use their resources more freely. They can decide independently in which policy sectors they want to create new forms of governance and with whom they should do it. Furthermore, in this type of system, cities become attractive partners as they have some degree of control over their resources and services, and some regulatory authority and are therefore more attractive as governance partners compared to cities with constrained autonomy. Thus, in the interactive governance perspective, autonomy is an institutional asset that can be used strategically to mobilize societal actors in the pursuit of the city's objectives. Another way of describing this pattern is that the effective horizontal autonomy of a city is linked to its vertical autonomy.

Transnational and domestic governance

The second aspect of vertical governance, which we will discuss in this chapter, is the relationship between domestic institutions and transnational structures like the EU. The literature does not agree on what the emergence of such transnational institutions means for the State. Some argue that international-ization has entailed a transformation of the formal and effective capabilities of the State (Mann, 1997; Weiss, 1998; Pierre and Peters, 2000; Sørensen, 2006) whereas others (see for instance Camilleri and Falk, 1992) maintain that globalization means a significant weakening of the state. Again, in an inter-active governance perspective, which is less focused on formal institutional authority and capability, it would make sense to argue that while globalization and the growing role of institutions such as the EU pose a challenge to the state, what it means, first and foremost, is a challenge to existing modes and models of domestic governance. And, those patterns of governance are more flexible and adaptive than formal institutions, particularly in the short and medium term.

In a globalizing world, networks and political entrepreneurship become more important than they are in domestic governance. Policymaking and administrative processes in the EU offer plenty of opportunities for national and subnational actors to extract resources and to influence regulation, as we will show later in this chapter. The EU governance process is less strict than the domestic policy process in most of its member states. Information and networks become important assets and attributes in a loose decision-making process, as the large number of lobbyists in the EU environment suggests. Indeed, networks and other forms of interactive governance are becoming increasingly important aspects of governance in the EU (Kohler-Koch and Eising, 1999).

The EU early on identified regions and local authorities more than the member states as the key targets for structural funds, agricultural support, and other financial resources. There is logic to that approach—structural and agricultural issues are regional more than national issues—but the strategy also defined EU governance as inclusive of all institutional levels, not just the interaction between the member states as such and the EU structure. The combination of this regional strategy and the fairly contextually defined style of policymaking, which is typical to the EU, has created a political landscape that is difficult to grasp for the outside observer but which promotes a particular style of governing, based less on transparency and formal procedures but more on networks and political entrepreneurship. It is a style of governing that easily lends itself to interpretation in an interactive governance perspective, highlighting a decoupling of formal structure from behavior and agency over institution.

The insertion of transnational objectives, instruments, and resources into the domestic governance processes and the growing role of transnational institutions in regulating domestic matters more broadly—current estimates suggest that about two-thirds of all domestic regulation in the EU member states is EU-harmonized—has brought a new dimension of governance into play in the member states. This leads us to the issue of interactive vertical governance in a multilevel institutional context.

Vertical governance as multilevel governance

In some ways, all governance is multilevel governance. It is very difficult to think of any governance process that does not include actors, institutions, or processes on at least two institutional levels. Even when governance appears to be firmly located on only one institutional level, actors' scope of action is often defined at other levels as a shadow of hierarchy, or perhaps of interactive governance, located at other institutional levels present in most of the governance process (cf. Scharpf, 1997). Similarly, formal issues of metagovernance are often settled at higher institutional levels. All of this suggests that in order to understand governance at any given level, we need to consider the extent to which agency is constrained and facilitated by institutional arrangements.

This pattern applies not only to governance in the political and administrative sphere. Local markets are embedded in national and global markets, and local market behavior is largely a manifestation of that embeddedness (Crouch et al., 2004). Furthermore, organizations devoted to some form of global governance such as the UN or the WTO see their latitude and capabilities defined, and constrained, by actors at the nation-state level. Embeddedness is thus not merely a matter of subordination to actors and institutions at higher levels; it also refers to the relationships with lower institutional levels. Agency and behavior at any given institutional level are shaped by interactions with other actors at institutions at both higher and lower institutional levels.

Thus, understanding contemporary governance is to a large extent a matter of understanding not only the institutions and networks of governance but also their embeddedness in society and other institutional structures. Multilevel governance is the vertically organized process through which actors, institutions, and resources at different institutional levels are mobilized toward specific, ad hoc projects (Bache and Flinders, 2004). It may be more or less institutionalized—as this chapter will discuss, there are numerous empirical cases of both low and high degrees of institutionalization—and it may also vary considerably with respect to which specific institutional levels are involved. The key defining features of multilevel governance are not that it involves actors and institutions from different institutional (subnational, national, and transnational) levels but that hierarchy is replaced by bargaining; that process and participation are contextually defined; that interactions take place directly between actors at the lowest and highest levels; and that it blurs distinctions that traditional approaches in intergovernmental relationships consider important, like jurisdiction, subordination, and control.

Readers with an expertise in intergovernmental relationships might be confused about the notion of "multiple" levels. In part, the multilevel concept suggests that the number of levels involved in any given governance processes often cannot be determined beforehand. Multilevel governance, put simply, refers to governance processes involving agency and institutions on more than one level. However, as we will argue later in this chapter, participation in this governance process—as in many others—is contextually defined and that means that it is also difficult to predict the number of levels involved in a multilevel governance process. For example, in the United States, the "New Federalism" implemented by the Reagan administration in the 1980s aimed at drastically reducing the federal bureaucracy, in part by decentralizing tasks from the federal level to the state level. However, many US cities depended heavily on federal grants for urban development and renewal. With the abolition of those grants—the so-called urban development grants or UDGs—cities had to approach the state capitol for financial support (Mollenkopf, 1983). Thus, a change in the relationship between the federal government and the states pushed actors at the local level into action at higher institutional levels.

The most prominent and elaborated case of multilevel governance is found in the EU. The institutional setup and policy process of the EU explicitly aim at creating strong linkages between its own transnational institutions and subnational institutions (regions and local authorities) in the member states. The bulk of the EU's budget goes to agricultural support and the structural funds, and in both cases regions and localities, not the states, are the obvious targets. Furthermore, the EU Commission frequently allocates funds on an ad hoc basis where states, regions, and cities are invited to apply for support. This policy style clearly illustrates the notion of opportunity structures in multilevel governance, which we will discuss later in this chapter.

The traditional view on intergovernmental relationships has problems conceptualizing local strategies to influence the political center or to bypass the center to pursue international arenas. With only minor exaggeration, we could say that in the intergovernmental relationships perspective, the focus was on institutions and rules illustrated by the handling of issues and programs, whereas in the multilevel governance perspective the focus is on process, programs, and agency and institutional variables are considered wherever they matter to explain those processes. A slightly different way of describing the difference between intergovernmental relationships and multilevel governance is that in the former approach institutional design is the dependent variable, whereas in multilevel governance institutions are independent variables explaining agency.

Multilevel governance, conceived of as a layering of governance processes, highlights the previously mentioned embeddedness (domestic and international) of institutions and actors. The multilevel governance perspective stands in distinct contrast to the more conventional intergovernmental relationships approach in terms of how it conceives of political and administrative authority. In the latter perspective, constitutional rules provide a map for relationships between central, regional, and local institutions. This is not to suggest that those relationships are carved in stone or that they unconditionally steer agency, but it does put an emphasis on the formal structure of the political system. Intergovernmental relationships are constantly evolving along with changes in the political agenda and the roles given to institutions at different levels in addressing societal problems. Also, metagovernance issues related to decentralization or strengthening federalism reshuffle relationships between institutional levels, as countries on both sides of the Atlantic experienced during the 1980s (Smith, 1985).

In the multilevel governance perspective, on the other hand, those relationships and institutional roles are seen as opportunity structures or arenas for agency. Entrepreneurial agents such as skillful local politicians, EU lobbyists, or state senators use the institutional setup as stepping stones to promote their interests at higher institutional levels. More than anything else, perhaps, the multilevel governance perspective allows us to conceptualize agency much better than the intergovernmental relationships literature. Given the contextualization of governance in this vertical dimension, understanding agency is the key to account for policy outcomes. Unlike traditional models of intergovernmental relationships, multilevel governance highlights the contextualization of institutional relationships and also the nonhierarchical nature of governance including multiple institutional levels.

However, the weak institutional framework for multilevel governance entails potentially major problems for cities and regions. This type of multilevel governance exposes nation states and subnational institutions to global pressures without the mediating effect that domestic institutions are often believed to provide as multilevel governance creates direct linkages between transnational and subnational institutions. But this argument cuts both ways; this type of governance is also a vehicle for cities and regions to escape the confines of nation-state subordination and to explore international opportunity structures.

Again, these relationships are negotiated more than constitutional. Hierarchical relationships of command and control still certainly exist, not least within the EU apparatus, but in the implementation of programs there is an emphasis on negotiation and mutual accommodation in order to mobilize the targets of the programs. Shared financial responsibilities between the EU and the program targets are one strategy of creating incentives for local or regional mobilization. Such mobilization is essential to successful implementation.

As is the case in much of governance theory, multilevel governance tends to under-conceptualize agency, although it does a better job in that respect compared to traditional models of intergovernmental relationships. If the latter perspective downplays agency because its influence on institutional behavior is believed to be negligible, the former approach is focused on agency, but the contextual nature of that agency makes theory-building difficult. In multilevel governance analysis, institutions become arenas and stepping stones for access to higher, or lower, institutional levels. Thus, analyses of multilevel governance should to a large extent focus on actors, and actors in these processes, not least in the EU, tend to focus on financial resources.

Central government institutions have traditionally used financial incentives like state subsidies and grants as a means to steer subnational government. More recently, either as a result of the neoliberal "turn" in many countries or because of the financial crisis, such incentives have become less popular policy instruments. Instead, central government institutions have tended to tie grants to specific tasks and sometimes to provide grants on an increasingly competitive basis. Within the EU, this has created a higher degree of symmetry between member states and the programs implemented by the Union. In both cases, it is now much more up to subnational government to actively search for financial resources rather than to receive grants automatically.

In the EU, financial resources are to some degree allocated ad hoc, for specific projects or tasks. The main exceptions to this pattern are the agricultural funds and the structural funds that are highly institutionalized. However, a large number of funds are created, and allocated, ad hoc with the intent of inviting cities, regions, or member state governments to apply for financial support for some specific purpose. This process of ad hoc allocation of funds opens up for political and administrative entrepreneurship and network formation. In 2007, the EU, following an initiative from the French government, launched a "Globalization Adjustment Fund" to aid countries suffering from massive delocalization of jobs. A massive €500 million went into the fund

(Parker, 2007). To date, only two countries have applied for support from the fund and only France has received support. Similarly, the EU's "Solidarity Fund" was set up to pool capital to be used to assist cities and regions that have been hit by natural disasters. In 2004, only one application was submitted, to cover costs for flooding in France.

The low number of applications could be explained either by too high criteria or too little information about the funds circulated within the Union, or both. There is currently a debate about if and how the eligibility criteria should be changed. Even with such changes implemented, however, the EU Commission, in its strategy to use funds to steer member states, regions, and cities, creates and allocates funds through a process where information and knowledge are essential. This is a very different type of process compared to those where transparency and due process are fundamental values and where information is shared more openly.

Multilevel governance, networks, and institutions

Before we close this discussion on intergovernmental relations and multilevel governance, we should summarize the section by reiterating a point made earlier in the chapter. The previous image of vertical governance among scholars and practitioners was dominated by the intergovernmental relations perspective. This image of vertical governance emphasizes the formal, constitutional relationships among institutions at different levels of the political system although it does not exclude the possibility of violations or transgressions of those formal rules in real-world politics and administration. The consolidation of the EU with its particular notion of vertical governance increased the interest in multilevel governance. The point here is that the differences between intergovernmental relations and multilevel governance are bigger than just adding an institutional level to the equation. With only very little exaggeration, we could say that multilevel governance, both as a theory and as an empirical account, is the vertical dimension of interactive governance while intergovernmental relationships as a framework offer an account of vertical governance in a rather strict institutional perspective. Thus, theory development has been driven by changes in vertical governance mainly in the EU but also more broadly as a result of globalization and the changing relationship between nation-state governments and transnational institutions.

The metagovernance of multilevel governance is messy. If we once again use the EU as an example, it comprises basically all conceivable governance arrangements, ranging from firm hierarchical control to networks and partnerships. A fair assessment could be that today there is no distinct metagovernance arrangement for the EU model of multilevel governance. This represents a distinct contrast to horizontal governance where traditional and emerging models of administration and service delivery represent different metagovernance models of administration.

The interactive model helps us understand vertical governance primarily because the practice of vertical governance is becoming increasingly interactive. There are several developments inside and outside the State that propel interactive forms of governance. One is the aforementioned increasing social complexity. Another important driver is the growing professionalization of local and regional government, which means that top-down models of policy steering make less sense and are met with increasing resistance from below. Perhaps the most important change over the past couple of decades has been the emergence of contextualized multilevel governance that draws on non-hierarchical forms of interaction among actors and institutions at different levels.

Horizontal governance: From political control to multi-agency governance

The constitutional storyline of horizontal governance is that of a strong, cohesive political center directing and coordinating the actions of subsidiary organizations in the process of policy implementation. Power, resources, control, popular input, and accountability all lead into that political center, which in turn redirects the flow into policy programs implemented by agencies and subnational government. Today, most if not all observers would agree that this is a highly stylized picture. It is based on the same image of the centrality of the State, which is typical to much of democratic theory; the notion is that of a State sufficiently strong to control its territory and to efficiently regulate behavior and to have the internal cohesion and concord necessary to execute those roles. The real world of governance is replete with organizational and societal complexities that provide formidable challenges to politicians and bureaucrats. Some of these challenges are societal in origin while others, as we will see, seem to be the results of administrative reform and institutional change within the State. Much of what was said earlier about network formation in the context of vertical governance applies very much to horizontal governance as well.

Thus, if the past couple of decades have witnessed the political center becoming increasingly challenged and entangled in multilevel processes of vertical governance, we can see a similar development toward contextualized interaction in horizontal governance as well; only here it is seemingly driven by forces other than globalization and internationalization. Multilevel governance redefines the role of the traditional political center both vertically and horizontally. In the horizontal dimension of governance, the past couple of decades have seen a widespread interest in separating policy from operations by creating autonomous executive agencies (see Pollitt and Talbot, 2003; Laegreid and Verhoest, 2010). Thus, if the multiplicity of levels is the defining feature of interactive governance in the vertical dimension, we could say that multi-agency governance is the interactive governance model in the horizontal dimension. The previous control by the political and administrative center is now challenged by the sheer multitude of actors and interests, which constitute either the targets or the actors of interactive governance, or both. Collaborative models of service delivery transgress the border between the public sphere and the market and define agency more according to interests and stakes than to formal roles and responsibilities.

This development has been part and parcel of a larger campaign of administrative reform, New Public Management (NPM), aiming at separating policy from operations and to put markets into operation within the public sector (Hood, 1991; Pollitt and Bouckaert, 2004). In line with this type of reform, we have seen extensive usage of the market not only in terms of privatization, contracting out, and partnerships but also as a resource allocation mechanism within the public sector. The driving idea in this reform has been to open up the public sector to the market not only in terms of internal markets and managerial expertise from the corporate sector but also in terms of public sector discourse (Pierre, 2011).

The proliferation of private contractors, public organizations, and NGOs delivering public service has generated a need for networks and partnerships that can define rules for the new markets and build trust where it is undermined by competition. The emphasis on strategic public management has forced managers to create networks with other public managers in similar institutions to their own in order to exchange experiences, ideas, and resources to reduce transaction costs and escape excessive competition. Thus, like all models of public management, NPM too entails new forms of interaction that may or may not have been part of the original reform plan.

To take this discussion further, we need to briefly point out some crucial similarities and differences between the Weberian bureaucracy model, NPM, and interactive governance. The Weberian bureaucracy and the NPM model both (albeit for different reasons) emphasize the distinction between state and society and between politics and administration. The key difference between the two models is that the Weberian model of bureaucracy is a model of public governance, whereas NPM draws on a philosophy seeking to bring public and private governance together in the context of public administration. Furthermore, NPM and interactive governance are uncomfortable with the secluded and closed nature of Weber's model. NPM wants to replace public monopolies with competitive markets while the interactive governance perspective suggests that Weber's bureaucracy model does not take growing social complexity and fragmentation into consideration and is unable to engage in collaborative and interactive forms of problem-solving.

Thus, the traditional (purported or real) tug-of-war between those who make policy and those who implement it has to some extent been complemented, or even replaced, by another tension in the public sector: that between publicness and public value on the one hand and the market on the other (Peters, 1978; Rosenbloom, 1998; Suleiman, 2003; Bozeman, 2007; Newman and Clarke, 2009). In terms of interactive governance, NPM could be seen as a metagovernance arrangement that defines who should be in charge of what functions and tasks and what should be the system of norms sustaining those functions. This metagovernance arrangement challenges the Weberian model of administration, which—again, as a metagovernance model—defined its norms and values of administration. In the NPM model, a new set of interactions are described, both in terms of the nature of the players and in terms of the nature of the exchanges.

Some observers see NPM as a depoliticization of the public bureaucracy. To them, public administration is an integral component in democratic governance and therefore tampering with its structure, processes, or its exchanges with its clients has ramifications for its governance role. The significance of publicness, as opposed to markets, is one part of this argument but there are also aspects related to values such as legality, procedural fairness, and impartiality that define the democratic governance role of the public administration.

Others describe these changes in governance as a diffusion of politics (Benz et al., 1992). The argument is that the joint effect of agencification and marketization has been a weakening of the core executive, which may explain the recent efforts in many advanced democracies to mobilize power to the center (see Dahlstrom et al., 2011). A common pattern among the countries that extensively introduced NPM has been a loss of coordination and these efforts of recentering have served to address that problem and to revitalize leadership in the political system. To some extent, government purchased efficiency gains in public service delivery at the price of coordination and accountability; the creation of executive agencies created new models of regulation and service, but it appears likely that policymakers realized that this diffusion of public authority will cause coordination problems down the road. Whether that was the case or not, it has been obvious that most governments are now busy redefining the center, or "rebalancing" the system (Australia), or "joining up" government (United Kingdom), or emphasizing "horizontality" (Canada) (see Laegreid and Verhoest, 2010).

Agencification and marketization have also driven a process in which policy is shaped in the interaction between policymakers and policy targets. NPM reform has driven fragmentation and entailed a loss of coordination. Interactive governance has to some degree emerged as a response to that fragmentation. Not unlike the corporatist model of policymaking (Schmitter, 1974; Katzenstein, 1984), an interactive policy process tends to lead to better compliance and smoothes the process of implementation. In the conventional governance view, this policy process is said to favor organized interests and to complicate redistribution and implementing policies that cater to interests other than those immediately involved. Interactive governance emphasizes that such interaction is typical to political life and government in general and that the distinction between special interests and the public interest is basically impossible to sustain.

Thus, interactive governance looks at horizontal governance as a non-linear process where the distinction between policymakers and policy targets has become blurred and where policies frequently emanate from implementation rather than from elected politicians (see SOU, 1983: 39; Crozier, 2010). The shaping of policy is a continuous process, which does not end until implementation is completed. Interactive governance thus challenges the Wilsonian idea of a strict division between politics and administration (Peters, 1978; Kettl, 2002) and portrays the policy process as a continuous dialogue between politicians, bureaucrats, and societal actors (Bang, 2007). In this dialogue, the constitutional blueprint discussed earlier defines the formal roles of politicians and bureaucrats but their actual capacity to control the policy process is contingent on a number of contextual factors.

What are the consequences of this drift in roles, tasks, and responsibilities in the policy process? In a functionalist perspective, the blurring of roles and continuous exchange between politicians and bureaucrats may somewhat paradoxically enhance the efficiency of the process as a whole. Elected officials and civil servants have different types of knowledge about policy and by pooling these different types of knowledge, that is, by allowing greater bureaucratic influence on policy than the constitutional blueprint prescribes, policy design may become more efficient in addressing particular problems. Similarly, some political presence in policy implementation may help generate consent among the targets of policy.

Diagonal governance

The emergence of the EU opened up a veritable Pandora's box of interactive governance in the previously rather tightly, hierarchically controlled countries in Western Europe, emphasizing a multilevel, contextually defined process of governance where elected officials and bureaucrats at all institutional levels interact with each other and where the public governance process tends to be open to lobbyists and parochial interests, to business and NGOs, and to regions and interest groups. Many of these actors move freely between the subnational, national, transnational, and sometimes even global levels of governance. In such a highly complex web of governance, upholding traditional values of governance such as representation, accountability, demos, elective office, and administrative ethos becomes a challenge in itself. Interactive forms of governance, where the focus of attention is more on results than who, or what, is represented, becomes a strategy to cope with such complexity.

As we have seen several times in this chapter, it is no easy task to maintain a tight distinction between vertical and horizontal governance. Vertical governance is replete with complex processes where political, administrative, and private actors participate. Vertical networks can be administrative or political. As the consolidation of the EU continues in what is referred to as the vertical and horizontal integration processes, some issues are (initially) primarily political whereas others are left to bureaucratic coordination. At the EU level, a cluster of new regulatory agencies have been created over the past ten to fifteen years, thus creating new administrative interfaces between the transnational and national levels. These constantly changing patterns of authority, resources, and formal competences provide new opportunity structures for entrepreneurial actors to extract financial resources or to influence EU policy and regulation.

Integrating vertical and horizontal governance

A key argument in this chapter is that governance is becoming increasingly interactive and therefore it becomes more difficult to sustain the distinction between vertical and horizontal governance. For instance, subnational institutions typically find themselves having to deal with the tension between policy sectors and territorial considerations. While this is a problem that has haunted politicians and bureaucrats for decades if not centuries and becomes apparent even in traditional institutional analyses, placing the problem in an interactive governance perspective opens up for a partially new understanding of the complexity. In this perspective, subnational institutions are less monolithic and instead resemble complex "multiorganizations" where each segment of the organization defines its own environment and external relationships (Montin, 1990). As the local authority organization collapses into several semiautonomous segments, each segment in the "multiorganization" accommodates and reconciles the tension between territorial and sectoral policy ideas and regulations. Furthermore, these organizational segments are much better equipped to engage in interactive governance compared to the local authority as a whole.

These problems have been particularly noticeable at the regional level where in many countries, state administration institutions often coexist side by side with elected regional institutions. Recent institutional reform in European regions has attempted to bridge this institutional gap and to create institutions that are adequately designed to be able to mobilize funds from the EU structural funds although it seems clear that there are still several problems with this reform (Newman, 2000). In particular, the results of the effort to design institutions that can create or revitalize regional governance have been mixed at best.

In a more decentered perspective it might be argued that formal authority and other constitutional arrangements are metagovernance arrangements that have little or no bearing on the actual behavior of public or societal actors. There is some validity to that statement; there is ample evidence that subnational authorities either ignore central government regulation or that there is some degree of constitutional "drift" whereby institutional roles gradually become redefined. That having been said, however, the constitutional blueprint matters also in an interactive governance perspective because it defines the resources that various actors bring to the collective governance effort.

Conclusion

Interactive governance is helpful to the observer in going beyond constitutional roles and to uncover the real-world relationships among politicians, bureaucrats, and societal actors. In vertical governance, institutional relationships in this perspective highlight mutual contingencies and interdependencies rather than command, control, and subordination. Governance reforms in many Western countries are proof of the growing recognition of this evolving partnership among institutions at different levels of the political system. In horizontal governance, the classic dichotomy between politicians and bureaucrats, which has long since given way to a more realistic understanding of the more complex relationship between these two roles in the modern state, is in the interactive governance seen as a shared responsibility. Policymaking and implementation are integrated parts of the same process.

This chapter has shown how the vertical and horizontal dimensions of governance are not separate but closely integrated dimensions of governance. In interactive governance, horizontal governance is a strategy to address coordination problems. Such problems are not solved by the exercise of formal hierarchical command; had that been possible there would not have been very many cases of lack of coordination. Instead, coordination is attained through webs of more informal interaction. Vertical governance, on the other hand, could be seen as a metagovernance strategy to facilitate and steer interlocal and regional cooperation. Subnational government today is as professional and capable as central government; what differs is the nature of the governance tasks. Central–local relationships have changed from a pattern of command and control toward a pattern of dialogue, interdependence, and division of labor. Again, traditional institutional analyses do not fully capture these developments. However, vertical governance could also take place in interactive forms of networks or exchanges of knowledge and resources in the process of addressing new policy problems.

6

Institutionalizing interactive governance

It is not difficult to recognize interactive governance processes once they are in place and functioning well, but it is more difficult to identify the process by which those governance structures are created, and become ordinary components of the policy process. Even the processes of "traditional governing" through formal actors must be created and institutionalized, and in some societies—for example, failed states—that has not really occurred (see Kjær, 2011b). Some of the traditional literature in political development, for example, argued that the most important aspect of development was building effective institutions for managing demands from citizens and thereby creating stability (Huntington, 1968).

Developing effective institutions for successful interactive governance may be more challenging. This would have to occur in several different locales and the failure of one may mean the failure of the process as a whole. The first requirement is developing an effective government apparatus, as described above. Further, institutionalizing interactive governance requires identifying, and perhaps creating and supporting, the nongovernmental actors that can function to provide governance beyond the more visible state actors. It will also require building linkages between state and non-state actors, and modifying the working ethos within and among public sector organizations themselves. As we will develop in greater detail below, one of the major challenges for building effective interactive governance capacity is the ability to build effective policy networks and to institutionalize their role in governing.

Institutionalizing governance, whether interactive or not, is an aspect of forming the governance process. Even the interactive model, which by its definition is more subject to change and is defined by the interactions of the participants, requires some degree of institutionalization if it is going to provide the stability and predictability needed by its members for effective governance (see Schmidt, 2010). Likewise, even if there is an attempt to be inclusive in involving social actors in processes of interaction, there will still be some need to establish boundaries defining who is a legitimate participant in the process and who is not.

Interactive governance processes, once institutionalized, may create some benefits, but they may well create the need to activate other levels of steering and control. That is, successes in interactive governance may generate control problems for government actors. The same processes of creating interactive governance structures must be identified in building metagovernance structures, and also in converting that metagovernance into standard parts of governing (see Meuleman, 2008). For politicians and administrators (as well as for scholars) committed to traditionalist forms of governing that are centered on the State, building the structures for interactive governance amounts to a significant reduction of their steering capacity. Although interactive governance might prove valuable for politicians and administrators, this apparent loss of central steering capacity will generate problems that in turn will create a need for recreating some form of central steering, albeit central steering of a substantially different sort (see Peters, 2008).

The argument is that this governance is conducted in "the shadow of hierarchy," meaning that formal institutions may retain the capacity to intervene and to impose their own priorities (Scharpf, 1993). Greater governance challenges may arise, however, in failed states (see Risse and Lehmkuhl, 2010) in which there is no such hierarchy available as a backup. There may, however, be other shadows that may provide some alternative governance. There may, for example, be a shadow of the market when multinational firms control many facets of social and economic life that might normally be controlled by the State, for example, mining companies in several African countries.

This chapter will examine the factors involved in creating and dismantling processes of governance and metagovernance. This examination will employ the concept of institutionalization as the central lens for understanding the construction of stable processes for managing policy and administration. Further, we will be examining the deinstitutionalization of these processes as well as their creation. Institutions, whether of governance or metagovernance, are not created once and for all, but rather take the form of continuous processes of institutionalization and deinstitutionalization. In this particular case, one hypothesis guiding the analysis might be that there would be an interaction between these two aspects of policymaking—governance and metagovernance—so that when one increases the other would wane. The alternative hypothesis might be that the two vary together, so that effective governance will require effective metagovernance.

While in general we will sing hymns of praise to institutionalizing processes of interactive governance, we will also raise some notes of caution about the possibilities of the over-institutionalization of these processes. Creating stability is positive, but excessive stability produces rigidity and the inability to adapt. Further, in democratic terms, excessive institutionalization may exclude some actors expressing new sets of demands on government. Naturally, over-institutionalization may also limit innovation in the governance processes and reduce their capacity to govern effectively. Thus, the processes of institutionalization and deinstitutionalization must be considered in the light of the need to find some balance between predictability and rigidity.

The concept of institutionalization

Contemporary political science has had an increased interest in institutional explanations for politics and government. Although there has been the increased interest in those explanations, there are multiple approaches to explanation, related to different versions of institutional theory (Peters, 1999) and those multiple perspectives to some extent confound the institutional explanations. For example, the normative approaches to institutions focus on the manipulation of values and symbols to produce compliance on the part of the members of the institution (March and Olsen, 1984). On the other hand, rational choice versions of institutions focus on rules and incentives that can be manipulated by institutional leaders (Ostrom, 1990). Historical institutionalists rely more on path dependency and the inertial effects of initial policy and organizational choices (Pierson, 2000b). Discursive conceptions in institutionalization emphasize the creation of a common set of understandings, and a common language within an institution, to some extent analogous to the logic of normative institutionalism (Schmidt, 2010).

Another of the crucial analytic questions about institutions, arising in part from the need for institutionalization, is the extent to which they differ from organizations. That distinction is to some extent a matter of interpretation, but the important difference appears to be that an institution can encompass a variety of actions and actors, while the organization is smaller and more constrained. Douglas North (1990) and Ibn Khalil (1995) have described institutions as the rules of the game and organizations as the teams that are playing the game. That analogy works well for markets in which firms play the role of the teams rather well, and for our purposes the organizational members of networks, and the networks themselves, clearly are the participants in the relatively institutionalized "game" of politics and governing.

This analogy of teams and the game also works well for networks and for interactive governance. The stable pattern of interaction among the groups, with some rules and some boundary principles, can represent the game. The networks then in turn represent the players in the game. Perhaps the major difference would be that although markets and politics are usually thought of as competitive games, the interactive governance mode is more cooperative so that a very different type of game is occurring.

Most of the scholarly literature on institutions treats the existence of institutions as a nominal dichotomy—an institution exists or it does not. That dichotomy may be easy to identify for some institutions—the US Congress clearly exists while the Interstate Commerce Commission ceased to exist once it was terminated by that same Congress that continued in existence. The nominal dichotomy may be acceptable for these rather formalized institutions, but may be deceptive for less formalized structures and for sets of organizations or individual actors who are in a process of change. For example, many smaller political parties may virtually cease to exist between elections, but they are able to come back to life when an election approaches, or they may return with a different name and somewhat different members (Tavits, 2005).

In governance research, we need to think about institutions not as a dichotomy, but rather as a continuum, with individual structures becoming more or less institutionalized over time. Thus, it is important to think of institutions not only as varying along that continuum but also as involved in a reversible process. In terms of institutional theory, social, economic, and political structures can both institutionalize and deinstitutionalize over time, and continue to change over time. For example, the presidency of the United States has been both constructed, and deconstructed, as an institution over time. Franklin Roosevelt, for example, built the institution (including the Executive Office of the President) and left it more powerful than it perhaps had ever been. On the other hand, the illegalities of Richard Nixon, the indiscretions of Bill Clinton, and the limited competence of George W. Bush deinstitutionalized the structure and its role in governing.

Selznick's sociological model of institutionalization

To be able to assess effectively levels of institutionalization of political structures will require in turn a clear conceptualization of the terms, as well as some possibilities of measuring institutionalization. One such approach is that offered by Selznick (1984) who argued that institutionalization involved "infusing a structure with values greater than those necessary for the mechanical achievement of its tasks" (1984: 37). Thus, in this view, an institution is an organization that has moved beyond simply performing its basic function—be it in the market or government—and also has meaning for its members. This definition is conceptually clear, but still requires substantial attention to issues of measurement if it is to be effective in doing comparative research on institutions. The implication is that to measure institutionalization we will have to find measures of the attachment of members to a particular structure, and establish some threshold of institutionalization.

In the sociological perspective represented by Selznick's statement, institutionalization involves the creation of meaning within the organization. This concept has been elaborated as meanings, myths, symbols, and routines within the structure that enable the members of the institution to understand and replicate expected behavior within the institution. In the rational choice perspective, institutionalization might mean the creation of rules, and the willingness of the members of organizations and institutions to comply with those rules. In this view the rules need not have any particular normative meaning for the members so long as there is adequate compliance. Institutionalization is almost inherent in historical institutionalism, given that the assumption of path dependency involves the creation of a stable organization or program that defies easy change.

While the sociological approach to institutionalization is the most appealing intellectually, it also presents a number of difficult questions from a research perspective. The most obvious is that it implies a rather monolithic conception of the values and symbols that are being internalized by the members of the institution. A good deal of the research on organizational culture (Martin, 2002) has pointed to the simultaneous existence of several strands of culture in most organizations, and the same logic applies to organizations. Further, some scholars have argued that these multiple strands can be eufunctional for the organization or institution. The presence of alternatives to the dominant organizational culture may enable the organization to relate more effectively to other organizations or institutions within its environment.

The sociological version of institutionalism also emphasizes the importance of emphasizing the environment of any particular institution, or in this case a system of interactive governance composed of governance networks (see Pierre and Peters, 2009). In interactive governance, the participants may want to ensure that the social actors whom they want involved are also well-structured, so they can participate effectively, and likewise that the government itself is sufficiently institutionalized to manage the demands that may be placed upon it by the networks. For most industrial democracies, these are not major challenges but they may be for less well-developed systems that may need to construct both civil society and government.

Huntington's political model of institutionalization

Samuel Huntington (1968) developed a political model of institutionalization that involves several dimensions that he argued were related to the structuring of organizations, and of the public sector more generally. These dimensions were developed primarily to understand the capacity of the State to govern in the context of political development, with the argument that if institutionalization did not proceed at least as rapidly as the creation of demands, then stable political development was unlikely. Likewise, the various components of institutionalization had to proceed at more or less similar paces if the system was to maintain its overall capacity to develop and function effectively.

Although designed for analyzing governing at the national level, these dimensions of institutionalization have been used to analyze the development of individual organizations. For example, Ragsdale and Theis (1997) have used these dimensions to understand the development of the Executive Office of the President in the United States, and Peters (2008) has used them for discussing the institutionalization of executive structures in a number of governments. If anything, these dimensions are more applicable for the individual public organizations than they are for whole political systems and interactive policy arenas.

Huntington's analysis identified four dimensions of institutionalization:

1. *Autonomy.* To be an effective institution, it must be autonomous from other institutions and have the resources available to perform its tasks. That autonomy is perhaps especially difficult to maintain for social actors that wish to influence the public sector but run the risk of co-optation.

2. *Adaptability.* A well-institutionalized structure must be able to cope with changes in its environment and changes in the demands being placed upon it. This criterion implies maintaining the fundamental nature of the institution while adapting to cope with changing problems and a changing environment.

3. *Complexity.* To be successful in governing an institution must be sufficiently complex to match the complexity of the policy problems being confronted. That said, the institutions can be overly complex and have difficulty in responding and adapting to those problems.

4. *Coherence.* Institutionalization also requires that the structures in the public sector are organized to cope with the workload they have been allocated and to work with other organizations to manage public affairs. To this, we might add an emphasis on work across internal divisions in government to create more coordinated policies.

These criteria from Huntington are extremely valuable for the study of institutionalization for at least two reasons. First, they appear more readily amenable to measurement than are most other approaches to institutionalization (or indeed institutions) that depend more heavily on less visible, attitudinal aspects of change within an institution. As already noted, several scholars have developed operationalizations of these continua. Further, the Hunting-ton criteria clearly imply underlying continua so that we can speak of dynamic processes with institutions becoming more or less institutionalized across time. Institutions can vary along these continua without any need to define a threshold at which they become institutionalized.

Although valuable, these dimensions of institutionalization do have some real problems in terms of measurement and the weighting of the dimensions and these are to some extent directly related to the strengths mentioned above. On the other hand, however, these continua do not include the very important dimension of ideas and culture among the members of the structure, and may only represent more or less mechanical changes within institutions.

The discussion above also implies that these four criteria may not vary together and indeed several dimensions may be inversely related. For ex-ample, complexity and adaptability may be inversely related, given that more complex institutional structures will, everything else being equal, encounter greater difficulties in responding to a changing environment. Simi-larly, in some settings, coherence and autonomy may not covary, given that matching the structure of an institution to its environment may undermine the autonomy of the various sectors from the structures that they shadow. In addition to the potential lack of covariance among the elements of institu-tionalization, we have no clear weighting schemes that would enable us to provide a summative measure of the degree of institutionalization.

Likewise, as indicated above, these dimensions of institutionalization can also be taken too far for effective government. For example, institutions can be overly autonomous and not adequately constrained. That constraint may be exercised by other formal institutions or in the case of interactive government that constraint may be through the social actors that comprise the networks. Effective interactive governance therefore implies that state actors cannot function without close connections to society. Therefore, effective interactive governance requires some balance on all these dimensions, as difficult as that may be to define.

Institutionalizing governance

To this point we have been discussing institutionalization largely in the abstract, and as a process that is shared equally by almost any institution. We now need to move to the more specific question of institutionalizing the structures and processes of governance. This question too can be seen from a rather general perspective, as a means of examining the capacity of the public sector, with or without the involvement of social actors, to steer economy and society effectively. Further, this general perspective would inquire about the ability to maintain internal consistency (coordination) and adequate linkages with conditions in the environment to be able to steer effectively when confronting changing social conditions.

Although the governance systems of most industrial democracies have been sufficiently institutionalized to provide adequate governance capacity, there are differences in that capacity across countries and across time. For example, using the criteria advanced by Huntington, we could argue that the countries of Northern Europe have achieved a relatively balanced level of institutionalization on all these dimensions while others, such as the United States, have gone perhaps too far on some criteria (complexity and autonomy) while perhaps not far enough on achieving adaptability. Likewise, some of the countries of Southern Europe may not have developed sufficient adaptability within many components of government to be effective in governing society.

In this chapter, we will be examining institutionalization of governance processes along three different dimensions. The first is institutionalizing the fundamental processes of governance, including institutionalizing formal government processes and structures. We will then consider how to institutionalize governance networks and other instruments that tend to function as the alternatives to the formal governmental processes. Finally, we will examine the institutionalization of the role of governance networks in broader governance processes. While considering institutionalizing networks in governance, we need also to consider the institutionalization of less benign forms of informal governance that are more common outside the wealthy industrial democracies (see Piattoni, 2001*b*; Peters, 2010). Although the description of some aspects of these processes may appear redundant, we need to differentiate these processes and also to understand how they are linked. In particular, it may be necessary for the institutions of government to achieve some level of institutionalization of more formal structures before networks, however well-institutionalized they may be, can be effective in governing. In other words, networks and other forms of interactive governance may be valuable instruments, but do need some structure within which to function.

As well as these basic discussions of institutional development in those three aspects of governance, there is an underlying question, often unasked when discussing any aspect of institutionalization, about the appropriate level of institutional development. There has been some tendency to assume that higher levels of institutionalization are superior to lower levels, and further that creating any form of stability may be superior to chaos. We will, however, be arguing that some care must be taken in assessing the impact of institutionalization on the performance of organizations and patterns of interaction that shape our analysis of governance. Determining any appropriate level of institutionalization *ex ante* is difficult if not impossible, but governance is a continuous process of searching for effective means of steering society with or without the involvement of social actors.

We will be arguing, first that structures and processes can easily become overly institutionalized and can therefore create rigidity and incapacity to adjust to changing circumstances in the relevant environment. This rigidity is a common negative stereotype of public sector organizations, but it may be even more relevant for interactive structures. In those structures the patterns of interaction and the relative power relationships may have been worked out after substantial negotiation, so any attempt to change will be very threatening. So, it may be that the interactive structures that are often argued to be innovative may actually be poorly situated to produce effective change. This is especially true when the individuals work together for extended periods of time and develop "groupthink."

The second part of the need to nuance discussions of institutionalization is that many social and governmental practices may become established that are dysfunctional for governing, and especially for governing effectively. For example, clientelism (see above) and other formats for linking state and society may serve the participants very well, but may undermine attempts to govern in more transparent and accountable ways. Likewise, institutionalizing corrupt practices within the public sector may solve some problems but may then create another set of problems for citizens and for actors in the processes of governing. Thus, we need to understand the content of institutionalized practices as well as the level of institutionalism in order to make any judgments about the impact of institutional developments.

Institutionalizing government

In the Western industrial democracies, this aspect of institutionalizing governance may require relatively little comment. Most systems have been in operation with relatively constant constitutional and operation rules for decades, if not centuries. Outside of the CEE (Central and Eastern Europe) countries, the last among the European, North American, and Antipodean countries to institutionalize their governing systems were the three Southern European systems that rid themselves of autocratic regimes in the 1970s. The CEE countries themselves now have had almost 20 years of experience in providing autonomous governance, and have been able to do so with relatively few significant disruptions in their institutional arrangements.

Although a government may have apparently stable government institutions, that does not, however, mean that the institutionalization process is complete and has come to an end. As already noted, institutions and the degree of their institutionalization continue to change and some new equilibrium must be reasserted after those changes. This raises the interesting analytic question of whether equilibrium and institutionalization are the same in the public sector. Much of the rational choice perspective on institutions focuses on maintaining equilibrium (Riker, 1980; Shepsle and Weingast, 1981), but institutionalization appears to imply more than a simple mechanical equilibrium. Thus, an equilibrium may be conceptualized as a necessary condition for institutionalization but not as synonymous with achieving. Therefore, governments face continuous challenges to their stable level of institutionalization and their continued capacity to govern effectively, with or without the involvement of social actors. Given that the individual social actors, as well as their interrelationships, will also inevitably face some institutional questions, the task of maintaining institutionalization in such governance arrangements will be more difficult (see below).

When considering the institutionalization of government institutions, we must be careful not to focus exclusively on the formal institutions themselves. We will bring in the role of social actors later in this chapter, but institutionalizing government structures also requires their acceptance by the public they are meant to govern. Building the legitimacy of institutions, and public trust in them, is a crucial aspect of institutionalization. This is analogous to Selznick's argument (1984) about "infusing a structure with value," and extends the members of the institutions to include the public in general. Further, as confidence of the public continues to wane in government institutions (Norris and Newton, 2000), we can argue that some deinstitutionalization of government has been taking place, a change that may open the way for the institutionalization of networks and other less formalized means of governing.

When thinking about the institutionalization of government, it is also important to think about institutionalizing the relationships among the actors as well as the individual organizations. These two processes of institutionalization may not proceed at the same pace, with some implications for change in these governments. In most instances, institutionalizing the individual institutions is easier to achieve than institutionalizing the relationships among them. There is a formal structure to which members have been selected and to which presumably they have some allegiance. For the political institutions of governing, the meaning of the institutions for the participants is reinforced by their legitimacy in governing, while for legal and bureaucratic institutions, involvement with the law is a prime source for providing such meaning.

As the above implies, the processes of governing require building and institutionalizing the interactions of individual institutions and actors if governance is to be successful. One of the fundamental notions of institutions is that there should be some regularity of behavior. Another of the basic premises of institutional theory is that the environment of any one institution is other institutions. Therefore, governance—and in this case governance through government—requires ensuring that the individual institutions develop mechanisms for coping positively with the other institutions that may be their rivals for power. Further, this institutionalization involves generating mechanisms that can reduce the friction and transaction costs among the participants in governing so that they can govern more readily.

The budget process represents a good example of institutionalizing those relationships and establishing stable patterns of interaction that are characteristic of any form of institution. For example, some years ago Aaron Wildavsky (1968) discussed (albeit not in those terms) institutionalizing interactions among Congress, the President, and administrative agencies in budgeting. Although there were formal rules for these interactions, the informal rules that governed the transactions were even more important. These informal norms and rules, for example, the importance of reliability and trust, reciprocity, etc., were at least as important as the formal rules and tended to determine the success of the players in the process. This description of the budget process was of the United States, but other studies of budgeting have demonstrated some of the same routinization (Heclo and Wildavsky, 1974).

If we conceptualize the public sector as being composed of a number of these smaller institutional understandings, then it is relatively easier to understand some aspects of governing. For example, individual policy areas tend to create their own understandings among the actors about what is acceptable policy, what are the appropriate sources of information, how decisions should be made, etc. In part, these patterns of decision-making may be more similar within policy areas across countries than for different policy areas within the same country (Freeman, 1985). Furthermore, actors within these policy areas have an incentive to maintain their exclusivity so that they can prevent their own priorities from being undermined by other considerations, for example, agricultural policymakers may well want to insulate their sector from pressures from environmentalists.

Given the above, it is clear that when we move away from formal institutions to examining processes of governing, that which is most commonly institutionalized is a set of *governments*, rather than a single government. Some political systems tend to institutionalize these subsystems and subgovernments more readily than others, and hence may encounter greater difficulties in producing more coherent patterns of governance. The presence of the "iron triangles" or at least their progeny in the United States is a clear example of the difficulties in creating coherence, but the importance of the *Ressortsprinzip* in Germany may also lessen the capacity to create and impose government-wide priorities. Many governments are emphasizing the need to institutionalize system-wide patterns of governance within government, if not within the overall processes of interactive governance. Parading under the banner of coordination or collaboration or strategic governing, these attempts to create more systemic approaches to governing confront the problem of institutionalization at the lower levels that minimize the systemic governance capacity.

Although it is rarely discussed in the literature on institutions, there is some danger that the structures within the formal public sector will become *over-institutionalized* (see Kesselman, 1970). This potential dysfunction may occur at the level of the individual institution as well as at the level of the relationships among actors responsible for managing one segment of governing the society. At the level of the individual institution, the members of that structure may become so committed to the values and routines of their institution that they have difficulty in cooperating with other institutions or noninstitutional actors. This may be especially true for presidentialist regimes in which the major political institutions are rivals for power and may not always be inclined to cooperate with one another.

Institutions have a natural tendency toward over-institutionalization. This can be seen more clearly when adopting the normative perspective on institutional theory, when structures with dominant routines and common values create something like a "groupthink" ('t Hart, 1994) within the structure so that relatively few alternatives may be considered when designing a response to a perceived problem. Over-institutionalized structures will have difficulty coping with new information and changes in the environment, tending to code novel circumstances as the familiar and failing to adapt successfully.

The issues about full institutionalization, or perhaps over-institutionalization, can also arise in the context of multilevel governance. While much of the literature on multilevel governance has tended to celebrate the development of this style of governing within the European Union (EU), when considered more generally there can be important managerial and governance issues. As we have argued elsewhere (Pierre and Peters, 2005), these systems of governing are not so open as might be thought but rather may be dominated by the actors with clearer policy preferences, often central governments. Thus, these structures may not be as successful in responding to the range of demands coming from the subnational actors as might be expected, and the more institutionalized actors that have tended to dominate the system may continue to do so.

For the institutional structures defined by stable relationships among actors, for example, a policy area or a particular process, the same logic may be apparent. The commitment to one policy area, or the immersion of an actor in a particular set of routines and norms, may prevent cooperation and coordination. As noted above, these subgovernments may be more readily formed, and more powerful, in some governments and may constitute

115

important barriers to effective governance seen as more coherent patterns of steering. Managing the potential over-institutionalization of these systems will be facilitated to the extent that some actors play boundary-spanning roles, linking different subgovernments or different institutions.

At even more of an extreme of organizational behavior in the public sector, some "rogue organizations" in the public sector can be conceptualized as over-institutionalized, having internalized their own values and priorities, even in the face of other available values that would be more widely shared within that public sector. For example, organizations such as the FBI under J. Edgar Hoover have been extremely well-institutionalized in their own terms (Blau, 1956), but were hardly institutionalized into the larger value system of the public sector. Thus, the full institutionalization of a contrary set of organizational values can inhibit governance taken more broadly, while at the same time contributing to the organizational goals of the single organization.

One means of managing the over-institutionalization of one component of a governance structure, or one policy area, can be politicians or civil servants whose interests or organizational responsibilities are related to more than one policy (Marchington et al., 2005). Further, civil servants who have broad organizational experiences within government are more likely to be able to contribute to managing across boundaries. Also actors in the private sector organizations can play the role of boundary-spanner. As we will develop in greater detail below, network actors can be extremely important in playing that role given that they and their organizations often participate in a range of networks in different policy areas and hence can provide the linkages across those policies from the bottom up.

For the political systems outside the blessed world of the more affluent democracies, the process of institutionalization of governments is more problematic, as indeed Huntington's initial analysis had argued. For example, it may be difficult for these institutions to gain autonomy from social groups (defined by ethnic or religious groups) or from international donors who define the goals for these structures. Likewise, achieving the resources to be sufficiently adaptable to a changing socioeconomic environment may be difficult, especially as those resources may be tied to global markets. The difficulty for these countries may be, as Migdal (1988) has pointed out, that these are weak states functioning within weak societies and hence any form of governance may be difficult to produce.

We can sing praises to well-institutionalized systems of governance, but it is more difficult to explain how to create such a level of institutionalization. Perhaps the most obvious answer to that question is that leadership is required. Political and institutional entrepreneurs may be necessary to provide the impetus for institutionalizing interactions. In addition, there may be virtuous cycles in the interaction of actors, both public and private, that generate increasing levels of institutionalization (see Peters, 2007a). That is, initial attempts to create governance arrangements will produce positive feedbacks that assist in creating greater institutionalization.

Similarly, the rewards of being within the governance system may be evident, especially to social actors, so that actors may become more willing to comply with internal controls in order to gain those benefits.

Institutionalizing interactive governance

In addition to the institutionalization of governance capacities in general, the central focus of this book is on the role played by networks and other forms of relationships between the public sector and social actors in providing governance. Therefore, we should focus on the more particular question of how the governance networks that have become increasingly central to governing become institutionalized. Much of the literature on network forms of governance assumes that these structures are self-organizing, with a generally implicit functionalist argument that the networks form in response to a social need to organize and control a sector of social activity that cannot be governed by a single actor. The theoretical literature on self-organization (Luhmann, 1984; 't Veld et al., 1991) argues that the dysfunctions of contemporary governments are sufficient to provoke social actors to organize and to assume some of the regulatory functions that might be required from an effective government. The functionalist assumption about the self-organization of networks is supported by some cases, but it does appear that many of the networks involved in governance are encouraged by actors in the public sector. As such, Rhodes (1996) and Sørensen and Torfing (2007) have argued that governance networks develop as a political and administrative response to failures of the formal actors in public sector.

Attempting to organize networks may confront problems of pluralistic ignorance (Shamir and Shamir, 1997) when neither the organizers nor the potential members of the networks are aware of the existence of other actors who may have the same values, or the same political aspirations. Further, individual groups may not recognize the benefits that may accrue to them and their members through involvement with the network and its connections to the public sector. Finally, the possibilities of influencing the public sector through concerted action may not be apparent to all potential members of network structures, although this is increasingly unlikely as networks become better institutionalized as components of governing.

The functionalist assumption about forming networks for policymaking and implementation can be supplemented by a more economic logic in which networks are formed in order to lower transaction costs among the participants, including participants from the public sector. Although members of networks may share some common interests, that is often insufficient to guarantee the formation of an effective and enduring network. If, however, there are gains to be made from institutionalizing the structures and creating effective networks, then the network may persist and may even begin to have meaning for the participants.

Whether they are produced by some functional logic or they are the product of strategic action from the public sector, networks will face several challenges as they are created and institutionalized. These are components of the "liability of newness" (Stinchcombe, 1965) that any nascent organization will face. The first challenge (Boin and Goodin, 2007) that the network will face is developing its own internal culture and internal manner of functioning. Given that most of these organizations tend to be formed without any specific template and perhaps without individual leaders who can devote full-time to managing the structure, this routinization of activities will be difficult. That said, as these are meant to be relatively informal structures, these demands might not be so great as they would be for a business or even one of the constituent organizations of a network.

Boin and Goodin (2007) were concerned primarily with the managerial elements of making a new organization function, but for networks there is also another and more subtle element. A network needs to establish internal values and a sense of belonging to the network. This challenge is, of course, analogous to Selznick's conception of institutionalization. The need to create these values may be greater for networks than for more formalized institutions because of their less formal nature, and their general inability to provide incentives for membership other than the moral, solidaric benefits of belonging. If networks are to fulfill their potential for bringing together potentially disparate social and economic interests, then there must be a means of building common values, not the least of which are the benefits (intrinsic and extrinsic) values of involvement with the networks.

The second challenge that a new organization or network will have to overcome is establishing effective relationships with the political environment. Networks need to legitimate their role in governance and to secure a legitimate place within the processes of governing. This task is somewhat easier in societies with a history of corporatist and corporate pluralist forms for interest intermediation, in which the role of social actors has already been legitimated. The assumption for organizations operating in these societies is that their involvement with the public sector is a natural aspect of their being organizations with some policy relevance. That said, many corporatist arrangements were dominated by state actors, so the shift toward greater equality of participation and the associated indeterminacy might still need some legitimation.

The above discussion is premised on an assumption that networks are indeed new, although some may have been in existence for some time and are only adapting their behavior to become more a part of governance. To some extent this adaptation on the part of existing structures should be easier, given that the initial challenges of institutionalization would all have been overcome. There should be some regular pattern of interaction as well as some shared meaning among the members that are necessary to maintain it. As a functioning organization, such a network should be able to transform its performance to cope with the new tasks, but this will require some deinstitutionalization and reinstitutionalization of its activities.

Although the existing networks may have the simple virtue of existing, that does not mean that they will necessarily have the capacity to adjust to changing pressures coming from their involvement with making policy. As noted, some members may be involved in network activities more for social reasons than for purposive reasons and may find the need for the network to play a more political role to be distasteful or at least unnecessary. Thus, these members must adopt different values or cease participating in the network. Further, the network structures may not have been able to achieve any effective level of institution on the criteria developed by Huntington to understand institutionalization. In particular, the networks may not have any effective autonomy from their members, nor indeed autonomy from the parts of the public sector with which they work.

Networks may also become over-institutionalized, as discussed above for organizations and institutions within the formal areas of governing. Network governance literature has the functionalist assumption that the networks are there to serve some purposive goal, while in reality they may be more interested in maintaining themselves rather than in achieving the goals. The tendency toward over-institutionalization will naturally increase as these institutions remain together longer and the social embeddedness of the actors becomes more crucial to them, an outcome that Schaap (2007) has defined in terms of closure.

Much of the same logic of institutionalizing networks applies to the other major instruments of interactive governance considered in this book. For example, partnerships by definition involve the interaction of actors that may have somewhat different values and goals. Thus, there is a need to create effective linkages among these actors. Quasi-markets also involve some levels of institutionalization although the more instrumental nature of the involvement of the actors may not depend so much on institutionalization.

Institutionalizing linkages

As well as addressing the question of how networks themselves institutionalize, we must also be concerned with the institutionalization of the linkages between the networks and the formal aspects of the governance system. This linkage is crucial for the success of network governance, but can also be highly variable. First, we would expect the linkages between networks and formal government institutions to be a function of their own internal institutionalization, and for this linkage to be non-linear over time. Newly formed and poorly institutionalized networks may find it difficult to work effectively with other actors, perhaps fearing that this will undermine their own developmental process (Boin and Goodin, 2007). Likewise, over-institutionalized structures will have lost some of their utility for governance.

We will also hypothesize that the success of the linkage between networks and the formal public sector is to be a function of their internal homogeneity. To the extent that the network can speak with a single voice concerning its demands for policy and involvement in governance, it is more likely to be able to create a stable relationship with its counterparts in the formal institutions of the public sector. That said, however, some internal heterogeneity within a network may enable it to function more effectively with a range of public sector organizations, which themselves may have different goals.

This argument is analogous to that in the organizational culture literature that says that members of an organization who are not committed to the dominant culture may play a positive role by linking that organization to other organizations in its environment. Those organizations in the environment may be important for the one organization that is central to this analysis but have somewhat different values. One of the common arguments in institutional theory is that the environment of one institution is composed of other institutions so that the capacity to work effectively with those other institutions is crucial. This linkage is perhaps even more crucial for interactive governance, given its very nature of the involvement of multiple actors.

Finally, we might expect these linkages to depend also upon the nature of the organizations and individuals within the public sector. We have already noted that some organizations within the public sector may become so institutionalized and committed to their particular perspectives on policy and government that they may not be open to influences from outside their own boundaries. Such closure within the organization may be especially true for groups whose policy perspectives are not in full agreement with the perspectives of the organization(s) in the public sector with which they must work. Various versions of organization theory have discussed the importance of boundary-spanning roles (Jemison, 2007) for the success of organizations and for interactive governance those roles may be all the more important.

Conclusion

This chapter has emphasized the role that institutionalizing relationships has in the process of governance. There are at least three sets of such relationships that must be institutionalized if interactive governance is to be successful: within government itself, within networks, and between networks and the formal components of the public sector. In general, we have been arguing that building well-institutionalized structures is a positive outcome of these dynamics for governing, whether those dynamics are controlled from society or from the public sector. Institutionalization is not, however, an end in itself, but rather should be understood in the context of enhancing the capacity for governance.

Institutionalization may, in some instances, also be an impediment to flexible and effective governance. If government organizations or networks are over-institutionalized and closed in on themselves, then they may not be effective in facilitating cooperation and securing flexible adjustment in public governance. This problem may be especially important given that so many contemporary policymaking situations require effective cooperation across policy areas and between the public and private (broadly conceived) sectors. Therefore, we need to consider the logic of institutionalization in a somewhat broader manner, recognizing not only the benefits of stability and predictability but also the potential dangers to policymaking.

7

Metagovernance: The art of governing interactive governance

The concept of metagovernance is increasingly important for understanding how modern governments—and other legitimate and resourceful actors—can govern contemporary societies in the face of the current surge in interactive governance. Quasi-markets, partnerships, and governance networks are proliferating in response to rising demands, the need for resource mobilization, and a growing complexity of societal problems (Heinrich et al., 2009). However, interactive forms of governance do not emerge spontaneously but are often facilitated, initiated, and even designed by public authorities. In addition, the interactive governance arrangements might fail to produce effective and legitimate ideas and solutions. Finally, elected governments must impose some kind of direction on the interactive policy processes in order to realize their overall objectives, enhance pluricentric coordination and policy alignment, and ensure democratic accountability. Hence, the attempts of governments at multiple levels to reap the fruits of interactive governance call for a reflexive and strategic metagovernance. Metagovernance can be defined as the "governance of governance" as it involves deliberate attempts to facilitate, manage, and direct more or less self-regulating processes of interactive governance without reverting to traditional statist styles of government in terms of bureaucratic rule making and imperative command.

Those politicians and public managers who fail to grasp that metagovernance is a new and important assignment for government will find it increasingly difficult to achieve their policy goals. Although public bureaucracies are still providing the lion's share of public regulation, goods, services, and transfer payments, a growing number of public goods and services are being delivered by private contractors in recently created quasi-markets, and the development of public policy is often a result of negotiated interaction in networks and partnerships. As such, governing interactive governance arenas is a crucial task for governments, and it requires the development of a new way of governing that aims to build, shape, and enhance the self-governing capacities of decentered governance arrangements, while giving direction to the policy process and holding the interactive policy arenas to account.

This chapter provides a comprehensive discussion of metagovernance that brings together different theoretical contributions and draws on empirical experiences from different countries and levels. The basic argument is that metagovernance is not only a new and important task for governments and other capable actors but also a difficult task that is prone to failure. The chapter begins with a brief assessment of the growing concern for metagovernance *avant la lettre*. As such, it is claimed that although the concept of metagovernance is new, it helps us to understand practices of "regulated self-regulation" that have played an increasing role in the last few decades. This introductory discussion is followed by an overview of different theoretical approaches to metagovernance. The central insights from these approaches are used to create a more elaborate definition of metagovernance. The next section aims to show how the concept of metagovernance can help us to avoid the misguided idea that interactive governance drastically reduces the role of the government and to secure the democratic anchorage of quasi-markets, networks, and partnerships in elected politicians. The main part of the chapter analyzes the various objectives, tools, and forms of metagovernance and critically reflects on the limits, challenges, and dilemmas of metagovernance. The chapter is concluded with a discussion of what it takes to become a metagovernor and a brief discussion of the future research agenda.

Metagovernance *avant la lettre*

The concept of metagovernance can help us to understand the new and emerging ways of governing interactive forms of governance and their relation to other forms of governance. However, many ideas and practices that we describe today as instances of metagovernance predate the notion of metagovernance that emerged in the second half of the 1990s. The attempts of federal governments to regulate interstate governance and the efforts of national governments to govern the interaction between local municipalities are clear examples of metagovernance as they involve reflexive and strategic attempts to alter the political, institutional, and economic conditions for interactive governance processes. The many and changing European Union (EU) treaties are also a case in point. The aim of the consecutive EU treaty reforms is not to solve particular policy problems but to enhance the capacities for democratic and effective problem-solving in the face of globalization and European diversity by means of facilitating sustained interaction between EU institutions, member states, and an array of private actors.

More recently, New Public Management (NPM) reforms have generated an acute need for understanding the regulation of self-regulation (Sørensen and Triantafillou, 2009). The NPM doctrine combines market competition with business-like managerialism, but despite this apparent marriage of opposites (Hood, 1991), the new ideas associated with NPM have swept like a tsunami across much of the OECD world (Pollitt and Bouckaert, 2004). David Osborne and Ted Gaebler (1992) have fleshed out the key principles of NPM that they believe will help governments to become more efficient and effective. First of all, politicians and their top managers should focus on "steering" (policy decisions) rather than "rowing" (service production). The latter should be the task of public administrators working either in self-governing teams or in quasi-autonomous agencies equipped with a clearly defined mission. Steering should take the form of strategic goal setting, which should be combined with an elaborate system of performance management that enables politicians and top managers to check whether or not the predefined goals are achieved. Second, the central executive agencies should not govern the local service delivery agencies by means of bureaucratic rules and commands but rather by a skillful combination of storytelling, economic incentives, and benchmarks that aim to unleash the entrepreneurial spirit of public managers and street-level bureaucrats within an increasingly devolved public sector. In short, public organizations should be result-driven rather than rule-driven. Third, public managers should contract out the production and delivery of standardized public goods and services to private providers who will enhance quality and spur innovation because they operate in cut-throat markets where only the best survives. The private providers should have considerable room for maneuvering, but their operation should be bound by contracts that define objectives, tasks, quality standards, and prices and establish procedures that can help to ensure negotiation and trust building. Fourth, public organizations should be transformed into public enterprises that operate on market terms and invest in future possibilities to earn money. This requires establishment of public enterprise boards in an arm's length from elected government. Finally, the users of public services should be redescribed as "customers" and customer satisfaction rather than the public interest should drive public service provision. To ensure this, the users should have both exit and voice options so that they can leave bad service providers or help to improve the quality of public services through participation in user boards.

All these normative prescriptions seem to hinge on the creation of spaces for relatively self-regulated practices. Public employees, quasi-autonomous agencies, private contractors, public enterprises, and customers are requested to use their competences, resources, and energies to achieve politically defined objectives in new, efficient, and creative ways. Ideally, the public and private actors should be governed neither by bureaucratic rules nor by top-down commands but have considerable autonomy within boundaries and constraints defined by political objectives, legal parameters, funding schemes, and budget allocations. In reality, NPM tends to keep the local actors in a strait-jacket of top-down control. Nevertheless, the new focus on regulated self-regulation immediately throws up the questions of how these self-regulating practices are facilitated, coordinated, and managed and how we can conceptualize the persistent attempts to govern these practices. The NPM discourse does not have much to offer when it comes to answering these pertinent questions, but merely refers to the use of management-by-objectives and the deployment of a large array of performance measurement techniques. These management techniques are not in themselves novel. What is new is the way that these techniques are used in attempts to manage more or less self-regulating organizational arenas in which public and private actors are called upon to develop and use their "entrepreneurial spirit" to improve public performance and create public value.

Some academic commentators have noticed the new ways that public management is exercised in the wake of the growing emphasis on self-regulation implicit to NPM reforms. For example, it has become quite common to talk about how governments are forced to swap direct for indirect controls and how governments must learn to govern in ways that help other organizational actors to achieve their objectives (Rhodes, 1997a). However, more elaborate attempts to understand the new governing practices have been few and far between. An exception is Nikolas Rose and Peter Miller who claim that governments are becoming "dependent upon technologies for 'governing at a distance,' seeking to create locales, entities and persons able to operate a regulated autonomy" (Rose and Miller, 1992: 173). This diagnosis captures the new emphasis on how principals should govern devolved agencies by means of hands-off governance, but it fails to conceptualize the gradual shift from the imperative command of subordinate agencies and employees to facilitation, management, and direction of self-regulated governing practices. This is exactly why the notion of metagovernance is important. It offers a way of conceptualizing the relation between devolved quasi-autonomous actors and agencies and the reflexive and strategic attempts to govern these actors and agencies in order to achieve particular goals, without reverting to traditional forms of bureaucratic control and sanctions. The concept of metagovernance helps us to understand not only the new governing practices associated with NPM but also how partnerships and governance networks, which are often formed as a strategic and practical response to the fragmentation caused by NPM reforms (Rhodes, 1997a), can be governed by resourceful and legitimate actors that we will call metagovernors.

Theoretical approaches to metagovernance

Today, there is a growing interest in the study of metagovernance. The expanding literature on metagovernance comprises both theoretical contributions (Kickert et al., 1997; Jessop, 2002; Kooiman, 2003) and empirical studies (Whitehead, 2003; O'Toole and Meier, 2004; Hovik and Vabo, 2005; Bell and Park, 2006; Kelly, 2006; Sørensen, 2006). However, the analytical vantage point from where interactive forms of governance and metagovernance are envisioned tends to differ between different groups of researchers. Hence, when organization sociologists analyze the new interactive governance arrangements, they tend to see them as ways of getting things done and promoting societal transformation. In line with this view, they raise important points about how to ensure good and constructive interaction through the exercise of a process-oriented leadership within networks and partnerships (Mandell and Keast, 2009). By contrast, public management researchers tend to see interactive governance arrangements as tools for dealing with different kinds of uncertainty (Koppenjan and Klijn, 2004). This leads them to consider how the public managers, who are dealing with networks and partnerships, can affect the functioning of these interactive arenas through different kinds of network management (Kickert et al., 1997). Finally, when political theorists look at networks, partnerships, and other interactive governance arrangements, they tend to perceive them as a new and attractive mode of governance that supplements public hierarchies and private markets. This prompts them to raise questions about when and how public authorities should use different interactive modes of governance and how government can hold interactive policy arenas and governance arrangements to account (Jessop, 2002; Meuleman, 2008; Sørensen and Torfing, 2009). Despite their different views of the role and character of interactive governance, the three groups of researchers all pose highly relevant questions about what metagovernance is and how it should be exercised. Still, the main difference when answering these questions regards how they envision and where they locate the metagovernor. As such, the metagovernor is variably portrayed as a leading network actor, a network manager who is simultaneously inside and outside the network, and the State aiming to govern the interactive arenas from a distance.

In the emerging scholarly debate on metagovernance, there are four different theoretical approaches that deserve special attention (see Sørensen and Torfing, 2007). *Interdependency theorists* such as Rod Rhodes (1997a) and Walter Kickert et al. (1997) focus on networks and partnerships, which contribute to joint problem-solving through negotiated exchange among interdependent actors with diverging interests. Successful network governance requires the inclusion of relevant and affected actors, the willingness of the participants to exchange or pool their resources, and the development of common conceptions of problems, solutions, and decision-making premises. However, many things can go wrong and lead to governance network failure. Social and cognitive closure may exclude relevant stakeholders from the interactive policy arena (Schaap, 2007). Competition and opportunistic behavior may foster defensive and noncooperative strategies and give rise to damaging conflicts. Finally, the failure to build mutual trust, communication processes resembling a dialogue of the deaf, and high transaction costs from networking may erode the basis for continued interaction (Koppenjan and Klijn, 2004). These permanent risks call for hands-on "network management" that aims to improve and stabilize the interaction processes among the network actors (Kickert et al., 1997). Network management involves a skillful combination of process management and process design.

Other interdependency theorists such as Bob Jessop (2002) provide a state-theoretical approach to metagovernance that tends to view metagovernance as a possibility for the capitalist State to exercise power by choosing and mixing different modes of governance, mitigating the risks of failure associated with each of these modes of governance, and determining the overall conditions for how they are functioning. This view, which also informs the recent work of Louis Meuleman (2008), adds a crucial power perspective on the exercise of metagovernance. Metagovernance is seen as a new way that the State can exercise power in the context of interactive governance. The state-theoretical approach to metagovernance also emphasizes the moment of reflexive choice where state authorities carefully consider the problem or task at hand and choose a particular combination of different modes of governance (hierarchy, market, or network) in order to achieve a desired outcome. No matter whether metagovernance is seen from the point of view of the State or the point of view of public managers, interdependency theorists tend to agree that metagovernance is a tool for facilitating interaction and resource exchange in the face of diverging interests and political conflicts. Governance networks are arenas for interest-based political struggles and metagovernance is a way of reducing the risk of disruptive conflicts.

Governability theorists such as Jan Kooiman (1993a, 2003), Renate Mayntz (1993a, 1993b), and Fritz Scharpf (1994) also perceive stakeholders as strategic actors with diverging interests, but they tend to downplay the role of conflict. Networks, partnerships, and other forms of negotiated interaction are seen as a functional response to the increasing differentiation of societal systems and organizational subsystems that tend to enhance the ungovernability of society. However, due to the propensity of network actors to pursue individual strategies and to defect from negotiated agreements, governance networks are continuously on the brink of collapsing as a collective form of governance. As such, metagovernance is strictly required in order to facilitate stable and efficient forms of interactive governance. Metagovernance involves efforts to clarify, emphasize, and even construct relations of interdependency between the interacting actors: the higher the level of interdependency between the actors, the greater is their willingness to search for shared goals and to take risks. However, clarifying interdependency through the illumination of the specific resources of the relevant actors, or creating interdependency by providing ad hoc funding of networked policy initiatives is not enough to secure smooth coordination in interactive governance arenas. Hence, metagovernance must also involve "game structuration" through institutional design of the conditions for negotiated interaction (Scharpf, 1994: 40; Kooiman, 2003: 155). Game structuration can be performed in many different ways (Scharpf, 1994). First, cooperative strategies can be furthered by institutional facilitation of positive-sum games in which the network actors gain from redistribution of material and immaterial resources within the network. Second, the search for joint solutions in a network or partnership can be stimulated either by providing positive incentives or by emphasizing that the interactive governance arena operates in "the shadow of hierarchy," which means that the capacity for self-regulation will be reduced or removed if the process of negotiated interaction fails to find a feasible solution to the problem or challenge at hand. Last but not least, unwarranted cost-shifting from the interactive arenas to third parties can be prevented by means of regulating the distribution of costs.

At a lower level of abstraction, Adrienne Héritier and Dirk Lehmkuhl (2008) discuss the use of contracts to regulate interactive governance arrangements that are involved in policy regulation (networks and partnerships) or service delivery (quasi-markets). Contracts typically define the scope of the tasks and competences of a particular governance arrangement. They also regulate the distribution of costs and benefits and they often provide "sticks and carrots" that will shape the actions of the public and private actors. However, the bounded rationality of the actors and the impossibility of including provisions for all future contingencies mean that contracts are necessarily incomplete. The incomplete character of governance contracts highlights the importance of specifying a set of procedural rules for adjusting the contract to changing conditions and resolving conflicts arising from the application of incomplete contracts.

Whatever the concrete tools and instruments of metagovernance, governability theorists tend to agree with Scharpf (1994) that the ultimate goal of metagovernance is to enhance positive coordination. At least, interactive governance arrangements should foster negative coordination, which is a situation in which the network actors avoid interfering negatively with each other's interest sphere and base their cooperation upon what is generally considered as the least common denominator. In more mature networks and partnerships, the goal is to facilitate positive coordination where the interdependent actors aim to exploit the possibilities for joint action by means of arriving at a common definition of policy problems and searching for joint solutions that are sustained and implemented even if they may incur certain costs.

Normative integration theorists such as James G. March and Johan P. Olsen (1995), Walter Powell and Paul DiMaggio (1983, 1991), and Richard Scott (1995) do not talk explicitly about metagovernance. Nevertheless, they have quite a lot to say about how to govern interactive governance arrangements that are formed either through a bottom-up process where contacts between interdependent actors are evaluated and extended on the basis of institutionalized logics of appropriateness (March and Olsen, 1995), or through top-down pressures to adopt new fashionable governance templates that can help to enhance legitimacy within an organizational field (Powell and DiMaggio, 1983). According to the normative integration theorists, social and political actors are not driven by rational calculations based on exogenous preferences and interests; rather, they act on the basis of interpretations of the rules, norms, routines, values, and cognitive schemes that make up the institutional context of their interaction (March and Olsen, 1995). Therefore, metagovernance is not so much a matter of stabilizing exchange in the face of conflict or of creating cooperative games through institutional design. Metagovernance involves the development of the identities and capabilities of the public and private actors and enhancing the accountability and adaptiveness of interactive governance arrangements (March and Olsen, 1995). The development of identities involves the shaping of the actors' perceptions of themselves, each other, and their joint missions. This is done through storytelling, the production and circulation of knowledge, and the creation of institutional rules, norms, symbols, and rituals. The development of the capabilities of the network actors is an attempt to empower the actors to act alone and together. Empowerment involves the construction and distribution of rights, resources, competences, and political know-how. The accountability of interactive governance can be enhanced through the production of narrative accounts of the way that the actors perceive particular problems and opportunities and the reasons they have for acting in a certain way. Last but not least, the adaptiveness of interactive governance arrangements can be further developed by building institutional structures that encourage experience-based and experimental learning. According to the normative integration theorists, the overall purpose of the various attempts to govern interactive forms of governance is to form a strong democratic community within and between interactive forms of governance. The means by which to do this is normative integration.

Governmentality theorists such as Michel Foucault (1991), Nikolas Rose (1999), and Mitchell Dean (1999) do not use the notion of metagovernance either, but the concept of "the regulation of self-regulation" plays a central role in their understanding of how advanced liberal societies are governed. Like the normative integration theorists, Foucault and his followers tend to see concrete governance practices as being shaped by institutionalized ideas, norms, and routines, but unlike the integration theorists the governmentality theorists tend to see the shaping and reshaping of identities and actions as a practice that involves both power and resistance. Governmentality theorists hold a decentered account of power, arguing that power does not emanate from the sovereign center of the State but is exercised in and through a mobile and heterogeneous network of relations and interactions (Foucault, 1990). Governmentality theory defines government as a power strategy that involves the "conduct of conduct" (Foucault, 1986b) and it aims to explore the historical conditions for how to govern and be governed. The historical conditions for government in the sense of the conduct of conduct are captured by the notion of governmentality that is defined as the institutionalized collective mentalities, rationalities, and technologies that shape the concrete acts of government. The attempt to "govern at a distance" is at the core of the liberal governmentality. In the advanced liberal societies that emerge as a result of an ongoing problematization of the modern welfare state and the neoliberal turn to the market, we are witnessing an increasing attempt to construct and mobilize free and responsible actors who are placed within specific conditions of possibility that tend to ensure a certain conformity with overall policy objectives. As such, metagovernance combines what Dean (1999) terms "technologies of agency" with "technologies of performance." While the former attempt to mobilize the energies, resources, and knowledge of free and self-regulating subjectivities through the formation of partnerships, governance networks, free choice, and participatory devices, the latter aim to regulate the conduct of the self-regulating actors by producing and disseminating a large array of norms, standards, benchmarks, performance indicators, and incentives. In other words, metagovernance can be seen as a subtle power strategy that involves both subjectification and subjection. Power always has a telos and in advanced liberal societies it is to govern the population in an efficient and legitimate way while limiting the deployment of resources and keeping the use of force and repression to a minimum.

The various approaches to metagovernance all provide valuable insights that can help us to qualify and elaborate the minimalistic definition of metagovernance as a second-order "governance of governance." Foucault (1991) draws our attention to the institutionalized discourses that regulate concrete forms and acts of governance. Jessop (2002) highlights the reflexive choice and mixing of different modes of governance and Kooiman (2003) insists that the choice of a particular institutional system of governance invokes a series of normative values and ideals. Scharpf (1994) and Kickert et al. (1997) provide a detailed insight into how to stabilize and improve the functioning of interactive governance arrangements and give them a certain direction. Combining these insights renders it possible to redefine metagovernance as a reflexive, higher order governance practice that involves (*a*) *the production and dissemination of hegemonic norms and ideas about how to govern and be governed*; (*b*) *the political, normative, and context-dependent choice among different modes of governing, or among different combinations of governing modes*; and (*c*) *the strategic structuring and managing of particular institutional forms of governance in order to facilitate sustained interaction, prevent dysfunctions, and advance particular political goals*. This elaborated definition of metagovernance sets out the main themes in the study of metagovernance as it captures the discursive, normative, and strategic aspects of the exercise of metagovernance.

Connecting government and governance through metagovernance

There has been a growing body of literature claiming that traditional forms of government have given way to a new form of "governance without government" (Pierre and Peters, 1998). Rod Rhodes (1996) argues that NPM has fragmented the public sector and fostered a growing demand for horizontal coordination through networks and partnerships that seriously challenge the Whitehall model of government. Ken Menkhaus (2002) shows that new governance arrangements beyond government are evolving in failed states like Somalia. Finally, at the international level, James Rosenau and Ernst Czempiel (1992) argue that the absence of a world government creates a space for negotiated governance within and among states, and Susan Strange (1996) contends that the autonomy and regulatory capacities of national states are under pressure from the global capital markets. While agreeing that interactive forms of governance prevent states at various levels from exercising the kind of control that they are assumed to have had in the past, we should be careful not to paint a picture of a totally incapacitated State that is rendered powerless by the advent of new forms of governance. The State is not being "hollowed out" as some people are suggesting (Milward and Provan, 2000). Many traditional state powers are still in place and new powers are developing in the face of the challenges from networks, partnerships, international governance arenas, and global markets (Pierre and Peters, 2000). The State in contemporary societies has in many cases and areas lost its ability to control political decision-making through unilateral action, but it still has the capacity to influence the different arenas of multilateral action. State authorities establish, monitor, and regulate quasi-markets; they form, manage, and participate in partnerships; and they play a central role in developing and framing different kinds of networks. In short, governments are capable of influencing policymaking in the decentered world of interactive governance through the exercise of metagovernance.

Metagovernance is an important concept for understanding how traditional forms of government and new and emerging forms of interactive governance are connected. Governments are still in charge of running large-scale regulatory and service-delivering bureaucracies, but they are also engaged in the metagovernance of interactive policy processes involving a number of public and private actors. Metagovernance aims to facilitate, manage, and direct multilateral policymaking, but as the various actors have their own rule and resource bases and can freely decide whether to exchange or pool their resources, metagovernance cannot take the form of imperative command. Attempts to metagovern by issuing orders and commands, providing a detailed set of authoritative and non-negotiable rules, or in other ways trying to eliminate the room for maneuvering in the interactive policy arena will either scare off the private stakeholders or provoke a fierce resistance giving rise to damaging conflicts. Metagovernance cannot revert to traditional forms of hierarchical steering as metagovernors must respect the capacity for self-regulation of the interactive governance arenas in order to preserve the commitment of the public and private actors. As such, the concept of metagovernance does not, as it has been suggested, endeavor to "bring the State back in" by insisting on its omnipotence and, consequently, reduce governance to "the tools, strategies and relationships used by governments to help govern" (Bell and Hindmoor, 2009: 191). Rather, the notion of metagovernance offers a way of balancing state-centered and society-centered views on how society and the economy are governed. It permits us to avoid erroneous ideas about the decline or death of the state and to appreciate the role of states and governments in influencing arenas of multilateral action, while insisting that traditional forms of control and command are rendered obsolete, or least reduced to "a shadow of hierarchy" (Scharpf, 1994), in areas where decentered forms of policy interaction are expanding.

The concept of metagovernance is also helpful in rethinking how the "primacy of politics" can be maintained in areas where interactive forms of governance play an important role. The "primacy of politics" refers to the ability of elected politicians to influence the authoritative allocation of values in society (Easton, 1965*b*). This influence is supposedly gained through politicians' pivotal role in law making and government's right to instruct public managers how the laws are to be implemented. Some scholars fear that politicians' ability to control public governance is threatened by the increasing use of contracting out, networking, and other forms of "third-party" governance. As such, Lester Salamon (1989) claims that interactive governance "puts government in the position of operating on remote control" (1989: 8–9) and declares that the US welfare state "is not run by the State at all, but by a host of nongovernmental 'third parties'" (1989: xv). By contrast, we claim that the exercise of metagovernance permits elected governments to maintain some kind of control over public governance in those situations in which they are no longer in charge of public regulation and service production (for empirical support of this argument, see Heinrich et al., 2009).

The problem with politicians' loss of control with public governance is an old one. The blurring of the demarcation between politics and administration enhanced the influence of the strong and permanent executive managers and professional street-level bureaucrats and reduced the power of elected politicians. The NPM doctrine has aimed to remedy this problem by trying to reestablish the Weberian and Wilsonian division of labor between goal-setting politicians and service-producing administrators. However, the surge of interactive forms of governance, which is partly induced by NPM, seems to render the elected politicians even more powerless. They are losing out not only to public bureaucrats but also to private firms, interest organizations, and social movements. The kind of management-by-objectives recommended by NPM provides a key tool for understanding how politicians can influence interactive policy arenas, but the notion of metagovernance is even more helpful as it expands the role of politicians to include the design of interactive policy arenas, reflexive monitoring and occasional intervention in political negotiations, and direct participation in the decision-making processes through which problems are framed, goals are redefined, and solutions are found and implemented. Hence, in contrast to the preaching of the NPM doctrine, metagovernance is not restricting the politicians' means of influencing the deployment of "hands-off" measures, and also involves crucial "hands-on" measures such as process management and direct participation. Limited resources in terms of time and energy and the fear of not being able to understand the complex relations and technical issues at stake mean that politicians often delegate the responsibility for metagoverning networks, partnerships, and quasi-markets to public managers who in the absence of clear and extensive instructions from the politicians will have to rely on intuition, institutionalized rules, norms, and values, and the anticipation of the politicians' reactions. However, to the extent that public managers are acting on behalf of elected politicians, their attempt to metagovern, interactive governance arrangements will, together with the efforts of the elected politicians themselves, contribute to uphold the ideal of the primacy of politics and ensure democratic accountability. Interactive governance arenas are notoriously difficult to hold to account when something goes wrong (Rhodes, 1997a; Pierre, 2000). The actors engaged in interactive governance might be accountable to each other (horizontal accountability), but in a representative democracy they should also be held to account by the elected politicians (vertical accountability). It is precisely here that the notion of

133

metagovernance shows its value. Metagovernance involves a reflexive monitoring of the processes and results of interactive policymaking as well as deliberate attempts to influence the interactive decision-making process and to evaluate and sanction the outputs and outcomes of interaction and collaboration. In other words, metagovernance provides a crucial instrument for ensuring democratic anchorage of interactive governance in elected governments (Sørensen and Torfing, 2005*b*).

Objectives, means, and forms of metagovernance

Having, thus, demonstrated the analytical value of the concept of metagovernance, we shall turn to discuss the *objectives* pursued in the exercise of metagovernance, the *means* deployed in order to achieve these objectives, and the different *forms* that metagovernance might take in different contexts. Such a discussion will add some flesh and blood to the concept of metagovernance and give a more detailed understanding of how and why it is exercised.

Metagovernance of interactive forms of governance may have different objectives and serve different purposes. The objective can be to create a relative stable arena for policy interaction, to manage conflicts among various stakeholders, or to give some political direction to the interactive policy process. Metagovernance may also aim to assess and improve the impact and performance of networks or partnerships invoking an entire range of normative criteria such as democracy, effectiveness, policy innovation, coordination, mobilization of private resources, equity, etc. (Provan and Kenis, 2008).

Whatever the objective or purpose of metagovernance, there seem to be two different means by which to exercise metagovernance. As such, metagovernance can either involve "the mobilization of bias" (Schattschneider, 1960: 71) in terms of invoking, maintaining, and shaping the political, organizational, and socioeconomic structures of society, or it can involve the deployment of a variety of tools that are chosen and manipulated in order to produce a particular impact on processes and outcomes of governance (O'Toole, 2007).

Metagovernance through the "mobilization of bias" will take the form of more or less conscious attempts to invoke, maintain, or gradually transform the structural context for interactive forms of governance. Drawing on the Kiser and Ostrom (1982) model, we can distinguish among three sets of rules that are likely to have a structuring effect on interactive governance: operational rules, legislative rules, and constitutional rules. Constitutional and legislative rules are harder to change than the operational rules that govern the day-to-day practices in particular policy areas. However, metagovernors might choose to rely upon, or even accentuate, particular constitutional or legislative rules that define the basic conditions for governance. They may also aim to gradually change either the actual content, or the role and character, of constitutional and legislative rules in order to redefine rules of the game for interactive policymaking. The increasing use of enabling laws and the proliferation of independent auditing agencies are examples of how metagovernors can enhance flexibility while strengthening accountability. Metagovernors might also count upon, or seek to transform, particular political traditions and socioeconomic structures that more or less indirectly determine the scope for success and failure of interactive policy arenas. Loosening the grip of the etatist state tradition in France might spur the formation of interactive policy arenas and augmenting local government spending in Norway might enhance the prospect for participatory governance at the local level as allocation of money draws a bigger crowd than making cutbacks.

Metagovernance through the mobilization of bias involves a particular combination of action and inaction and can be exercised by metagovernors that are distant from a particular interactive governance arrangement. Metagovernors that are closer to interactive governance arrangements may also exercise metagovernance by means of deploying different managerial tools that may contribute to improving the performance and impact of particular governance arrangements. *Institutional design* of rules, norms, and procedures determines the basic functioning of interactive governance arrangements by means of influencing their scope, character, and composition. *Goal and framework steering* gives purpose and direction to interactive governance and facilitates systematic auditing by means of defining the overall objectives, the fiscal basis, the legal parameters, and the discursive storylines and setting up procedures for monitoring and evaluating the performance of interactive governance arenas. *Process management* helps to reduce tensions, resolve conflicts, selectively empower particular actors, and lower the transaction costs of networking by providing different kinds of material and immaterial inputs and resources. Finally, *direct participation* in interactive policy arenas makes it possible for metagovernors to influence the policy agenda, the range of feasible options, the premises for decision-making, and the negotiated policy outputs by means of leadership, argumentation, and coalition building.

While the first and second of these managerial tools are examples of "hands-off" metagovernance, which is performed at a distance from the relatively self-regulating quasi-markets, networks, and partnerships, the third and fourth tools are examples of "hands-on" metagovernance, which is exercised in and through a relatively close interaction between the metagovernors and the individual stakeholders. In contrast to the NPM doctrine that prescribes the use of hands-off metagovernance only, we believe that metagovernance of interactive governance arrangements is most successful when the metagovernors combine hands-off and hands-on metagovernance tools. Hands-off metagovernance often needs to be supplemented with hands-on metagovernance, permitting the metagovernors to influence policy interaction in a more direct and proactive manner. Institutional design and goal and framework steering might be sufficient in the initial phase, where the stakeholders are recruited and empowered and the basic parameters for policy interaction are defined. Later, when there are signs of failures in terms of conflicts, deadlocks, and the exclusion of key actors from the policy deliberations, or when the negotiated policy output strays too far from what is deemed acceptable by the metagovernors, there will be a need not only for redesigning or reframing the network but also for a more hands-on metagovernance through process management and direct participation.

The choice of would-be metagovernors between hands-on and hands-off metagovernance is also likely to vary from policy issue to policy issue. Hence, hands-on metagovernance will be deemed essential in policy areas that are closely related to the core functions of the State, such as the safeguarding of the national interest vis-à-vis the interest of other states, the preservation of law and order, the protection of public health, and the allocation of fiscal means. In these policy areas, where governance failure is likely to have fatal consequences, close interaction with the stakeholders is required in order to facilitate a more fine-grained, day-to-day regulation of the network or partnership based on precise knowledge of the interactive processes. For much the same reason, hands-on metagovernance will also be considerable in relation to interactive governance arrangements operating within policy areas defined by the political decision-makers as strategically important. Governance networks and partnerships established in response to the mounting pressures from economic globalization are a case in point. This explains why local networks in the field of active employment policy (Torfing, 2007*b*) and governance networks in the field of EU regulation of GMOs (Borrás, 2007) tend be subject to considerable hands-on metagovernance. However, a notable exception to this rule is those cases in which the relative autonomy of the governance network is a political goal in itself. A good example of this is the transnational network of central bankers that produces and disseminates rules and norms for monetary regulation (Marcussen, 2007). Politicians all over the world tend to believe that too much interference with the network of central bankers will potentially damage the efficient functioning of the global monetary system.

Challenges, limits, and dilemmas of metagovernance

Although the research on metagovernance is not so well developed as the research on governance, a number of empirical studies and practical guides aiming to show how interactive governance arrangements are, or should be, metagoverned have already been proffered. Robert Agranoff (2003) draws some important lessons for metagovernors who must recognize the shared expertise-based authority in networks and operate through agenda orchestration, incentive creation, and the deployment of interpersonal skills. Brinton Milward and Keith Provan (2006) define different kinds of networks (knowledge sharing networks, problem-solving networks, implementation networks, and capacity building networks), and insist that public managers should understand what type of network they are managing and what its purpose is before they can metagovern it effectively. Erik-Hans Klijn and Geert Teisman (2000) call for a combination of goal-oriented project management and process-oriented network management in the governing of public–private partnerships aimed at innovation and improvement of public services. Ludo Struyven and Geer Steurs (2005) draw our attention to the need for designing and redesigning quasi-markets for the reintegration of jobseekers. Finally, Steve Goldsmith and Bill Eggers (2004) offer an "accountability framework" that permits metagovernors to achieve results from network-based contracting with private firms and voluntary organizations. All these guides, checklists, strategies, and frameworks can be seen as a response to the growing need for reflecting on how metagovernance is exercised at a practical, managerial level.

However, in the light of the many attempts to "manualize" the exercise of metagovernance, it should be emphasized that metagovernance is a difficult and complicated endeavor, which is facing a series of challenges, limits, and dilemmas. The challenges that make metagovernance a necessary, but tough assignment are many. Hence, would-be metagovernors must respond to a series of problems arising from interactive governance (Peters, 2007*b*). First, it is often difficult to secure participation of the relevant and affected actors and maintain their commitment to continued interaction and common search for joint solutions. Second, the demand for coordination among a large number of public and private actors with different values, norms, interests, and strategic horizons is immense, while collective action problems such as "negotiators dilemma" and "free-riding" are ever-present risks. Third, interactive governance of wicked problems tends to generate a tremendous need for coping with substantive, strategic, and procedural uncertainties that make political paralysis and indecision a constant danger (Koppenjan and Klijn, 2004). Fourth, strategic games among the involved stakeholders tend to favor policymaking by the lowest common denominator and this might threaten the output legitimacy of interactive policy arenas. Fifth, the metagovernors face a classical principal–agent problem as they will often lack sufficient knowledge about the competences, capacities, efforts, and possible reactions of the stakeholders. Sixth, the metagovernors might be tempted to pursue their own short-term interests through a combination of instrumental cooptation of adversarial stakeholders, strategic manipulation of the policy interaction, and blocking of controversial proposals, rather than pursuing their long-term interest in enhancing the input and output legitimacy of public governance (Scharpf, 1999). The challenges come with the territory and the only way to meet them is through a skillful combination of different metagovernance strategies.

However, even the most well-intended, innovative, and context-sensitive metagovernance might fail due to the structural limitations to the exercise of metagovernance. In the attempt to respect the self-regulating capacities of interactive governance arrangements, the metagovernors must abandon the usage of tools that aim at exercising direct control by means of mandatory participation, centrally fixed remits, binding objectives, and prescribed procedures. Instead they must rely on allegedly "soft" instruments like institutional facilitation of participation, agenda setting, storytelling, and active participation—sometimes backed by more or less explicit "threats" of changing the composition of the interactive arena, narrowing its scope, limiting its public resources, or replacing it with either hierarchical command or the reign of the free market.

Evidently, the lack of direct control puts severe limits on what can be achieved through metagovernance. Nevertheless, the soft instruments can be quite effective when the new identities, norms, and vocabularies have become properly disseminated and internalized by the actors. In a way, the soft instruments, like voluntary standards, best practice, and other sermons, are quite "hard" as they aim at influencing the knowledge, perceptions, and preferences of the social and political actors rather than the range of feasible options (defined by using the stick) or the reward matrix (defined by offering carrots). This is confirmed by recent studies of the so-called Open Method of Coordination (the OMC) within the EU. In the OMC, a transnational policy network, consisting of member states and key stakeholders, negotiates and agrees upon a common set of guidelines that are supposed to regulate the policy performance of national governments and governance networks. The national compliance with the EU guidelines is voluntary, but backed by procedures for "naming and shaming" member states that stray too much from the transnational standards. Although the OMC does not result in any significant policy convergence at program level, there is a clear convergence at the level of policy discourse that might stimulate mutual learning and future convergence in problem definitions, policy objectives, and policy instruments (Jacobsson, 2004; Nedergaard, 2005; Lopez-Santana, 2006; Triantafillou, 2008). The backdrop of this apparent effectiveness of soft instruments is that their effects are rather unpredictable and that it might take a long time to produce a significant impact.

Would-be metagovernors must content themselves with the soft metagovernance tools and learn how to make the most of them. When exercising metagovernance in relation to interactive governance arrangements, they will soon come up against a number of dilemmas that call for hard choices and difficult balancing acts. One of the key dilemmas concerns the question of how to avoid either excessive or insufficient metagoverning (Kooiman, 1993*b*). If the metagovernance is too tight and strait-jackets the interactive policy arenas, it will give rise to resistance and conflicts, pacify the network actors, and reduce their willingness to participate and invest themselves in the joint problem-solving. This will reduce the benefits gained from the self-regulated policymaking or policy implementation. To illustrate, Damgaard (2006) shows that the public metagovernance of the employment policy networks in the Danish municipalities is so interventionist that it either marginalizes the role and influence of the local networks or reduces them to implementation instruments for the local government. If, on the other hand, the exercise of metagovernance is too weak and vague, it might lead to underperformance, stalemate, and disintegration, because the interactive policy arena does not receive proper support in terms of discursive framing, funding, and conflict resolution. There are many examples of insufficient metagovernance, but they are not well documented by researchers because the interactive arenas tend to perform badly and have a short life time.

Another important dilemma is captured by the question of how to strike the right balance between hands-off and hands-on metagovernance (Sørensen, 2007*b*). On the one hand, a strong reliance on hands-off metagovernance, aimed at facilitating and framing interactive governance, might result in political conflicts between the governance network and the democratically elected government, because the absence of close interaction between the various stake-holders and the public metagovernors hinders the construction of joint ownership of the policy outputs and policy outcomes. On the other hand, strong reliance on hands-on metagovernance aimed at resolving internal conflicts and influencing the content of actual policy solutions tends to bind the public metagovernors tightly to the policy output, leaving little scope for subsequent policy changes. If the compromise obtained through negotiations with the public metagovernors is not respected by the government, then implementation resistance will rise and the prospect of continued policy interaction will be dim. This is exactly what happened with the Water Management Committees in New South Wales (Bell and Park, 2006). The participants in the regional committees were appointed by the government that was also itself participating in the governance networks. The private stakeholders worked closely together with the government representatives and they expected to have considerable influence on water sharing policy in New South Wales. Therefore, when the government overruled the water-sharing plans that had been developed by the regional networks, it created a lot of frustration and the disillusionment has apparently ruined the prospect of future network governance.

Finally, public metagovernors are facing a number of dilemmas in relation to the competing objectives of metagovernance. As such, there might be a trade-off between democracy and effectiveness as a more inclusive participation of relevant stakeholders might make governance arrangements more democratic, while simultaneously reducing their ability to formulate clear and sustainable compromises based on negative and/or positive coordination (Scharpf, 1994). Another potential trade-off exists between policy innovation and consensus-building as interactive arenas that develop a shared understanding of the world tend to give way to "groupthink," which is detrimental to innovation. As such, there is a constant danger in epistemic networks, dealing with global issues such as AIDS, poverty, and global warming, that attempts to define a common ground and create consensus prevent the network actors from developing new and creative ideas by means of exploiting diversity and challenging each other's ideas. Last but not least, a trade-off might occur between resource mobilization and equity as attempts to include strong and resourceful stakeholders such as big business and large interest organizations might undermine the possibility for weaker and less resourceful actors to be heard and to gain recognition.

In sum, metagovernance is a necessary but inherently imperfect governing practice, which is facing a range of challenges, limitations, and dilemmas. Metagovernors must exploit the opportunities they have for influencing the interactive policy processes and come up with pragmatic and innovative responses to the challenges and dilemmas they encounter. Yet, they must be prepared to accept, and hopefully learn from, metagovernance failures (Jessop, 2002).

What does it take to become a metagovernor?

In principle, all political actors that fulfill Christopher Hood's NATO-criteria by having sufficient nodality, authority, treasure, and organizational capacity can act as metagovernors (see Hood, 1986). However, the central position, formal authority, and democratic legitimacy of public authorities make them particularly suited for exercising metagovernance (Klijn and Koppenjan, 2000a). The public metagovernors may be located either at the same or at a higher level than the interactive policy arena, which they are metagoverning (Esmark, 2007a; Jensen and Kähler, 2007; Sørensen, 2007b). In some cases, public authorities will have continual fights with each other about who is the principal metagovernor. Such cases provide a good indication of the considerable power and influence that can be achieved from metagoverning interactive governance. To save them the trouble of detailed monitoring and hands-on metagovernance, public authorities sometimes choose to delegate the task of metagoverning networks, partnerships, and quasi-markets to third-party organizations that are specialized in the oversight and management of interactive governance arrangements in which they are not themselves a member. An example of this is found in the state of Texas that has signed a contract with a third-party organization recruiting, managing, and evaluating a large number of child care providers (Goldsmith and Eggers, 2004). Another example is the British government's delegation of the responsibility for monitoring and regulating local governance networks to the independent Audit Commission (Kelly, 2006).

Metagovernance might also be exercised by resourceful and legitimate private organizations that are themselves a part of the quasi-market, partnership, or network in question. In Denmark, there are examples of large trade-union confederations that have both the political skills and organizational capacities to metagovern local networks in the field of social inclusion (Andersen and Torfing, 2004). Quasi-markets, partnerships, and networks might also be metagoverned by policy objectives, standards, and guidelines formulated and enforced by networks operating at a higher level within a multilevel governance system. As such, we may talk about "multilevel metagovernance" (Jessop, 2004: 69–73) when interactive policy arenas at the local, regional, and national levels are designed, framed, and regulated by interactive arenas and public authorities at higher levels. This is to a large extent what is happening in the OMC in the field of active employment policy where a transnational governance network in and around the Employment Committee metagoverns national governance networks that are responsible for formulating and reporting on national policy initiatives and for metagoverning regional and local governance networks that are implementing the national policy initiatives (Torfing, 2007*b*).

A limit case of metagovernance is when governance networks, partnerships, and even private contractors are required to elicit, and take into account, the opinions and preferences of the users of public service and regulation, for example, as a part of Total Quality Management. Although such a requirement is a result of hands-off metagovernance from above, it provides an example of metagovernance from below as it permits citizens, users, and customers to influence what is happening in the interactive policy arenas.

It has also been suggested that interactive governance arenas can metagovern themselves (O'Toole, 2007). This allegedly happens when networks, partnerships, or quasi-markets engage in systematic reflections on their own performance and find ways of improving it. Some governance networks carry out periodic reviews of their own functioning and achievements. Such reviews might spur processes of mutual learning and foster strategic attempts to change the pattern of interaction. However, the conceptual difference between self-metagovernance and self-governance is small and difficult to maintain in empirical analysis.

A special problem concerns how global governance networks are metagoverned. Global networks and partnerships may attempt to metagovern themselves and they may become metagoverned by international organizations like the United Nations, the World Trade Organization, and the World Bank, which will often act as convenors of global networks, provide various support functions, and define some basic institutional parameters (O'Brien et al., 2000). However, the absence of a world government means that there is no shadow of hierarchy cast on global networks and partnerships. Regional powers and hegemonic nation states might try to fill the void left by the absence of an overarching political authority, but they cannot threaten to dismantle the network and solve the global problems through unilateral action. Even the strongest of nation states are dependent on interaction with other nation states and a plethora of private actors in order to find global solutions to global problems. Hence, at best hegemonic states tend to be *primus inter pares*. The situation is slightly different in the case of the transnational governance networks in the EU that are metagoverned by the European Commission and the European Council. In those areas where the EU has a clear legal competence, both the European Commission and the European Council are capable of casting, and tend to cast, a shadow of hierarchy over the transnational networks (Borrás, 2007; Esmark, 2007a).

As public authorities are naturally born metagovernors, it is crucial to examine their willingness and ability to exercise metagovernance. Politicians often appear less willing to metagovern interactive governance arrangements than public managers who are facing the need for exchanging knowledge, resources, and energies in their daily practices. Many politicians cling to the traditional image of politicians as sovereign rulers. They tend to see interactive forms of governance as messy, undemocratic, and a threat to their political authority and prefer to remain at a safe distance from networked policy interaction. Nevertheless, the political and discursive pressures on public authorities at all levels to facilitate, manage, and direct interactive policy arenas gradually force politicians to take on the responsibility for metagoverning these arenas, although in many cases they will delegate the task to public managers.

Politicians and public managers are well versed in planning, budgeting, and concrete decision-making. As metagovernors, however, they will also require proficiency in other tasks, such as forming, activating, arranging, stabilizing, integrating, and developing networks (Goldsmith and Eggers, 2004: 157). To perform these crucial tasks, the public metagovernors must possess a range of strategic and collaborative competences. The strategic competences include negotiated goal alignment, risk assessment, procedural and means–end flexibility, project management, and the ability to tackle unconventional problems. The collaborative competences include communication skills, storytelling capacities, and talents for coaching, cooperation, and trust building. The lists of strategic and collaborative competences can be further expanded, and some of the competences are also relevant for carrying out tasks other than those narrowly related to networks, partnerships, and quasi-markets. However, the important thing to realize is that the metagovernance of governance networks brings some particular strategic and collaborative competences to the fore.

At the other end of the line, we can distinguish between different reactions to the exercise of metagovernance depending on how invasive it is. Social and political actors facing a highly intrusive hands-on metagovernance will protest and fight back the strait-jacketing in order to protect the space for self-regulation. If the metagovernance is less invasive but still rather strict and constraining, the actors might try to exploit ambiguities and inconsistencies to advance a selective interpretation of the metagovernance strategy, or adopt a decoupling strategy, according to which they pretend to go along with the new metagovernance measures while they are actually going about as if nothing had happened. Metagovernance strategies that aim at facilitating and enhancing self-regulation will be readily accepted and will often be exploited to advance the scope, competence, and policy proposals of the network, partnership, or contract-based collaboration in question. Given the asymmetrical distribution of information between the metagovernor and the metagoverned arenas and actors, there is a large room for gaming. The use of hands-on metagovernance will reduce this space considerably. Discussing the reactions to metagovernance, we should not forget that the most important reaction is neither dissent nor consent but anticipation. The actors in a network will anticipate the metagovernors' reaction to their actions and inactions and adjust these accordingly. This is precisely the situation that the idea of metagovernance "in the shadow of hierarchy" refers to. Interactive policy arenas will do their best to deliver what they are supposed to deliver because they fear that the metagovenor will otherwise restrict their scope and authority.

Conclusion

Metagovernance is a relatively new concept with a large analytical potential. It helps us in understanding the efforts of federal governments to regulate interstate governance and the attempts of national government to support and direct local governments. It may also help us in conceptualizing the endeavor of the protagonists of NPM to create and sustain spaces of bounded autonomy in which public managers and private providers, infused with an entrepreneurial spirit, can take responsibility for developing the public sector and providing or delivering low price and high quality services. Last but not least, it provides a tool for understanding the role of government and other legitimate and resourceful actors in facilitating, managing, and directing the increasing number of interactive governance arenas. It captures the attempt of local municipalities and third-party organizations to manage and assess networks of private contractors and voluntary organizations in the field of preventive health care. It covers the efforts of national governments and strong interest organizations to influence the procedures, processes, and outputs of policy communities and issue networks, and it sheds light on the endeavor of international organizations, hegemonic nation states, and other would-be metagovernors to govern the negotiated interactions in global networks and partnerships.

Metagovernance involves "the governance of governance" and the fundamental challenge for would-be metagovernors is to facilitate, manage, and direct interactive governance arrangements without reverting to top-down command and without undermining the self-regulatory capacity of networks, partnerships, and quasi-markets. Theories of interactive governance can help us to understand different aspects of metagovernance and to develop a more elaborate definition of metagovernance that perceives metagovernance not only as a hegemonic discourse on how to govern but also as the choice and development of particular governance arrangements. The metagovernors' toolbox contains a variety of hands-off and hands-on tools that can be used to pursue different objectives. In this sense, metagovernance can be seen as a means for governments to influence interactive forms of governance. However, as argued above, metagovernance failure is an ever-present risk due to tough challenges, structural limitations, and inherent dilemmas facing would-be metagovernors.

Being a new concept, metagovernance calls for further studies. The theoretical research agenda is quite full. It includes exploration of the conceptual links between the concept of metagovernance and the literature on the "enabling state" and the "regulatory state." It also includes detailed comparisons of the contributions of the different theoretical approaches to metagovernance in order to identify common insights and complementarities. Finally, it includes a further analysis of the reasons for choosing particular governance arrangements and of conflicts and trade-offs between different objectives and tools of metagovernance.

8

New roles and role dilemmas in interactive governance

The role images of public governors have been an important issue in political science debate ever since Plato (1991 [c. 360 BC]) advanced his ideal conception of public rulers as Philosopher-Kings. Max Weber's prescriptive analysis (1978 [1920]) of the role of public administrators in modern bureaucracies is a crucial milestone in the debate, and so is Gabriel Almond and Sidney Verba's categorization (1963) of different types of citizens. Implementation research challenged these neat role images by pointing out how the actual role distribution among politicians, public administrators, and citizens was much more complex and overlapping (Pressman and Wildawski, 1973; Lipsky, 1980). More recently, the New Public Management (NPM) distinction between "steerers" and "rowers" (Osborne and Gaebler, 1992) has sought to redraw the boundary between the roles played by politicians and public administrators, and recast citizens as consumers and private firms as providers of public services. These new role images have become important points of reference in laying out how different groups of actors are expected to act, although the boundaries between the roles have proven difficult to uphold in actual governance processes (Svara, 1999a, 1999b; Provan and Milward, 2000). The analysis of role images is important because public governance is shaped by social and political actors who are acting on the basis of more or less sedimented images of the role they are supposed to play.

Role images in public governance are contingent and subject to frequent transformation. This is not least the case in advanced liberal democracies in which traditional role images are currently being challenged by new perceptions of what it means to be a politician, a public administrator, a citizen, and a private business or an NGO. New role images are taking form and are offering themselves as points of identification as the interactive governance paradigm manifests itself in an increasing number of governing practices and reform programs in the Western democracies.

Table 8.1. Traditional role images and new roles, dilemmas, and coping strategies in the interactive governance paradigm

	Government paradigm	Interactive governance paradigm	Dilemma	Coping strategies
Politicians	Sovereign political ruler Responsive political authority	Board of Directors Boundary spanning participant	Involvement or independence	Forming strong metagovernance alliances and developing shared ownership between them and interactive governance arenas
Public administrators	Sovereign executive bureaucrat Responsive street-level bureaucrat	Executive manager Boundary spanning and facilitating manager	Power or legitimacy	Forming strong metagovernance and developing shared ownership between them and interactive governance arenas
Citizens	The entrepreneurial citizen The passive subject and/or voter	Consumer Coproducer Everyday maker	Influence or avoidance of responsibility	Downplaying their actual engagement and influence in interactive governance
Private actors	The lobbyist The passive object	Service producer Project partner Policy producer	Publicity or privacy	Downplaying their engagement and influence in interactive governance

An Italian survey of local government roles shows that politicians identify most strongly with the role as facilitators who seek to bring together different individual and collective interests and least strongly with the role as policymaker that involves initiating and formulating new policies (Liguori et al., 2010). In Denmark, a new codex for executive public managers insists that a major objective for executives consists of "negotiating their degree of discretion with their political leader" (Danish Ministry of Finance, 2005), while a similar codex for mid-level managers underscores that a central task consists in motivating "relevant actors to involve themselves," and in making sure that "all employees view citizens and users of public services as collaboration partners with relevant resources and a right to influence decisions that affect them" (Management Greenhouse, 2008). In the United Kingdom, the government's policy service program *Working Together—Public Services on Your Side* advocates that "front line employees and citizens are given the autonomy they need to improve the productivity and quality of public service delivery" (British Government, 2010), and the British Home Office (2010) has launched a huge reform program *Policing our Communities Together* that aims to increase the effectiveness of policing by "involving citizens and private actors directly in making priorities and taking action in making communities more safe."

These and many other programs and guidelines for public governance are more or less explicitly remodeling our notions of what it implies to be a politician, a public administrator, a citizen, or a private for- or non-profit actor. Such changes in role images are significant, not because they are bound to change the behavior of key policy actors, but because they provide new reference points that actors can activate in their efforts to find a place for themselves in different policy arenas and to justify and legitimize their actions in the eyes of other actors.

In the previous chapters, we described how the surge of a new interactive governance paradigm has gone hand in hand with the institutionalization of a variety of governance arrangements such as quasi-markets, partnerships, and governance networks. This chapter focuses on the impact that these paradigmatic and institutional changes have on the role images that condition and frame efforts to justify or criticize actions taken by politicians, public administrators, citizens, and private actors. Furthermore, we analyze the dilemmas that are likely to emerge when these role images guide action, and discuss the coping strategies that can be applied in dealing with emerging dilemmas. A study of role images, dilemmas, and coping strategies is valuable because it helps us to understand how paradigmatic and institutional changes at the meso and macro level influence actions at the micro level, which in turn will transform and/or reproduce the patterns of social and political interaction.

As such, the study of role images can contribute to explaining the complex interrelation between structure and agency.

In order to grasp the complex relationship between paradigmatic and institutional change and patterns of social and political action, we distance ourselves from the traditional functionalist or systems-theoretical conceptualizations of roles that tend to define roles as a set of relatively fixed norms resulting from the sedimentation of collective expectations to context-specific action (Linton, 1936: 114ff.; Parsons, 1951: 25). Instead, we take our departure in a relational understanding of roles that emphasize the actors' active involvement in shaping, applying, and developing role images (March and Olsen, 1989; Powell and Dimaggio, 1991).

In a relational perspective, there are a number of reasons why actors are not only role takers, but also role makers. First, role images are viewed as sets of rules and norms conditioning how a certain group of actors are supposed to act in particular situations. They take the form of institutionalized "logics of appropriateness" (March and Olsen, 1989). Actors become role makers because rules and norms implicit to a given logic of appropriateness are ambiguous and undecidable and their application calls for situated interpretations of their content and nature. Second, actors become role makers because role images are multiple, complex, and conflict ridden and confront actors with dilemmas and trade-offs that can only be tackled through the invention of creative coping strategies. Third, those role images that offer themselves at a given point in time draw on a complex and dynamic mix of old and new archaeological layers of role fragments that fit different situations and contexts. Actors become role makers when they actively construct their own particular role profile in concrete situations. Finally, there are blurred boundaries between the institutional domains of different logics of appropriateness. This means that actors, in some situations, can legitimize their actions with reference to logics of appropriateness that are dominant in other institutional domains. In sum, a relational approach views role performance as a complex process in which actors involved in public governance seek to legitimize their actions with reference to an ambiguous, conflictual, dynamic, and multilayered plurality of overlapping logics of appropriateness and role fragments.

Consequently, it makes little sense to try to identify a clear causal relationship between governance reform, paradigmatic transformations, and changes in role images. The role images that are at play at a given point in time represent a complex mix of points of identification that draws on a combination of old and new role fragments, and the choice of points of identification is in the end made by the individual actors. This relational understanding of roles further supports the argument made in Chapter 1 that current transformations in the way Western societies are governed should not be sketched out as a neat shift from government to governance but as an untidy process in which new ways of governing become mixed up with old ones as a result of complex strategic choices inspired by a variety of available role fragments.

The aim of this chapter is to draw the contours of an emerging set of interactive role images, to analyze some of the role dilemmas that confront actors who draw extensively on these emerging role images, and to consider what coping strategies are available for actors who seek to deal with these dilemmas. However, first we give a short description of the role images, dilemmas, and coping strategies that are associated with the traditional government paradigm. This description is followed by a brief analysis of how the governmental role images are challenged by the emergence of the interactive governance paradigm.

Role images in the government paradigm

The ideal typical role images at play in the liberal-democratic government paradigm were formulated in nineteenth- and early twentieth-century political science and public administration theory (Mill, 1820; Wilson, 1887; Weber, 1978 [1920]). These ideal types construct an image of politicians as *sovereign political decision-makers* who rule by passing laws; public administrators as *bureaucrats* who implement laws; citizens as *voters* and *subjects* in between elections; and private firms and organizations as *objects* of regulation.

From the very beginning, however, these ideal typical role images were integrated with fragments of earlier archaeological layers of thought. These fragments include Friedrich Hegel's image (1967 [1821]) of public administrators as actors with a particularly high moral standing and privileged access to identifying the common good, and John Stuart Mill's perception (1991 [1861]) of politicians as particularly capable of identifying the common good, and citizens as being capable of developing into moral beings given the opportunity to participate. These and other role fragments building on a premodern conception of the common good have moderated the ideal typical role images characterizing the modern government paradigm.

The traditional liberal-democratic role images have been further recast in the course of the twentieth century. A growing technocratization of the governing of society founded on a strong belief in scientific knowledge promoted the image of the public administrator as an expert (Haber, 1964). Moreover, the emergence of pluralist and corporatist strands of thought and new insights from implementation theory assigned public authorities the role of being responsive but firm coalition partners capable of dealing with political pressures from citizens with strong preferences and organized interest groups with considerable resources (Schumpeter, 1976 [1943]; Waldo, 1948; Dahl, 1961; Schmitter, 1974; Lindblom, 1977; Lipsky, 1980). Finally, as pointed out in several comparative studies, the ideal typical image of what it means to be a public authority and a citizen has been affected by contextual factors such as national political culture and institutional setup (see Almond and Verba, 1963). Liberal democracies with an authoritarian political culture and centralized political institutions, such as France, have developed one version of the liberal-democratic role images in which the reference to the common will is central, whereas countries with a more participatory political culture and decentralized political institutions such as those located in Scandinavia have developed a somewhat different version in which negotiation is a key virtue (Rhodes, 1999).

In light of these modifications, we can conclude that the role images offered by the government paradigm are ambiguous, conflictual, and heterogeneous. Rather than placing the involved actors in the position as role takers that act in line with a clear, homogeneous, and pregiven role image, the social and political actors act as role makers who make conditioned choices among a plurality of context-dependent role fragments in a constant search for ways to cope with the dilemmas that go hand in hand with role performance.

The ambiguous role images offered by the government paradigm raise dilemmas for all the involved actors: Politicians are called upon both to make sovereign decisions and to be responsive to the views and interests of active citizens and interest groups. Public administrators are simultaneously expected to follow the rule of law, act in accordance with their perception of the common good, and bargain with active citizens and interest groups. Citizens are assigned the role as subjects in between elections, while they are at the same time expected to participate in local decision-making processes. Moreover, while private business firms and NGOs are mainly viewed as objects of governance, they are also expected to do what they can to lobby public authorities.

In coping with these dilemmas, a certain differentiation into subcategories of role positions has taken place. The role as sovereign political and administrative rulers has primarily been assigned to national authorities and in particular to high ranking politicians (A-politicians) and executive bureaucrats. The role as responsive authority has, then, been assigned to public authorities placed at lower levels, such as ordinary politicians (B-politicians) and street-level bureaucrats (SLB). This distinction between the sovereign and the responsive has created an image of leading politicians and executive bureaucrats as a joint political-administrative leadership team with a shared task and destiny (Svara, 1999a, 1999b). Such a team, which has been so eloquently portrayed in TV shows such as *Yes, Minister*, down-tones the Weberian and Wilsonian call for a clear distinction between the politicians' role as policy-maker and the public administrators' role as policy implementer.

Turning to the differentiation of the images of what it means to be a citizen and a private actor, one can identify a similar distinction between "the capable and interested elite" and "the common man." While the former role category serves as a legitimacy basis for entrepreneurial citizens and lobbying firms and NGOs, the latter serves to legitimize citizens who take on the role as passive subjects and/or delimit their political involvement to voting, and small firms and organizations, which take on the role as objects of government that abstain from lobbyism.

Challenges to traditional role images posed by interactive governance

The emerging interactive governance paradigm challenges the traditional government role images and role differentiations by introducing role fragments and new ambiguities and conflicts that further complicate and transform the traditional ideal typical role images. The transformations in role images are triggered by the way in which the interactive governance paradigm destabilizes three constitutive distinctions of the government paradigm.

First, it blurs the distinction made between the governing and the governed. In viewing governance as a complex process in which public authorities and private stakeholders interact in the pursuit of negotiated goals, it becomes more difficult to define some actors as governing and others as governed. Instead, the relevant question becomes how, when, and where different actors are expected to contribute actively to the governing of society.

Second, seen from the perspective of the interactive governance paradigm, the distinction between public and private actors is less relevant as a point of reference for determining whether or not an actor should be viewed as a legitimate participant in a governance process. Hence, the legitimacy of the various actors has less to do with their sector belonging than with the extent to which they are affected by the governance processes or possess knowledge and resources that are relevant for contributing to defining or solving the governance tasks in question.

Third, the interactive governance paradigm challenges the well-established distinction between political and administrative governance tasks and the idea that the former precedes the latter. By pointing out that all phases in a governance process involve political as well as administrative tasks, it becomes much more complicated to draw a distinction between the kind of norm-based actions that are to be performed by politicians and public administrators, respectively. Although it still makes some sense to view politicians as policymakers and public administrators as policy implementers, it is increasingly difficult to set up a clear division of labor between the two parties.

The destabilization of these three distinctions in the government paradigm has initiated a search for new role images of what it means to be a politician, a public administrator, a citizen, and a private actor. In the next sections, we shall see how the interactive governance paradigm shapes a new ambiguous, conflicting and heterogeneous set of role images for each type of actor. First, however, we shall conclude this section by giving an overview of the traditional role images characterized above and an outline of the new and emerging roles, dilemmas, and coping strategies available to politicians, public administrators, citizens, and private actors.

It should be noted that the emergence of new role images does not render the different role images provided by the government paradigm obsolete. Rather, the interactive governance paradigm adds a new archaeological layer of role fragments on top of the old ones, thus widening the repertoire of possible governance roles. This new archaeological layer further radicalizes the call for interaction voiced by the corporatist and pluralist versions of the government paradigm. As such, the aim of Table 8.1 is not so much to draw a sharp demarcation line between past and present roles as it is to clarify the complex plurality of role fragments that currently offer themselves to actors in the intersection between the government paradigm and the emerging interactive governance paradigm. As argued by March and Olsen (1995: 69), what determines the legitimizing power of role fragments is the frequency with which they are activated and applied. It is, in other words, an empirical matter to uncover the articulation and impact of different role images and role fragments as they take form in different contexts at a given point in time.

In the following, we present the new archaeological layer of role images that are emerging in the wake of the interactive governance paradigm; the dilemmas that they establish; and the coping strategies that actors activate in their efforts to deal with these dilemmas. Let us first turn our attention toward the politicians.

Politicians: Roles, dilemmas, and coping strategies

Seen from the perspective of the interactive governance paradigm, the role of politicians is to design, manage, and direct interactive governance arenas through the exercise of metagovernance. Gone is the image of politicians as either sovereign rulers or responsive authorities. Politicians still play these roles, but they are under an increased pressure to take on the role as metagovernors who create, monitor, and steer interactive governance arenas in which they themselves may or may not participate. As mentioned in the introduction and further outlined in Chapter 7, governance theorists define metagovernance as the governance of governance, and this particular form of governance can be exercised in a variety of ways ranging from a macro-level "hands-off" shaping of the objectives and rules of the game to a micro-level "hands-on" process management of and participation in interactive governance processes. Hands-off metagovernance involves the institutional as well as political, financial, and cognitive framing of the conditions under which public and private stakeholders interact. Hands-on metagovernance is exercised through the direct involvement of the metagovernor in the interactive governance processes either as facilitator of or as participant in interactive governance processes.

Metagovernance can, however, be performed by any one actor who has the necessary and relevant resources to frame, monitor, and manage interactive governance arenas such as quasi-markets, partnerships, and networks. Nevertheless, role fragments deriving from the traditional role of sovereign politician place politicians in a privileged position as democratically legitimate exercisers of hands-off metagovernance through a legal, political, and financial framing of interactive governance processes. Politicians can pass reflexive laws that determine which stakeholders should be involved in making what kind of decisions (Teubner, 1989), define the overall political goals that the interactive governance arenas must pursue, and distribute financial resources between different interactive governance arenas (Sørensen and Torfing, 2009). This privileged role as a hands-off metagovernor is more or less identical with the role of Board of Directors that the NPM doctrine assigns to the politicians (Hood, 1991; Osborne and Gaebler, 1992; Pollitt and Bouckaert, 2004). As Board of Directors, politicians are expected to maintain a certain distance to interactive governance arenas and thus refrain from engaging themselves in hands-on forms of metagovernance.

Generally, politicians are in a less privileged position to play the role as hands-on metagovernors in relation to interactive governance arenas. This is partly because their direct contact with society has traditionally taken place on the input side of the political system in connection with elections and not on the output side that has been the domain of public administrators. The resulting distance between the politicians and citizens as well as private stakeholders found at the output side has been further sustained by the aforementioned image of politicians as equal to a Board of Directors. However, some scholars have advocated for an alternative image of politicians as hands-on boundary spanners that engage more directly as participants in interactive governance processes (Williams, 2002; Sørensen, 2006).

As we shall see, the new role as metagoverning politicians is in the governance literature described a little bit differently in relation to different new forms of governance, but the basic message is the same: politicians should take one step back and maintain some distance to interactive governance processes. In relation to *quasi-markets*, the role that is granted to politicians is explicitly spelled out as that of a Board of Directors in a private firm. The relationship between the politicians and the production unit—be it a private contractor or a public special-purpose agency—is understood in terms of a principal–agency relationship in which the politicians act as a principal who hires an agent to perform a particular task (Stoker, 1998: 22), and the exchange between the two parties is outlined in a business contract. In order to work, this contract must contain a detailed description of the task that is to be carried out at a given price. The interaction between the parties to the contract is supposed to be kept at a minimum. Public employees have, however, criticized this rigid fixed contract model for leading to a postbureaucratic standardization nightmare with very limited flexibility. This critique finds support from a number of scholars who argue that successful contract relationships tend to call for a relatively high level of ongoing interaction between the parties to the contract (Williamson, 1985; Provan and Milward, 1991; Greve, 2007). This is particularly the case in relation to the governance of complex tasks, which run over a long period of time. A recent growth in relational contracts that set up rules for how issues and disputes are settled in ongoing negotiations between public authorities and public and private providers of public services emphasizes the need for such interactions (DeHoog, 1990; Greve, 2007).

The term *partnership* refers to a specific form of collaboration between public authorities and for- or non-profit organizations that relies on more or less formalized agreements. Compared to quasi-markets, partnerships do not view politicians as parties to a contract but as agenda setters and activators who provide a legal, political, and financial framing that encourages public agencies and private actors to engage in a shared effort to provide public services. Since partnerships are expected to have some degree of autonomy in defining the precise character of their assignment, politicians are also in this context expected to stay at an arm's length from the interactive governance processes. As this arm's-length principle is central for legitimizing the involvement of private actors in governance processes, the interactions that do in many cases take place tend to be kept at an informal level (Provan and Milward, 2000; Baker et al., 2009).

While, in relation to quasi-markets and partnerships, the role of politicians is restricted to that of exercising hands-off metagovernance, they are expected to use all available means of metagovernance in governing *governance networks*. As governance networks rely on a considerable degree of autonomy, a central task for politicians consists in defining the precise character of this autonomy through different forms of political and economic framing. To perform this task, however, politicians must engage in an ongoing dialogue with governance networks, as such a dialogue is expected to give politicians both strategic knowledge that can qualify their efforts to frame governance networks and an opportunity to influence the network activities (Klijn and Koppenjan, 2000b; Sørensen, 2006). The view that politicians need to engage more directly with self-governing actors is not only found among governance network theorists. It also finds some support in principal–agent theory that points out how the relationship between principal and agent is characterized by a high degree of interdependency. Agents do indeed depend on choices made by the principal, but principals are also dependent on the agents' specialized knowledge. By participating in governance networks, politicians get an opportunity to retrieve this knowledge and to gain information about the complex motives that drive the actions of the involved stakeholders (Stoker, 1998: 22).

Summing up, politicians are called upon to take on the role as metagovernors in relation to quasi-markets, partnerships, and governance networks. They are, however, expected to do so in slightly different ways. While they are first and foremost expected to rely on the exercise of hands-off metagovernance in the governing of quasi-markets and partnerships, they are also expected to engage in hands-on metagovernance in relation to governance networks.

The role of metagovernors is, however, not without dilemmas. Politicians who maintain themselves at an arm's length of interactive governance arenas are in danger of losing their ability to control what is going on, to make qualified and informed decisions, and to gain support for their political program among relevant and affected stakeholders. In contrast, politicians who participate in interactive governance arenas risk losing their position as independent authority capable of making overall and long-term political decisions. Accordingly, one of the problems that needs to be addressed by the emerging interactive governance paradigm is how politicians can exercise metagovernance in a way that grants them both a certain level of involvement in and a fair amount of independence from interactive governance arenas.

How then can politicians cope with these dilemmas? There is little doubt that many politicians find it difficult to cope with their new role as metagovernors. Those who have chosen the role as hands-off Board of Directors as advocated by the NPM reforms are frustrated because they experience a loss of influence. Those who engage themselves in hands-on metagovernance have a hard time balancing the role as superior authority against the role as participant in horizontal interactions (Klijn and Koppenjan, 2000b; Sørensen, 2006). As many have pointed out, politicians need capacities to function as boundary spanners – a capacity that is ever more important to possess in an interactive governance context (Williams, 2002). However, two overall coping strategies seem to be used among politicians. One strategy consists in exploiting the already well-established distinction between A- and B-politicians. A-politicians take on the role as Board of Directors while B-politicians take on the role as boundary spanners. A second coping strategy consists in delegating the role as boundary spanners to the public administrators. This frequently used strategy is strongly inspired by some of the coping strategies employed by politicians within the government paradigm (Peters, 1987). A study of interactive governance processes in the small Danish town Skanderborg envisages how this strategy was applied with great success by a major and a public administrator (Sørensen, 2007b). As illustrated by this study, the success of such coping strategies depends on the ability of those involved in metagoverning an interactive governance arena to form a strong alliance and work as a team. A- and B-politicians must be on the same mission, and so must be politicians and the involved public administrators. Alliances are needed if those involved in exercising metagovernance are to do so efficiently. Without strong metagovernance alliances, the capacity to metagovern interactive processes is seriously weakened.

Public administrators: Roles, dilemmas, and coping strategies

Turning now to the public administrators, the interactive governance paradigm challenges the traditional images of public administrators as sovereign administrative rulers and responsive authorities are fading and become less powerful and new role images emerge and are activated and accepted as points of reference for legitimizing and justifying the doings of public administrators. The most powerful way of legitimizing action is no longer to point out that it is legal, is in line with the common good, is advocated by leading experts, or can be seen as an expression of responsiveness on the part of public administrators. Not to say that these criteria are suddenly irrelevant or have lost all their credibility. Most of them still play an important role in shaping the expectations about and self-perceptions of public administrators, but they tend to emerge in a less distinct fashion and face competition from new norms and standards (see Peters, 1987; Moore, 1994; Peters and Pierre, 2003).

The traditional role images are supplemented by new images of public administrators as metagovernors capable of managing and facilitating interactive governance processes. These new role images tend to rank effectiveness over legality, flexibility over regularity, and dialogue over authority, and are in many ways parallel to those offered to the politicians. But while the politicians are mainly expected to metagovern through the exercise of political, financial, and legal framing of and/or participation in interactive governance arenas, public administrators are first and foremost designated to metagovern through the institutional design and facilitation of these arenas. Public administrators are in other words recast as managers of interaction. Executive public managers are offered the role as designers of interactive arenas while lower ranking public managers are designated to facilitate such arenas. As was the case with the politicians, these new role images fit well into the overall logic of the NPM reform program: Executive public managers steer and assist the politicians in their role as Board of Directors while the lower level public managers row by taking on the role as boundary-spanning moderators, mediators, and facilitators of interactive governance arenas (Wiig, 1997; Williams, 2002; Marshall and Buske, 2007).

The new role as manager of interactive governance arenas is sketched out a little bit differently in relation to different governance arrangements. Seen in relation to *quasi-markets*, the role of the executive public manager consists in designing competitive markets that grant public and private providers of public services a clear incentive to produce politically defined outcomes as efficiently and effectively as possible. Delivery of health care services and social services, and infrastructure projects are areas in which quasi-markets have proliferated. The kind of metagovernance required to regulate such markets depends heavily on an arm's-length development of shrewd budgetary models and refined evaluation systems that make it possible to reward those who are performing well and punish those who are not. Among this kind of performance measurement systems, we find bench-marking programs and a variety of naming and shaming schemes (Power, 1997; Pollitt and Bouckaert, 2004; Wright and Ørberg, 2009). While hands-off metagovernance is mainly exercised by executive managers, lower level managers are offered the role as hands-on metagovernors who provide administrative support systems and help to clarify the rules of the game for those involved in the interactive governance processes. The exercise of hands-on metagovernance is important as it has limited impact to have designed a smart funding scheme if the relevant actors are not notified of the new possibilities or are in need of help in order to be able to take action.

In the case of *partnerships*, executive public managers are expected to design rules of the game and formulate programs and funding schemes that stimulate collaboration between public and private actors in an effort to solve wicked policy problems such as unemployment, education, and regional development. While executive public managers metagovern quasi-markets through the design of rules of the game that triggers competition between potential service producers, their task in relation to *partnerships* is to design conditions that motivate public agencies and private organizations to pool resources, coordinate their actions, collaborate, and share risks and gains (Lee, 2001). This is done through the strategic construction of interdependencies between public and private agencies under the motto: "If you work together in order to promote solutions to politically defined policy problems, funding is available." Just as the impact of competitive games depends on the degree to which it is supported by boundary-spanning facilitators so does the impact of collaboration designs. The role of these lower level public managers does not least

157

consist in bringing potential public and private partners into dialogue with each other.

Finally, public managers are required to design the room for maneuvering available to *governance networks* and to assist them in their efforts to collaborate in ways that add to the production of public governance. There is a potential tension between a governance network's widespread need for autonomy and public authorities' desire to control and regulate its actions. Just imagine situations in which public authorities involve governance networks in developing a plan for urban development just to acknowledge that the plan that is being developed by the governance networks is incompatible with their own ideas and plans. This tension between the wish to control and the desire to involve the governance networks is of course particularly strong in situations where politicians have high ambitions and the realization of these ambitions depends on the active involvement of governance networks. In order to deal with such tensions, the metagovernance of governance networks benefits from a considerable degree of interaction between metagoverning public administrators and the affected governance networks. Through this interaction, public managers can sometimes provoke a proactive alignment of the policy goals pursued by politicians and the governance networks. They can also take on the more interventionist role as policymakers and campaigners that sell a catchy policy narrative to politicians and governance networks and thus bring them together in a shared endeavor to reach a common goal. That this role as policy campaigner has become popular among public administrators is among other things illustrated by the enormous amount of policy documents that are being produced by public administrators. While the role of the executive managers is to design communication processes, formulate strong policy narratives, and sell them to the politicians, the role of the boundary-spanning managers consists in facilitating communication and/or disseminating these policy narratives among the network actors.

Public administrators face a series of dilemmas when taking on the role as metagoverning managers. Executive public managers at all levels of governance are confronted with the difficulty of differentiating their role from that of the A-politicians. Hence, metagovernance exercised through a legal, political, and financial framing of interactive governance arenas is not that distinct from metagovernance performed through the institutional design of interactive governance arenas. In practice, the distinction is further undermined by the A-politicians' attempt to cope with their role dilemmas through the formation of strong alliances with public administrators. The unclear division of labor between A-politicians and executive public managers places the latter in a dilemma. On the one hand, they might be able to increase their ability to metagovern more effectively if they exploit the lack of clarity to gain more power. On the other hand, by doing so they might reduce the politicians' ability to gain public support for the political goals and strategies that in the end legitimize the exercise of metagovernance. The lower level managers face a slightly different dilemma between their role as boundary spanners between public authorities and interactive governance arenas, and their role as facilitators of these arenas. While the role of boundary spanner calls them to push interactive governance arenas in a direction desired by politicians and executive public managers, this activity might at the same time weaken their credibility as trustworthy, loyal, and disinterested facilitators of these arenas.

Empirical studies show that public administrators involved in interactive governance arrangements employ a host of coping strategies in dealing with these dilemmas (Marshall and Ozawa, 2004; Sørensen, 2004). Many executive managers have followed more or less the same path as the politicians and formed strong metagovernance alliances with leading politicians. The strength of these alliances relies on the degree to which it is possible for executive managers and leading politicians to formulate a shared vision and strategy and on whether or not they are able to agree on how to divide the role as metagovernors between them. This pragmatic coping strategy is explicitly advocated in a Danish codex for top level managers (Danish Ministry of Finance, 2005). The result of this strategy is likely to be a centralization of political power at the national as well as local levels of governance in the political system. Hence, it takes considerable courage for a B-politician to go up against A-politicians who have formed strong alliances with executive public managers. Lower level managers on their side need to find ways to neutralize the dilemma between their role as boundary spanner and their role as facilitator. This can be done by promoting communication between hands-off metagovernors and the many self-governing actors that are involved in quasi-markets, partnerships, and governance networks. This kind of vertical communication makes it possible for them to bypass the conflicts and confrontations that might undermine their position as facilitator of the interactive governance processes.

Citizens: Roles, dilemmas, and coping strategies

The emerging interactive governance paradigm has also triggered a reinterpretation of the role of citizens. The image of citizens as voters at the input-side and subjects at the output-side of the political system has increasingly been challenged by the view that citizens have a legitimate right to have a say in governance processes that affect them and that this right should be institutionally guaranteed. As pointed out in Graham Smith's *Power beyond the Ballot* (2005), the changing image of what it means to be a citizen is fueled by a plurality of local and regional experiments with new forms of participatory governance. There have also been debates within the government paradigm about the forms and degrees of citizen involvement, but these debates have mostly concerned citizen involvement on the political input-side in between elections (Barber, 1984). The interactive governance paradigm is significant because it turns the focus of attention toward citizen involvement on the output-side of the political system, and changes the role of citizens from being subjects to being coproducers of governance. Hence, citizen involvement is no longer seen merely as a means to ensure citizens' democratic influence. It is also seen as a crucial means to enhance the efficiency and effectiveness of public governance by tapping into the experiences, demands, and ideas of different user groups (Warren, 2009).

The citizens' new role as co-governors, however, differs in relation to quasi-markets, partnerships, and networks. In *quasi-markets*, the co-governing citizen takes the form of the competent customer that makes informed choices between competing producers of public services. Consumers vote with their feet by exiting producers who fail to meet their demands and quality standards. Parents choose between a variety of teaching institutions for their children, and elderly people or their relatives choose between different providers of elderly care. The aggregated outcome of consumer choice is a demand-driven improvement of the quality of public governance (Osborne and Gaebler, 1992). However, as pointed out by Albert O. Hirschman (1970), the effectiveness of demand-side pressures depends on a balanced combination of exit and voice mechanisms. When customers are exiting, there is a huge loss of information because the service institutions they exit will not know why they do so. Therefore, exit options provided by consumer choice must be combined with voice options such as those provided by user satisfaction surveys, focus groups, and user boards.

In relation to *partnerships*, the role of citizens is less pronounced although it has considerable implications for the way citizens are viewed. These implications are, however, different in relation to different kinds of partnerships. Hence, in relation to public–private partnerships such as those involved in the field of infrastructure provision, the citizens are placed in the role as customers paying tolls to cover the costs of new roads, bridges, and tunnels. In relation to partnerships between public agencies and non-profit organizations who work together on projects aiming to improve living conditions in deprived neighborhoods by offering specialized local services, individual citizens are expected to become elite activists (Bang and Sørensen, 1998) who deliver voluntary labor and thus take on the role as coproducers of public governance. Individual citizens are also sometimes placed in this role as coproducers who form some sort of partnership with public authorities. This is most often seen in relation to employment and rehabilitation programs, where citizens agree to change their behavior in return for specific benefits

(Andersen, 2008). As such, the role that partnerships assign to citizens is both vague and diverse. In some contexts, they offer citizens a role very similar to that offered to them by quasi-markets, and in other contexts they are granted the role as coproducers of public governance.

The new role offered to citizens participating in *governance networks* is more explicit, and further promotes the view of citizens as active partakers in the provision of public governance indicated by some partnership constructions. Hence, although governance networks are often caputed by experts and interest organizations, they frequently aim to engage relevant and affected citizens directly in the formulation and implementation of public governance. While the consumer role grants citizens the opportunity to evaluate public governance by means of exit and voice options, and partnerships in some cases expect them to contribute to realizing certain policy objectives, governance networks also involve citizens in the formulation of these policy objectives (Fung, 2004). In governance networks, citizens are placed in the role of so-called "everyday makers" who engage themselves in governing issues of immediate relevance to them through ad hoc participation in interactive governance processes (Bang and Sørensen, 1998; Rhodes, 2000*b*).

Although they do so in different ways, the emerging images of citizens as consumers, coproducers, and everyday makers undermine the traditional notion of citizens as voters and subjects. They are active co-governors that interact more or less intensely and directly with public authorities. In choosing between the new role images, citizens face a serious dilemma: Involvement grants them influence, but at the same time it makes citizens responsible for governance outcomes. While the consumer role might be problematic in that it grants citizens a relatively "thin" influence, it is attractive because it does not burden them with responsibility. The role of contributor grants citizens more influence but simultaneously increases their responsibility. Finally, network participation carries the potential of substantial influence, but with it comes an extensive amount of responsibility. Every role entails gains and losses.

Now, what strategies are available to citizens in coping with this dilemma between the desire for influence and the wish to avoid responsibility? One route to take is to cling to the traditional role of voter and subject although it is increasingly viewed as illegitimate to refuse the role of co-governor in one form or other. Another coping strategy for citizens is to argue that the influence that they have is not really of a kind that obliges them to engage in larger scale considerations like those dealt with by politicians and public authorities. This line of argumentation is well known among members of school boards, neighborhood councils, local employment councils, and consumer committees who maintain that their involvement is not political and that they cannot be expected to consider larger political and financial prioritization issues. It seems, however, to be increasingly difficult to keep up this argumentation in those interactive governance arenas that engage in a close and ongoing dialogue with political authorities (Fung, 2004). A third, and often successful strategy applied by citizens consists in covering up their engagement and actual degree of influence in order to be able to maintain influence while at the same time avoiding the suitable amount of responsibility.

Private actors: Roles, dilemmas, and coping strategies

Turning finally to the private actors little is left of the image of private business firms and NGOs as passive objects of government. Today, private actors are increasingly viewed as co-governors that possess competences and resources, crucial for formulating and implementing strategies for solving wicked governance problems. Business firms are viewed as indispensable contributors to the promotion of economic growth, job creation, and the reduction of global warming, and the active participation of NGOs is perceived as vital for empowering and activating civil society in solving social problems, youth crime, and lifestyle-related health problems.

Quasi-markets offer business firms and NGOs an active role as producers of public goods. A public authority employs them to perform a certain task for a certain contracted price and to offer it to citizens who step into the role of consumers. While both firms and NGOs are on home ground when it comes to performing different functional tasks, quasi-markets place them in a situation that is quite different from the private market and civil society contexts they are used to operate in. Hence, in a quasi-market they are supposed to assist public authorities in realizing politically defined objectives and to observe a range of rules and norms pertaining to the public sector in doing so. Although quasi-markets aim to establish an arm's-length distance between politics and production, the private providers are called upon to legitimate their actions with reference to these political objectives and public sector values (Andersen, 2000). Consumers of public goods and services expect the same kind of ethical values and standards regardless of whether the provider is public or private.

The preservation of the idea that private actors are "private" is even more difficult to maintain in relation to *partnerships* where public and private actors work closely together in a shared effort to realize particular policy goals. In partnerships, private actors play a highly responsible role, not only as producers of public tasks but also as partners who contribute actively to the design of concrete governance practices in close collaboration with public authorities. This is particularly the case in partnership arrangements that are of a certain size and run for a considerable period of time. One example of such partnership arrangements is huge infrastructure projects, but the same long-term partnerships exist in relation to the running of cultural institutions and schools. As a consequence of the active involvement of the private partners in forming concrete policies and services, the pressure grows on them to be willing to account for their actions and legitimize them with reference to public values and political standards.

The transformation of business firms and NGOs into co-governors is taken one step further in the case of *governance networks* where the private actors are directly involved not only in providing and developing new services but also in defining policy problems, in formulating policy goals, and in developing, implementing, and disseminating concrete policy strategies. In other words, private actors and other network participants are active in all phases of the policy process, which makes it even more difficult to draw a clear distinction between public and private actors.

The role of private actors as active and increasingly visible partners in interactive governance processes confronts them with serious dilemmas. Business firms face the dilemma that the more active a role they play in processes of public governance, the more they are held to account for their actions and inactions with reference to standards defined by a public ethos and contingent political objectives (Andersen, 2000; Hebson et al., 2003). Particularly, the cost of involving themselves in partnerships and governance networks can be high. Multinational businesses involved in corporate social responsibility projects cannot maintain production facilities in Burma, or overlook bad working conditions in Chinese factories, and they have to sacrifice some of their profits in order to make sure that local actors are empowered and communities are developed when they make investments in Africa.

With regard to NGOs, they face a slightly different dilemma that has to do with their traditional reliance on voluntary labor and their general position as civil society actors. The reliance on voluntary labor is problematized when NGOs involve themselves in quasi-markets and their activities are being redefined as commodities that can be bought and sold. Accordingly, NGOs that engage themselves extensively in the provision of public services such as sports activities for public schools, cultural entertainment for elderly people, or social programs for immigrants face the prospect of gradually turning into firms that rely on the employment of a paid workforce. Engagement in partnerships and governance networks also raises dilemmas as close collaboration with public authorities involves the risk of cooptation, which might imply that NGOs lose their footing in civil society and become partakers in the exercise of public authority in ways that undermine their independence and critical potential (Selznick, 1948; Lewis, 2005).

How can private actors cope with these dilemmas? The variety in coping strategies is considerable. Some business firms and NGOs choose to stay at a safe distance from interactive governance processes and accept the loss of the potential profit, influence, and prestige that could have been harvested through the involvement in quasi-markets, partnerships, and governance networks. Other private actors take the full step into the new world of co-governance and brand themselves as responsible societal actors with a normative agenda and a willingness to share responsibility for the common good. However, a third strategy consists in claiming that the involvement is of a particular technical nature and does not involve policymaking of any kind. Thereby, they can avoid taking full responsibility for the outcome of interactive governance processes. That strategy is, however, more difficult to pursue in relation to governance networks than in relation to quasi-markets and partnerships as the former often involves making choices between different policy options and making commitments to politicians.

Conclusion

The surge of the interactive governance paradigm has challenged established role images, and brought along new ones. The traditional, but still rather multifaceted images of what it means to be a politician, a public administrator, a citizen, and a private actor have been supplemented with a new layer of role images that social and political actors can refer to in order to legitimize and add meaning to their behavior. Politicians and public administrators are increasingly viewed as metagovernors that exercise their authority through the metagovernance of interactive governance arenas, while citizens and private actors are expected to play an active and responsible role in the formulation and implementation of public policies. These emerging role images vary to some degree between quasi-markets, partnerships, and networks, but the similarities across the different interactive governance arrangements are larger than the differences. New interactive role images are taking form.

However, as we have seen, it is not an easy task for the involved actors to navigate in this messy complexity of old and new role fragments and to cope with the dilemmas that they produce. As such, the new interactive governance paradigm does not leave politicians, public administrators, citizens, and private actors with any clear-cut manual that they can follow when interacting with each other. Rather, they are placed in a situation where they are forced to become role makers. As noted earlier, there is always a fair degree of role making involved in performing a role, but the need to act as role maker is particularly acute in times characterized by paradigmatic and institutional changes, as is currently the case. Old role images appear as less relevant and applicable and the new layer of role fragments has not yet been fully developed and become sedimented. Those who are involved in public governance today are pioneers who are forming a new layer of role fragments as we speak, and as such they play a crucial part in conditioning role performance in the years to come.

Then, to what extent have the different groups of actors taken on the position as role makers? Public administrators, citizens, and private actors have shown considerable willingness and capacity to develop new interactive role images for themselves and each other, and to deal with the dilemmas that these role images produce. This willingness and capacity to develop and apply new role images have been promoted by deliberate and intensive attempts by reform makers to address these issues and by governance researchers who have taken heed to study and debate the implications for these actors of the surge of interactive governance processes. The widespread interest in these issues has among other things triggered training programs for public administrators that give them the competences needed to develop new roles, and to cope with the many dilemmas that occur when public administrators, citizens, and private actors interact.

The capacity and willingness to deal with dilemmas related to the role of politicians in interactive governance processes have been much less apparent among the involved actors, as well as among reform makers and governance researchers. The limited interest in the role of politicians in interactive governance processes and the nature of the dilemmas they face are problematic because the challenges politicians face and their need for new role images are considerable. If politicians are to become more than distant and somewhat marginalized participants in interactive governance arenas, efforts should be made among public sector reformers as well as among governance researchers to consider how politicians can become active and influential participants in interactive governance arenas, and to develop training programs that promote politicians' capacity to develop new role images and cope with the dilemmas they unavoidably produce.

9

Assessing and improving effective interactive governance

When it comes to enhancing the legitimacy of the regulatory standards of the EU, resolving conflicts over national social policy reforms, facilitating innovative regional planning, and providing tailor-made local welfare services to elderly people, public authorities increasingly turn to interactive forms of governance that involve negotiated exchange, coordination, and collaboration among a plethora of public and private actors (Rhodes, 1997a). Consequently, interactive forms of governance appear to proliferate at all levels and within or across most policy areas (Bache and Flinders, 2004).

The proliferation of interactive forms of governance has prompted growing research focusing on the role of networks, partnerships, and quasi-markets in public governance (Heffen et al., 2000; Hajer and Wagenaar, 2003; Sørensen and Torfing, 2007). Looking back at the last two decades, it is possible to identify two generations of research in relation to interactive governance. Whereas the *first generation* was mainly preoccupied with describing different kinds of networks, partnerships, and public–private collaboration and showing how they function as mechanisms of governance (Marin and Mayntz, 1991; Marsh and Rhodes, 1992; Marsh, 1998), a new *second generation* aims to assess the normative and political impact of interactive governance arrangements and explore how to improve their performance (Koppenjan and Klijn, 2004; Sørensen and Torfing, 2005b; Benz and Papadopoulos, 2006). The attempt to assess and improve the functioning and impact of interactive governance may invoke an entire range of normative criteria in terms of equity, democracy, efficiency, goal-attainment, stability, conflict resolution, mutual learning, etc. The question of how to choose appropriate criteria for assessing network performance has been dealt with elsewhere (Kenis and Provan, 2009).

Here, we shall focus on the impact of network-types of governance on effective governance defined as a coordinated mobilization and deployment of resources, ideas, and energies that contribute to the solution of policy problems or the provision of new opportunities. The assessment of whether networks and other forms of interactive governance contribute to an effective governing of contemporary societies is important since the formation of networks and partnerships is often justified with reference to the need for making public governance more effective (Goldsmith and Eggers, 2004). Since networks and partnerships are typical ways of organizing interactive forms of governance, the discussion in this chapter has a general relevance for governance in the generic sense of defining and realizing collective goals through sustained interaction among relevant policy actors.

Interactive governance arrangements are not inherently effective or ineffective. Networks and partnerships may succeed in breaking policy deadlocks, providing negotiated solutions to emerging problems, or turning socioeconomic challenges into new opportunities. However, they may also fail to do so. Governance failure is just as likely and frequent as government failure and market failure. As shown in Chapters 7 and 8, there has been an increasing focus on how politicians and public managers can prevent governance failure and improve the performance of networks and partnerships through different kinds of metagovernance (Kickert et al., 1997; Rhodes, 1997a; Kooiman, 2003; Koppenjan and Klijn, 2004; Kelly, 2006). However, the attempt of the public metagovernors to enhance the contribution of networks and partnerships to effective governance must be guided by a clear assessment of their effectivity. In this chapter, we claim that in order to measure the effectivity of networks and partnerships, we must move beyond the traditional notions of cost efficiency, operational effectiveness, and allocative efficiency. Alternatively, we propose that the effectivity of network-types of governance is measured in relation to a set of criteria that aims to capture the specific promises in terms of effective governance that are identified in the burgeoning literature on networks and partnerships. The discussion of how to conduct a criteria-based assessment of the effectivity of networks and partnerships is followed by a brief discussion of how different metagovernance tools can help to improve the effectivity of interactive governance arrangements.

Assessing effective governance

As Robert Agranoff and Michael McGuire rightly conclude, "the issue of collaborative effectiveness is fundamental yet has been incompletely addressed" (Agranoff and McGuire, 2003: 191). Interactive forms of governance are often praised for their contribution to making public governance more effective in policy settings characterized by a multiplicity of social and political actors, vague and incomplete problem definitions, the need for specialized knowledge, conflicting policy objectives, and a high risk of political antagonism (Koppenjan and Klijn, 2004). However, we lack a clear and adequate understanding of what "effective" means in relation to network-types of governance. The few public administration researchers who have addressed the question of the effectivity of interactive governance have been more interested in explaining the differences in effectivity across networks and partnerships than in scrutinizing the concept of effectivity and developing a systematic framework for assessing the effectivity of network-types of governance (Provan and Milward, 1995; Provan and Sebastian, 1998; Riccio, Bloom and Hill, 2000; Provan and Kenis, 2008). A major exception is Provan and Milward (2001) who provide an elaborate set of criteria for measuring the effectivity of community-based networks in terms of their costs and benefits for the community, the network, and the participating organizations. Although the criteria proposed by Provan and Milward are biased toward measuring the effectiveness of service delivery networks in a particular policy area, they certainly provide a valuable source of inspiration for the attempt to assess effectivity of governance networks per se.

It is commonly asserted that governance networks and partnerships provide a distinct mechanism for governance based on pluricentric negotiations rather than unicentric command or multicentric competition (Kersbergen and Waarden, 2004). This means that we cannot define or assess the effectivity of these interactive forms of governance in the same way we define and assess the effectivity of hierarchies and markets (Jessop, 2002: 236).

The effectivity of hierarchical forms of government is normally evaluated in terms of either the *cost efficiency* of public policy programs, defined as the total costs of producing a certain policy output, or the *operational effectiveness* of such programs, defined as their ability to attain some predefined goals through the operative mobilization and deployment of particular resources (Etzioni, 1964: 8–9; Lane, 1995: 242–3). In public bureaucracies, there is an ever-present tension between cost efficiency and operational effectiveness. Whereas the former requires focus, discipline, and control, the latter is predicated upon experimentation, loose discipline, and relaxed control (March, 1995: 5). According to Nancy Roberts (2000: 228), however, the move toward collaborative forms of governance through networks and partnerships may permit public managers to achieve both efficiency and effectiveness. Networking with stakeholders in the identification and use of common means will tend to increase efficiency, and networking with stakeholders in the pursuit of common objectives will tend to enhance effectiveness.

Nevertheless, the standard notions of efficiency and effectiveness are not appropriate for evaluating the performance of governance networks. First, there are serious problems with measuring the *cost efficiency* of networked policy processes. The output of interactive governance arrangements can be very difficult to quantify, since it often includes intangible results such as joint problem understandings, common values, future visions, enhanced coordination, empowerment of private actors, cooperative processes, etc. Moreover, it is exceedingly troublesome to measure the total costs of networked policy outputs, since the governance networks in question are seldom in control of the production of the tangible and intangible policy outputs, which are often partly the responsibility of the network actors and partly the responsibility of a broad range of government agencies that are not part of the network. Even if we somehow managed to measure the outputs and estimate the costs of producing them, it would not be very interesting to measure whether governance networks produce and deliver policies in a cost efficient manner. Despite Nancy Roberts' optimistic assertions about the effectiveness of governance networks, we should not expect collaborative governance to be highly cost efficient, since there is nothing particularly efficient about making decisions jointly (Agranoff and McGuire, 2003: 191). Collaboration with stakeholders might help to mobilize additional resources, and negotiated coordination might help make better use of the available resources; however, we should not forget that the transaction costs of networking are often high and hard-won agreements might not amount to more than the least common denominator (Scharpf, 1988). Hence, although the commitment of public and private resources is a critical issue in public governance, cost efficiency is not an appropriate norm for measuring the effectivity of network-types of governance.

The attempt to evaluate the *operational effectiveness* of governance networks does not fare any better. The assessment of policy outcomes, and thereby goal achievement, is complicated by the fact that the definition of the policy goals is subject to ongoing conflicts and negotiations among the network actors leading to imprecise and competing goal formulations. The presence of diffuse and multiple objectives is a standard problem in the assessment of goal attainment in public programs (Etzioni, 1964: 14–16; Riccio et al., 2000: 167). However, there is an additional problem in the case of the networked policy processes, since the policy objectives are constantly changing due to mutual learning and shifting power relations among a larger number of actors. Indeed, a flexible adjustment of policy objectives to changing preferences and circumstances is often one of the primary reasons why interactive forms of governance are invoked. The occasional and momentary presence of relatively clear, stable, and coherent objectives might facilitate the assessment of a governance network's capacity for goal attainment, but since governance networks and partnerships often share the operational responsibility for reaching the specified goals with a host of government agencies, it would be wrong to hold the networks accountable for the failure to achieve particular goals. Moreover, while the capacity for goal attainment of governance networks is surely important, the real strength of governance networks will often lie in defining a complex set of objectives that reflects the complexity of the policy problems rather than in delivering the outputs that produce the desired outcomes (Kooiman, 1993a; Koppenjan and Klijn, 2004). This observation seriously challenges the appropriateness of the notion of operational effectiveness for evaluating the effective performance of interactive governance.

The evaluation of the kind of "quasi-markets," which recently have been created and expanded as part of the fashionable New Public Management reforms, is normally carried out in terms of cost efficiency (Cutler and Waine, 1997). Hence, the contracting-out of public services is most often motivated by the hope that competition among private providers will lower the costs of standardized public services. Hence, despite the secondary ambitions of the politicians to encourage the development of new innovative methods and tailor-made solutions, and despite the negotiated character of the interaction between the public procurers and the private providers, the key focus of performance management reports is on quality and costs of the services produced and delivered by the private contractors. However, in those cases in which the production of goods and services relies on the construction and operation of allegedly "pure markets," effectivity is assessed in terms of *allocative efficiency*, defined as a Pareto-optimal allocation of costs and benefits that ensures that the marginal utility equals the marginal costs for all actors (Downs and Larkey, 1986: 7). Compared to the notion of operational effectiveness, the Pareto criterion has the advantage of permitting an individual assessment of costs and benefits rather than assuming the presence of a collective utility function. However, the production of a Pareto-optimal solution does not provide an appropriate yardstick for measuring the effectivity of governance networks either. In governance networks, the economic competition among an infinite number of independent market actors is replaced by conflict-ridden negotiations among a limited number of interdependent stakeholders, and the political struggles based on institutional rules and coalition building are unlikely to result in a Pareto-optimal solution. Although win-win situations are not an infrequent outcome of networked policy processes, the existence of asymmetrical power relations will tend to produce both winners and losers, and without the presence of an overarching state authority, the compensation of the losers is unlikely.

In the search for an appropriate means of measuring the effectivity of networks and partnerships, we must move beyond the traditional notions of cost efficiency, operational effectiveness, and allocative efficiency. We need an alternative way of assessing the effectivity of governance networks that reflects their distinctive form, functioning, and contribution to the governing of society.

A simple and frequently chosen solution to the problem of evaluating effective network performance is measuring the perceived effectiveness of governance networks through a quantitative or qualitative survey of the *ex post satisfaction* with networked policy solutions (Koppenjan and Klijn, 2004). The target of such ex post surveys can either be the different groups of citizens affected by the networked policy solutions (Hasnain-Wynia et al., 2003) or the public and private stakeholders who are participating in the governance network (Teisman, 1992). The respondents are asked whether they believe the governance network has been effective in producing and delivering particular outputs and whether they are satisfied with the content and impact of these outputs. In order to test the comparative advantage of governance networks, the respondents may also be asked whether they think that collaborative network governance is "better" in the sense of producing solutions and results that otherwise would not have occurred (Agranoff and McGuire, 2003: 191). Such a counterfactual assessment helps reveal whether relevant citizens and stakeholders prefer the networked solution to solutions provided either by hierarchical government or competitive markets.

However, there are several problems with measuring ex post satisfaction with networked policy solutions. The first problem is that the respondents are not likely to provide particularly reliable answers, since the citizens are usually ignorant of how and by whom particular solutions and services are produced, and since the stakeholders will be strongly inclined to paint a far too rosy picture of the process and results because they have invested a lot of resources in finding joint solutions. Another problem is that the individual assessments of the effectiveness of the network will tend to reflect the relative gains of the respondents rather than the effectiveness of the governance network as a whole, for example in breaking policy deadlocks. Last but not least, the evaluation of ex post satisfaction will not tell us anything about why citizens and stakeholders are more or less content with networked policy solutions. There might be a thousand reasons for preferring a networked policy solution to other solutions, and we need a systematic understanding of these reasons in order to provide an adequate measure of the effectivity of governance networks.

The norms invoked by citizens and stakeholders participating in their evaluation of effective network governance in quantitative ex post satisfaction surveys can be studied through a qualitative, bottom-up analysis based on interviews and document studies. This has been attempted by Denise van Raaij and Patrick Kenis (2005) who have explored the explicit and implicit norms of effective network governance that were articulated in four Dutch health care networks. Although such an inductive approach improves our understanding of the underlying reasons for being satisfied or dissatisfied with the performance of particular governance networks, it does not provide a systematic and comprehensive account of what effectivity means in relation to governance networks.

In order to provide an appropriate measure of whether interactive forms of governance are effective or not, we suggest that networks and partnerships be assessed in terms of whether they actually deliver what the literature on interactive governance holds out as the particular promises of networks and partnerships in terms of effective governance. The assessment criteria listed below aim to capture the particular virtues and merits, in terms of effective governance, that are commonly ascribed to well-functioning partnerships and governance networks. These criteria include substantive as well as procedural aspects of interactive governance. In order to avoid confusing the effective performance of network-types of governance with the underlying conditions for this performance, the effectivity assessment criteria are formulated in terms of a set of norms specifying the desired impact and result of networked policy processes, which together measure the effectivity of partnerships and governance networks.

As suggested by Keith Provan and Brinton Milward (2001: 416), the assessment of the effectivity of interactive governance should pay attention to the quality of network-based policies; the actual ability of governance networks to solve relevant problems; the costs of the networked solutions and their distribution; and the enhancement of program legitimacy. To this list of points of attention should be added the ability of interactive governance arrangements to provide a flexible adjustment of policy solutions (Jessop, 2002: 228–30) and to build capacities for future cooperation (Koppenjan and Klijn, 2004: 122–9). As such, we shall suggest that the effectivity of network-types of governance be measured in terms of their capacity to:

1. produce a clear and well-informed understanding of the policy problems and policy opportunities at hand;

2. generate innovative, proactive, and yet feasible policy options that match the perception of the problems and challenges facing the network actors;

3. reach joint policy decisions that go beyond the least common denominator while avoiding excessive costs and unwarranted cost shifting;

4. ensure a smooth policy implementation based on continuous coordination and a high degree of legitimacy and program responsibility among the involved actors;

5. provide a flexible adjustment of policy solutions and public services in the face of positive and negative policy feedback and changing conditions, demands, and preferences; and

6. create favorable conditions for future cooperation through cognitive, strategic, and institutional learning that construct common frameworks, spur development interdependency, and build mutual trust.

The assessment of the effectivity of interactive governance according to these six criteria provides a broad and relatively comprehensive picture of the capacity of networks and partnerships to provide effective and comparatively better policy solutions. However, not all types of networks can be expected to deliver on all these dimensions. Hence, governance networks that are mainly preoccupied with policy implementation and service delivery might not be able to deliver on criteria 1 and 2. Likewise, governance networks that are primarily concerned with policy formulation might not be able to deliver on criteria 4 and 5. As such, the application of the effectivity assessment criteria in empirical analysis of particular governance networks, and our evaluation of the possible trade-offs, must take into account the role that the networks are playing in public governance.

Explicating the six effectivity assessment criteria

The application of the six effectivity criteria in empirical analysis of networks and partnerships in different policy areas and at different levels calls for a qualitative analysis of interactive policy processes. As such, in the explicit attempt to analyze the overall contribution of a whole network to an effective governing of a particular policy field, the researcher will have to compare information, narratives, explanations, and judgments obtained from actors inside and outside the governance network, from official documents and reports, and from observations of meetings and other arenas of interaction and negotiation (Bogason and Zølner, 2007). Such a qualitative analysis of the performance of actual networks and partnerships will not be able to produce an exact quantifiable measure of their effectivity; rather, the analysis will aim to establish the degree to which the network-types of governance deliver on the six effectivity assessment criteria.

In the final instance, everything depends on how each of the six criteria are interpreted and translated into a set of empirical indicators that can be applied in empirical analysis. It is, therefore, necessary to establish the precise meaning of the different assessment criteria and provide some further indications of what to look for in empirical assessments of effective network governance. This will be done here by elaborating a series of propositions that further explicate the content of the different assessment criteria in relation to governance networks.

The *first assessment criterion* concerns the production of a clear and well-informed understanding of the policy problems or policy opportunities at hand. It is well recognized in the literature that governance networks have their comparative advantage as mechanisms of governance in relation to "wicked problems" arising in policy formulation or policy implementation

173

(Koppenjan and Klijn, 2004). This means that the governance network faces a diffuse and ill-defined problem that can only be further clarified by drawing on the specialized knowledge of a wide range of actors among which there is an imminent risk of conflict. The immediate dilemma is that the network actors need to come to agreement about the precise nature and character of the problems and opportunities at hand, while, at the same time, the attempt to push through a clear problem definition is likely to stir conflicts and may result in discontented actors withdrawing from the governance network. A possible way forward for the network actors is, therefore, to begin with the formulation of a broad and vague, but relatively inclusive problem conception, and postpone the detailing of a more precise policy agenda to a later occasion, when the network actors have built some degree of trust and come to agreement about some of the basic aspects of the problem. A storyline that in broad, and even metaphorical, terms captures and defines the problems and opportunities at hand, and signals their urgency, is an excellent means to create commitment and unify the governance network (Hajer, 1993; Torfing, 2007*a*). However, in order to provide a basis for joint problem-solving, the storyline needs to be translated into a more precise policy agenda that specifies a more detailed set of problem definitions, policy objectives, and policy tasks. The formulation of a qualified policy agenda for a governance network is time consuming as it should be based on the specialized knowledge and insights of the different actors who may also use their contacts to bring alternative accounts and counterevidence to the table. These assertions bring us to the first proposition.

The *second assessment criterion* concerns the governance networks' ability to generate innovative, proactive, and yet feasible policy options that match the complex problems and opportunities at hand. Policy innovation is about

---

Proposition 1: Governance networks' ability to produce a clear and well-informed understanding of the policy problems and policy opportunities can be assessed by posing the following questions:

- To what extent has the governance network formulated a broad and inclusive storyline that captures the problems or opportunities at hand and signals their urgency?

- To what extent has the storyline been translated into a more precise policy agenda that specifies a detailed set of problem definitions, objectives, and tasks?

- To what extent has the policy agenda been informed and qualified by the specialized knowledge of actors from inside or outside the governance network?

generating new and creative ideas by means of articulating new and exciting forms of knowledge, experience, and practice. Governance networks that include a diversity of actors and have a high density in the interactions are often capable of crafting innovative solutions by bringing together actors with different perceptions and ideas and facilitating the development of mutual and transformative learning (Dente et al., 2005). A high degree of mutual trust, generated in and through sustained interaction, is also important as it reduces the risk-aversive behavior of the network actors. Preferably, the policy options generated by governance networks should be proactive in the sense of taking into account future conditions and trends. Bringing together a plurality of actors with different conjectures about what the future may hold in a trust-based community facilitates the crafting of sustainable policy solutions that not only reflect the present policy preferences but also take future developments into account. Scenario building, for example, through the organization of joint workshops and the use of serious games, can be a good way of exploiting the potential for proactive policymaking in governance networks. Nevertheless, it is not enough that policy options are innovative and proactive. They must also be feasible in the sense that they can be implemented in a way that ensures the achievement of the main objectives. Dreaming up ingenious forms of public policy and governance that do not work in the real world of economic and legal constraints, veto powers, bounded rationality, and complex policy interactions is not of much worth. Hence, the involvement of multiple actors in a joint assessment of the feasibility of different policy options is a crucial way of enhancing the problem-solving capacity of governance networks. On the basis of these stipulations, the second proposition can be set out.

Proposition 2: Governance networks' ability to generate innovative, proactive, and yet feasible policy options can be assessed by posing the following questions:

- To what extent have the interactions among the network actors produced innovative policy options by exploring alternative options, further developing initial policy proposals, experimenting with new ways of doing things, and integrating ideas from other countries, organizations, sectors, or networks?

- To what extent has the governance network constructed scenarios for the future development of relevant parameters in the policy field and are these scenarios informing the formulation of policy options?

- To what extent are the judgments of the relevant actors from inside or outside the governance networks reflected in the joint assessment of the feasibility of different policy options?

The *third assessment criterion* concerns the ability of governance networks to reach joint decisions that go beyond the lowest common denominator while avoiding excessive costs and unwarranted cost shifting. This criterion reflects one of the key problems in governance networks known as the "negotiator's dilemma" (Lax and Sebenius, 1992). Interdependent actors need to cooperate in order to facilitate the exchange of resources and find common solutions, but the absence of a joint utility function tends to produce conflicts and competition among the actors. In the attempt to avoid potentially damaging conflicts and cut-throat competition, governance networks tend to reach joint decisions that merely reflect the lowest common denominator. They settle for an uncontroversial solution that may not satisfy any of the network actors, but is what everybody can agree upon. This is a situation that Fritz Scharpf (1994) calls "negative coordination" since the actors merely aim to avoid stepping on each other's toes. More mature governance networks based on mutual trust, shared values, and dialogue-based learning may aspire to produce "positive coordination" where the ambition is to arrive at common solutions through a combination of hard-nosed bargaining and open-minded deliberation. Joint fact-finding may provide a good starting point in the aspiration to achieve positive coordination as it tends to establish a common ground for policy deliberation. The road to positive coordination is long and troublesome, but there is a well-known shortcut that should be avoided. Decisions that go beyond the lowest common denominator are often reached by means of selecting a policy solution that is ambitious and highly expensive, but paid for by actors who are not part of the governance networks (national or local government, different user groups, future generations, etc.) rather than by the network actors themselves. Cost shifting may be warranted or unwarranted. It is warranted if a public or private funding body has signaled its ability and willingness to provide adequate funding. By contrast, it is unwarranted if those who are going to pay the costs would have declined to do so, if they had had the chance to speak up. On the basis of these reflections, the third proposition can be presented.

Proposition 3: Governance networks' ability to reach joint decisions that go beyond the lowest common denominator while avoiding excessive costs and unwarranted cost shifting can be assessed by posing the following questions:

- To what extent has the governance network managed to produce a rough consensus about major policy decisions as a result of significant changes in the values, perceptions, and preferences of one or more network actors?

- To what extent has the governance network paid attention to the observable and hidden costs of different policy options in its decision-making process?

- To what extent are network actors prepared to contribute to the financing of the costs implied by the major policy decisions of the governance networks and to what extent are the costs shifted to external actors who are either unaware of the future costs or unwilling to shoulder the burden?

The *fourth assessment criterion* concerns the ability of governance networks to ensure a smooth implementation of policy decisions so that problems are solved, opportunities are exploited, and goals are achieved. Hence, it is one thing to produce suitable policy options and reach joint decisions about which policies to pursue, and quite another thing to ensure that these policies are implemented in such a way that major obstacles are removed, serious blunders are avoided, and the expectations of the various actors as to the outcomes are met. There are three main reasons for expecting governance networks to be able to ensure a smooth implementation and create acceptable results. The first reason is that governance networks provide opportunities for a continuous coordination of collective and individual actions, tasks, and plans among the key actors in the policy field. Such a continuous coordination helps to ensure the coherence, sequencing, and timing of different policy-related activities and facilitates the creation of positive synergies and the prevention of wasteful duplications of efforts. It also enhances the exploitation and pooling of specific resources and competences in the network. The second reason is that negotiation and collaboration may facilitate resolution of practical and political conflicts arising throughout the coordination process. Negotiated collaboration may also increase the compatibility of different goals and prevent trade-offs between different objectives. The final reason is that the participation of the relevant policy actors in the governance network tends to enhance the legitimacy of the policies and thereby create a higher level of program responsibility that serves to reduce the risk of implementation resistance. Policy actors who have invested time and energy in crafting a new policy and feel that they have been capable of influencing the policy decisions will tend to feel ownership to the policy output and tend to take responsibility for ensuring that the policy output produces the desired outcome. These assertions can be used in formulating the fourth proposition.

> *Proposition 4:* Governance networks' ability to ensure a smooth policy implementation can be assessed by posing the following questions:
>
> - To what extent have the jointly formulated policies been implemented in a way that has reduced the number and size of obstacles, avoided serious blunders, and created acceptable results?
> - To what extent has the governance network managed to coordinate the different aspects of the implementation process so that synergies are created and duplications of efforts are avoided?
> - To what extent have practical and political conflicts been resolved through collaboration?
> - To what extent have implementation resistance and veto powers been mitigated by the production of program responsibility and joint policy ownership obtained through participation in negotiated policy interaction?

The *fifth assessment criterion* concerns the ability of governance networks to provide a flexible adjustment of public policies and services in the face of positive and negative policy feedback and changing conditions, demands, and preferences. In a complex, fragmented, and dynamic society, public policies and services need to be adapted to political responses from relevant actors and to new developments and ideas. Top-down government through public bureaucracy is often slow to adjust policies to critical feedback voiced by experts and user groups and to new circumstances experienced by street-level bureaucrats. By contrast, near-perfect markets are rather quick to adapt to fluctuations in demand and supply but since the customers in the marketplace tend to use the exit rather than the voice option when they are dissatisfied, a lot of valuable information about the reasons for wanting to exit are lost (Hirschman, 1970). In addition, the collective action problems among private firms prevent them from controlling the field in which they are operating. Compared to both hierarchies and markets, governance networks have the advantage of combining the ability to make quick and concerted policy adjustments with the ability to respond to criticisms voiced by a broad range of actors and the capacity to control, or at least influence, the external environment. The medium for flexible policy adjustment is negotiated interaction among the network actors who provide a range of different inputs concerning policy performance and reflect on how to respond appropriately to policy feedback and new societal developments. The negotiated interaction leading to more or less profound policy adjustments might take the form of either incremental learning or a conceptual reframing where taken for granted assumptions are being problematized (Agyris and Schön, 1978). These assertions help us to advance the fifth proposition.

Proposition 5: Governance networks' ability to provide a flexible adjustment of policies and services can be assessed by posing the following questions:

- To what extent has the governance network regularly assessed policy performance on the basis of reports from actors from inside or outside the network?

- To what extent has the governance network identified emerging problems and translated these into minor adjustments of policies and services?

- To what extent is the governance network capable of engaging in more profound learning processes that might lead to major policy revisions?

The *sixth assessment criterion* concerns the ability of governance networks to create favorable conditions for future cooperation through cognitive, strategic, and institutional learning among the network actors. Governance networks are capable of providing a flexible adjustment of policies and a flexible adaptation of the network itself, but the flexibility gain is constantly threatened by the lack of stability (Milward and Provan, 2006: 12). Governance networks do not have the same kind of institutional stability that public hierarchies and private markets usually enjoy and this means that attempts to stabilize governance networks and improve the conditions for future cooperation become an important feature of network-governed policy processes. Fortunately, the strategic reflexivity and learning capacities within governance networks are often deployed to improve the conditions for both continued and future cooperation among the network actors. As pointed out by Koppenjan and Klijn (2004), there are three critical factors in the effort to produce favorable conditions for sustained cooperation in governance networks: cognitive learning, strategic learning, and institutional learning. Cognitive learning refers to the network actors' development of a joint vocabulary and frame of reference that will help them to communicate about new policy problems and how they are to be solved. Strategic learning refers to the network actors' understanding and enhancement of their mutual dependencies and their consequential recognition of the need for sustained cooperation. Finally, institutional learning is about the creation of institutional rules,

179

norms, and procedures that build and sustain mutual trust among the network actors. The listing of these factors leads us straight to the last of the six propositions.

Proposition 6: Governance networks' ability to improve the conditions for future cooperation can be assessed by posing the following questions:

- To what extent have the network actors developed a common vocabulary and frame of reference that facilitate communication across different levels, sectors, and organizational domains?

- To what extent has the negotiated interaction within the governance network helped to clarify and enhance mutual dependence and to create a positive valuation of interorganizational cooperation despite conflicts and failures?

- To what extent has the governance network formed institutional rules, norms, and procedures that build and sustain mutual trust?

The six propositions offer a broad set of indicators that can help researchers and practitioners to assess the effectivity of governance networks, partnerships, and other interactive governance arrangements. Governance networks cannot be expected to do well in relation to all the eighteen indicators that all together set the bar very high. Nevertheless, assessing the effectivity of a governance network on the basis of the eighteen indicators, using an ordinal scale (weak, moderate, and strong) to measure its performance in relation to the indicators, permits us to assess the degree to which a particular network or partnership contributes to effective governance. The role and function of the governance networks will determine whether we will be satisfied with the result of the empirical assessment.

The application of the various indicators of effective network governance in empirical analysis requires that a governance network is delimited in time and space. The identification and delimitation of the governance network in question may either take a formally organized governance network as a starting point, or proceed from a backward mapping of the social and political actors involved in the production of a particular policy output. When the network actors, the governance arenas, and the policy process are determined, the assessment of effectivity of the governance network can be made on the basis of different types of qualitative data.

Metagoverning governance networks

The assessment criteria explicated above help to measure the degree to which governance networks actually are delivering what they promise to deliver according to the vast literature on network governance. However, the problem is that governance networks—just like hierarchies and markets—are prone to failure (Jessop, 2002). Governance networks rely on precarious social and political processes that are easily disturbed by external or internal events. The sociopolitical context might be unstable and subject to profound changes, and the centrifugal forces within the network emanating from conflicts and power struggles might be stronger than the centripetal forces rooted in mutual dependency and institutionalized norms and identities.

Attempts at increasing the effectiveness of public governance through reliance on different kinds of networks are thus conditional upon the form and functioning of these networks. In order to be effective, governance networks must be able to adjust to changes in their environment (March and Olsen, 1995) and provide a relatively institutionalized framework for sustained negotiations that facilitate the alignment of goals, values, and cultures and produce a stable coordination of actions in the face of diverging interests (Goldsmith and Eggers, 2004). Ensuring the conditions for effective governing by networks requires a careful governance of the self-regulating governance networks. In short, governance networks must be *metagoverned* in order to enhance their contribution to the effective governing of society (Kickert et al., 1997; Jessop, 2002; Provan and Kenis, 2008).

As we have seen in Chapter 7, metagovernance is a reflexive and strategic endeavor through which a range of legitimate and resourceful actors aim to combine and facilitate particular forms of interactive governance and shape and direct the way they are functioning in accordance with specific rules, procedures, and normative standards. The centrality, formal authority, democratic legitimacy, and organizational resources of public authorities make them particularly suited for exercising metagovernance (Klijn and Koppenjan, 2000a). As such, elected politicians and public managers can employ different tools in their efforts to metagovern governance networks: (a) *institutional design* that aims to influence the scope, character, composition, and procedures of governance networks; (b) *goal and framework steering* that seeks to determine the political goals, fiscal conditions, legal basis, and discursive storyline of governance networks; (c) *process management* that attempts to reduce tensions, resolve conflicts, empower particular actors, and lower the transaction costs in governance networks; and (d) *direct participation* that endeavors to influence the policy agenda, the range of feasible options, the premises for decision-making, and the negotiated policy outputs of governance networks.

The four metagovernance tools can in various ways be used to promote and enhance effective network governance. Table 9.1 provides a number of stylized examples of how the tools of metagovernance can be employed to enhance effective and democratic network governance. The list is not exhaustive, but it provides an overview of a broad range of options available to public metagovernors.

The first metagovernance tool is *institutional design*, which is not only important in the initial phase where the governance network is formed but also involves subsequent adjustments to the institutional design. Institutional design can help enhance effective network governance in several ways. First, a governance network should be formed around a number of clearly defined policy objectives. Focusing on policy goals rather than policy programs immediately brings up the question of which actors can contribute to goal attainment (Goldsmith and Eggers, 2004: 56–60). Reliance on well-established connections with "the usual suspects" is a common source of ineffective problem-solving, as it tends to exclude crucial policy actors capable of making a significant contribution to the governance network while including policy actors who might have little to offer in relation to the task at hand. To further stimulate effective interaction and decision-making processes in the network, the metagovernor might want to set, either unilaterally or through

Table 9.1. Metagovernance of effective network governance

	Different ways to enhance effective network governance
Institutional design	Keep a strict focus on objectives and innovative capacities when composing the network
	Define or negotiate clear deadlines for different forms of policy output from the network
	Terminate superfluous and unsuccessful networks
Goal and framework steering	Ensure coordination and goal alignment through political framing and storytelling
	Create strong interdependencies among the network actors in order to stimulate resource exchange
	Share effectiveness gains arising from network governance with the network and network actors
Process management	Provide adequate resources that lower the transaction costs and empower the network actors
	Reduce destructive tensions through agenda control, arbitration, joint fact-finding and cross-frame learning
	Signal that a flexible adjustment of ends and means is acceptable in order to encourage innovation
Direct participation	Facilitate sustained cooperation by producing quick victories and creating joint ownership of them
	Show trust in order to gain and build trust
	Institutionalize processes that work well and learn from those that do not

negotiation, a number of deadlines for the delivery of different kinds of policy outputs. Hence, a number of milestones can be defined in order to keep the network actors focused on the production of outputs in terms of reports, conferences, plans, policy proposals, and direct interventions. Finally, the design of appropriate procedures for cooperation and negotiation will enhance effective governance, as it helps lower the transaction costs of networking and may reduce the risk of damaging conflicts caused by uncertainty and lack of coordination. There is obviously a limit to how much the initial design of interactive governance arrangements will impact future effectiveness. It is therefore crucial that the metagovernors are prepared to either terminate or sever the links to governance networks that, after careful goal and framework steering and process management, continue to prove to be superfluous or unsuccessful. Terminating or banishing governance networks is troublesome, as it might be met by fierce resistance from the network actors. However, cutting down funding, gradually withdrawing delegated powers, or replacing obsolete networks with new ones is a viable path in most cases.

The second metagovernance tool is *goal and framework steering*, which is an ongoing process aimed at shaping the arena for networked interaction through the use of indirect means such as the formation of the overall goals, the specification of the fiscal and legal conditions, and discursive storytelling that defines the joint mission of the network. Effective network governance can be enhanced by framing the overall policy objectives in ways that help align the individual goals of the network actors and convince them that there is an urgent need for coordination and joint action (Termeer and Koppenjan, 1997). Storytelling through the dissemination of "best practices" can also be used to influence the means by which the network actors aim to reach particular goals. The metagovernors might also attempt to strengthen the interdependencies among the network actors in order to stimulate resource exchange. This can be carried out either by clarifying or shaping the interests, roles, and capacities of the participating actors or by offering to fund activities and policy solutions that all of the network actors can agree upon (game theorists will know this as a "split-a-dollar" game, see Gintis, 2000: 99). If, finally, goals are aligned, resources are exchanged, and effective policies are formulated and implemented, it becomes important that the effectivity gains arising from the networked policy process are shared with the network and the network actors in order to create an incentive for further cooperation and effectivity gains. The governance network can be rewarded by extending its remit and autonomy, enhancing its prestige and influence, or increasing its funding. The network actors may be rewarded by upgrading their political status, granting them access to other policy arenas, offering them better service, or compensating them for the time and energy invested in the governance network.

The third metagovernance tool is *process management*, which involves interaction and dialogue with the network, though not direct participation in the negotiations in the network. Process management can boost effective network governance by lowering the transaction costs of networking through the provision of adequate support and resources and by empowering the network actors through the funding of individual or collective learning in terms of participation in courses, seminars, and conferences, the invitation of guest speakers to network meetings, or the organization of future workshops with external moderators. Process management can also contribute to the reduction of destructive tensions through agenda setting, arbitration, the initiation of joint fact-finding, and the facilitation of cross-frame learning (Koppenjan and Klijn, 2004: 160–83). Finally, the metagovernors must clearly signal that a flexible adjustment of ends and means is acceptable if backed by sound arguments, results from a political compromise among the key actors, and non-involvement of heavy cost shifting. A stubborn insistence on predefined ends and old-fashioned means will tend to strait-jacket the governance network and prevent mutual learning and policy innovation.

The final metagovernance tool is *direct participation* which tends to create a complicated situation in which the metagovernor becomes one among many network participants but retains a reflexive gaze on the governance network in order to monitor and improve its functioning. Effective network governance can be furthered by facilitating sustained cooperation among the network actors. By participating actively in the network, the meta-governor can help produce the kind of quick victories obtainable by picking the lowest hanging fruits and creating a sense of joint ownership for such victories through a repeated emphasis on the contribution of the participating actors. Quick victories with joint ownership demonstrate that networking matters, which in turn fosters further commitment and willingness to share resources and risks. The sustained cooperation among the network actors must build on some degree of trust. The strategic behavior of the individual network actors will often depend on the other network actors. Everybody waits to see what the others are doing and which game is being played. In this situation, the public metagovernor will occasionally be able to gain and build trust among the network actors via a unilateral display of trust in the network and the different players. When first one actor has opened up and displayed trust, other actors might follow suit, and the result might be the development of a generalized trust whereby everyone expects everybody else to abstain from exploiting an opening in the negotiation game to their own advantage. Sustained, trust-based interaction might produce successful public governance, but it might also lead to failures and policy disasters. Here, the role of the metagovernors is to encourage the network to institutionalize the processes that worked well and learn from those that failed. Interactive governance is based on a good deal of trial and error, but it is crucial to ensure the codification of the processes and procedures that appear to work well.

Conclusion

Despite the world-wide celebration of the merits of governance networks, their contribution to effective public governance is seldom subjected to systematic analysis. In order to compensate for this neglect, this chapter has aimed to further advance the debate on effective governance through networks. The endeavor has been achieved through the elaboration of criteria for assessing the extent to which governance networks contribute to an effective governing of particular policy fields. As such, it has been argued that effective network governance cannot be assessed using the well-known concepts of cost efficiency, operational effectiveness, and Pareto-optimal allocations that are normally applied in evaluations of hierarchical government and private markets. Therefore, a distinctive set of effectivity assessment criteria have been developed and each of them has been further detailed through a series of propositions that provide empirical indicators to be used in the concrete analysis of the actual performance of governance networks. The extent to which governance networks contribute to effective governance is a matter of degrees and it can be improved through careful metagovernance. The chapter demonstrates how different metagovernance tools can be used to enhance effective network governance and considers the dilemmas that are facing the public metagovernors. At a more general level, the chapter shows that the assessment and improvement of effective planning, problem-solving, and service delivery in a context of decentered governance provides a crucial challenge for both researchers and practitioners. Empirical studies following the lines of argument presented above will help to meet this challenge.

10

Assessing and improving the democratic quality of interactive governance

Over the last ten years, debates concerning the democratic implications of interactive forms of governance have been gaining more and more momentum (Sørensen and Torfing, 2007). While governance researchers tend to agree that the surge of interactive governance arenas such as quasi-markets, partnerships, and networks have implications for the role and functioning of democracy, there is less agreement about what these implications are (Klijn and Skelcher, 2007). Some argue that interactive forms of governance are democratically problematic because they undermine political equality, and the transparency in governance processes that makes it possible for the public to control and hold political decision-makers to account (Hansen, 2007; Papadopoulos, 2007; Bexell and Mörth, 2010). Others claim that interactive forms of governance give new life to a disenfranchised representative democracy because they provide new arenas for empowered participation on the output side of the political system (Fung and Wright, 2003; Warren, 2009).

The aim of this chapter is to argue that there are no clear-cut answers to the question of how interactive forms of governance affect democracy. Interactive forms of governance are neither intrinsically undemocratic nor intrinsically democratic. Their impact on democracy depends on their particular form and functioning in a given context. By taking this point of departure, we hope to add nuance to the current debate about the relationship between interactive governance and democracy. Instead of discussing, in abstract and general terms, the likely impact on democracy of interactive forms of governance, the focus is shifted toward empirical studies of the democratic quality of concrete governance arenas. Such studies, however, call for the development of empirically applicable criteria for assessing the democratic quality of such arenas. This chapter offers a model for assessing the democratic anchorage of interactive governance arenas, which provides a means to draw a democratic profile of concrete interactive governance arenas and inform strategies aiming to make them more democratic.

The chapter proceeds as follows: First, we justify the claim that interactive governance arenas are neither intrinsically democratic nor intrinsically undemocratic by showing how they can be both. This complexity is apparent when viewing interactive governance arenas through the lenses of traditional and new theoretical approaches to representative democracy, respectively. Then, we present a model for assessing the democratic anchorage of interactive governance arenas that takes into account both critical concerns and high hopes, and discusses how the model can be put into use in empirical studies of interactive governance arenas. Finally, it is considered how the democratic anchorage of interactive governance arenas can be improved through different forms of metagovernance.

Viewing interactive governance in light of theories of democracy

The proliferation of interactive governance arenas such as quasi-markets, partnerships, and networks has first and foremost been seen as problematic for democracy but voices are raised claiming that they have democratic potential. The premise for the debate is that the degree to which interactive governance arenas are to be deemed a threat or a potential for democracy depends on their ability to organize political decision-making in ways that manifest a set of norms hailed more or less unanimously by modern theories of liberal democracy, that is, political equality, political competition, democratic accountability, and individual liberty. The hegemonic position of the institutions of representative democracy in the Western world rests on the widely recognized view that this institutional model is more able than any other available model to guarantee these norms. Political equality is accommodated through the citizens' equal and legally guaranteed right to vote; political competition and democratic accountability are ensured through frequent elections and the presence of a free press; and individual liberty is provided by the existence of a private sphere in which individuals and local communities enjoy a considerable degree of autonomy.

Seen from the above outlined understanding of democracy that perceives the institutions of representative democracy as highly successful and sufficient means to ensure democracy, interactive forms of governance are highly problematic because they tend to undermine this institutional setup. Four major critiques are advanced against interactive forms of governance. First, individuals belonging to the territorially defined citizenry are not guaranteed equal access to political influence as interactive governance arenas privilege functionally affected stakeholders and tend to privilege strong and capable actors over those with fewer resources (Hansen, 2007). Second, public control over decision-makers is restricted because those participating in interactive governance arenas are seldom elected. Third, because decisions in interactive forms of governance are made in opaque and secluded negotiation processes, which depend on a considerable degree of bargaining and coalition building among involved parties, interactive governance arenas are difficult to hold to account (Katz and Mair, 1995; Pierre and Peters, 2005). Finally, the systematic involvement of private actors in governance processes threatens to undermine or diminish the sphere of individual liberty as there are no clear limits for what societal activities such governance arenas can attempt to regulate (Habermas, 1996; Bang, 2003). All in all, there are good arguments for suspecting that a surge of interactive forms of governance will undermine representative democracy.

Although the above noted dangers for democracy posed by interactive forms of governance are recognized, a new strand of democratic theory points out that interactive forms of governance also hold certain democratic potential. Hence, they can supplement the institutions of representative democracy in ways that might help to remedy some of their shortcomings. Hence, these theories explore the ways in which interactive forms of governance might democratize the output side of the political system by further strengthening the connection between "what governments do and what citizens receive" (Hirst, 1994, 2000; Dryzek, 2000; Young, 2000; Etzioni-Halevy, 2003; Fung and Wright, 2003; Fung, 2004; Sørensen and Torfing, 2005a; Keane, 2009; Warren, 2009). The new theories of democracy highlight three ways in which interactive governance arenas can democratize the output side of representative democracy.

First, it is argued that interactive governance arenas can bring us even closer to realizing the constitutive democratic norm that influence should be distributed more equally with reference to affectedness than the institutions of representative democracy have been able to do on their own (Held, 2006).

Democracy entails self-government; that is, those who are affected by decisions are able to influence these decisions. Institutions of representative democracy pursue this goal by linking affectedness closely to the status as citizen within a given territorially defined polity, and their important contribution to reaching this goal is indisputable. While general elections provide a superior means to distribute influence equally among these citizens, however, the method does not take into account that citizens are not equally affected by decisions made by an elected government. Federal and decentralized political systems that grant local communities the right to govern themselves can be seen as an expression of this idea that democracy privileges those who are particularly affected with more influence than those who are less affected in ways that do not collide with the organizing principles of representative democracy.

However, patterns of affectedness do follow not only territorial but also functional patterns: Those who have children in school are more immediately affected by school reforms than those who have not, and those who use public transport are more affected by changes in route plans and prices than those who do not. Interactive forms of governance might supplement the institutions of representative democracy in ways that make democracy even more sensitive to levels of affectedness among the members of a given population.

This argument is similar to the point made by Robert A. Dahl (1989) that a pluralistic representative democracy should allow for variations in the channels of influence available to citizens in light of variations in the intensity of citizen preferences. Since interactive governance arenas are often organized around a specific function or policy issue, they open the door for such extra channels of popular influence to those who are particularly affected by certain decisions (Dryzek, 2007; Warren, 2009). By introducing functional affectedness as a supplement to territorial notions of affectedness, the debate about how to promote political equality becomes more nuanced, and attention is drawn to the fact that interactive governance arenas might under certain conditions contribute to further enhance the equal distribution of political influence provided by the institutions of representative democracy among citizens.

It should, however, be kept in mind that the introduction of decentralized as well as functionally organized channels of political influence hold certain dangers for democracy. Hence, such arrangements might lead the populations' political attention away from general political issues and concerns related to the overall governing of society. If citizens are more occupied with local and specific functional issues, how is it, then, possible for politicians to gain support for broad strategies that aim to deal with issues related to the overall governance of society? What is at stake here is that interactive forms of governance can end up undermining the "public" in public governance. That is, if those most affected by programs are given special rights, then there is a risk that less directly affected citizens lose the capacity to shape public policies in the conventional democratic manner. In effect, public governance becomes a series of particularistic and narrow-minded subgovernments described so well by Schattschneider (1960). A final problem has to do with the question of how it is to be decided who should be regarded as affected by a governance process. There is a certain risk that those with the greatest verbal and organizational skills will decide who will be included and who will be excluded. For these reasons, the interactive governance paradigm maintains that representative democracy is paramount to ensuring a well-functioning democracy.

Second, interactive governance arenas provide an intermediate level of subelites between elected politicians and citizens. Although this systematic institutionalization of arenas in which subelites such as leaders of NGOs and private firms, as well as entrepreneurial and particularly knowledgeable citizens, can involve themselves in governance processes raises concerns about how to ensure the democratic legitimacy of such arenas, the presence of such subelites might under certain conditions enhance the level of participation and accountability in representative democracies (Barber, 1984; Hirst, 2000; Fung and Wright, 2003). Hence, interactive governance arenas can provide supplementary arenas that might help to enhance the political mobilization of larger parts of the population in political discussion and participation, to further spur political competition, and qualify the scrutiny of accounts given by governments and other influential political elites (Etzioni-Halevy, 1993; Esmark, 2007b).

Traditionally, the mobilization of citizens has first and foremost taken place within the confines of political parties, but the introduction of alternative paths into politics is likely to bring more citizens into the game. Moreover, the presence of political subelites could increase the pressure on politicians and other public authorities to give qualified accounts for their actions. Although the institutions of representative democracy are doing an important job in ensuring democratic accountability, problems remain (Schumpeter, 1946; Behn, 2001; Keane, 2009). Interactive governance arenas consisting of well-informed and capable subelites have the capacity to put more pressure on political elites to give solid accounts than do ordinary citizens. Examples of this are the important role played by Amnesty International in pressing governments to account for their use of torture, and school boards or parent organizations that identify and confront municipal councils with discrepancies between political promises and actual outcomes.

The downside to an increased involvement of subelites is, however, that in situations in which certain subelites tend to dominate the interactive governance arenas, it can be difficult to prevent them from subverting the policy process for their own ends. Given that most interactive governance arrangements lack the formal checks and balances provided by the institutions of representative democracy, the capacity of these arenas to restrain such actors is limited.

Third, by blurring the institutional boundaries between the public and the private sphere, new governance arrangements such as quasi-markets, partnerships, and governance networks promote a higher level of variety in policies and services within the public realm. By fragmenting public service delivery into a variety of competing and collaborating public and private service producing agencies, consumers of public services have obtained a direct influence on the character of the public services they receive. They can choose between different service providers and they can go into dialogue with service providers about the nature of such services. They have obtained what Albert O. Hirschman (1970) calls voice and exit options. The other side of the coin, however, is that citizens might end up focusing more and more on micro-politics while losing interest in the macro-level political battles and policy-making which they, often mistakenly, perceive to be of limited importance for their daily lives.

In sum, new theories of democracy make the point that although interactive governance arenas raise serious concerns for democracy, they might also have something to offer in supplementing representative democracy in ways that can further strengthen democracy. The different conclusions drawn by old and new approaches to representative democracy attest to the fact that interactive governance arenas can undermine as well as further develop democracy. The model for assessing the democratic anchorage of interactive governance arenas outlined below aims to guide empirical studies that seek to assess to what extent concrete interactive governance arenas do the one or the other. Do they de facto weaken representative democracy or do they supplement it? Moreover, the model aims to offer advice to those who seek to improve the democratic quality of concrete interactive governance arenas.

Assessing the democratic anchorage of interactive governance

The basic idea behind the model of democratic anchorage is that the democratic impact of interactive governance arenas depends on the degree to which they are anchored in a number of relevant territorially or functionally demarcated political constituencies and a set of rules for democratic interaction that lend them democratic legitimacy (see also Sørensen and Torfing, 2005b). The term anchorage is a metaphor for the presence of linkages between an interactive governance arena and different constituencies and norms so that each in its particular way grants democratic legitimacy to that arena. In representative democracies, it is evident that a primary anchorage point must exist between interactive governance arenas and elected politicians. However, as suggested by other models of democracy, additional anchorage points can further strengthen the democratic legitimacy of interactive governance arenas. As such, we shall claim that interactive governance arenas are democratically anchored to the extent that they:

1. are monitored by democratically elected politicians;
2. represent the membership basis of the participating groups and organizations;
3. are accountable to a territorially defined citizenry;
4. facilitate negotiated interaction in accordance with a commonly accepted democratic grammar of conduct.

The first anchorage point expresses the need to establish a close linkage between representative democracy and interactive governance arenas, which through various forms of delegation and decentralization ensures that decisions made by democratically elected politicians are not undermined by interactive governance arenas. Thus, the potential contributions of interactive governance arenas can be harvested without undermining representative democracy more than other forms of political decentralization and delegation. However, since this positive relationship between representative democracy and interactive governance arenas relies on the democratic quality of these arenas, this first anchorage point must be supplemented by other anchorage points. Hence, they can derive democratic legitimacy from the membership basis of the groups and organizations that are involved in the interactive governance arenas, from the citizens affected by the decisions made in these arenas, and from a democratic grammar of conduct that regulates the way in which those involved in these governance arenas interact with each other.

The model builds on the assumption that none of the four anchorage points alone can ensure the democratic quality of interactive governance arenas. The four anchorage points compensate for each other's shortcomings and only in unison can they provide a strong source of democratic legitimacy. As such, interactive governance arenas should be responsive to inputs from elected politicians, the membership basis of the participating groups and organizations, and the general public affected by decisions that are made in these arenas. Moreover, the interaction within the governance arenas should follow the rules specified by an explicitly formulated democratic grammar of conduct defining how legitimate decisions are to be taken. As we shall argue later, it is not to be expected that actors participating in interactive governance arenas will have an inclination to establish such anchorage points of their own accord. They must be enforced through different forms of metagovernance. Let us first consider, however, each of the four anchorage points in turn.

Anchorage in elected politicians

The rationale for anchoring interactive governance arenas in democratically elected politicians takes its point of departure in the basic idea found in traditional theories of representative democracy that government control over delegated policy decisions is paramount in order to make sure that these decisions are in line with the popular will expressed by the political majority of elected assemblies (Schoenbrod, 1993). Hence, elected politicians can lend democratic legitimacy to interactive governance arenas in so far as they control the formation, functioning, and impact of interactive governance arenas.

But what kind of control over delegated governance processes do we expect politicians to have in a democracy? As described in Chapter 4, it is commonly argued that the actual ability of politicians to control governance processes in any deep meaning of the word is relatively restricted. This counts for hierarchical bureaucracies (Lindblom, 1959; Lipsky, 1980; Behn, 2001) as well as for political systems that have been subject to New Public Management reforms (Pollitt and Bouckaert, 2004: 99). What politicians can do is to metagovern what they have delegated. As described in Chapter 7, a skillful exercise of metagovernance of interactive governance processes constitutes a forceful way in which top-down control can be exercised through strategic framing, shaping, and monitoring of interactive governance arenas. As such, the role as metagovernor is no less ambitious and powerful than the role as sovereign ruler. Taking on this role might help to reduce some of the deficiencies characterizing traditional forms of delegation through the enforcement of what Archon Fung (2004) calls "autonomous accountability" upon interactive governance arenas.

As outlined in Chapter 7, metagovernance of interactive governance arenas can be exercised through (*a*) an institutional design of the rules, norms, and procedures that condition interactive governance processes; (*b*) goal and framework steering that sketches out, and evaluates performance with reference to political, fiscal, legal, and discursive room for the maneuvering of interactive governance arenas; (*c*) process management that attempts to reduce tensions, resolve conflicts, empower and activate particular actors, and lower transaction costs; and (*d*) direct participation in interactive governance processes in an endeavor to influence the policy agenda, the range of feasible options, the decision-making premises, and the negotiated outputs and outcomes.

The efficient and effective exercise of metagovernance calls for a mix of the different forms of metagovernance. Not least, it is important that hands-off forms of metagovernance *a* and *b* are supported by hands-on metagovernance *c* and *d* and vice versa. As a case in point, efforts to metagovern quasi-markets, partnerships, and networks through an exclusive use of hands-off forms of metagovernance have tended to lead to all sorts of decouplings caused by factors ranging from pure misunderstandings to strategic behavior such as creaming. These problems could be reduced though an investment in hands-on forms of metagovernance. In the same vein, efforts to exclusively metagovern interactive governance arenas by means of hands-on metagovernance often prove to be obsolete if they are not supported by hands-off metagovernance that models the structural conditions that motivate the involved actors to interact in the desired ways.

There are also good reasons to mix more and less interventionist forms of metagovernance in order to avoid both over-regulation and under-regulation of interactive governance arenas (Kooiman, 1993*a*: 255). There are no ways of precisely determining the tipping point between the two. In the case of over-regulation, metagovernance is experienced as an unbearable strait-jacket for the relatively self-regulating interactive governance arenas. In the case of under-regulation, metagovernors lose their grip on the overall direction of the governance process. Nevertheless, if the metagovernors combine and balance the more interventionist forms of metagovernance *a* and *d* with the less interventionist forms *b* and *c*, the chances of avoiding over- and under-regulation will tend to increase.

Then, according to what criteria can we assess the degree to which interactive governance arenas are controlled by metagoverning politicians? Here, it might help to think about when and how things can go wrong. First, the elected politicians might not be aware of the existence of a particular governance arena, which will make it impossible for them to exercise metagovernance. Second, the politicians may fail to clarify whether or not a governance arena is involved in "high politics" and therefore needs a careful metagovernance, or whether it is engaged in "low politics" bordering on administrative coordination or private activities and therefore needs less, or even no, metagovernance. Third, limited knowledge about what is going on in an interactive governance arena can prevent the exercise of effective democratic metagovernance. Last but not least, overburdened politicians might be tempted to leave the metagovernance task to public administrators and thereby seriously reduce the level of democratic control with decentered governance processes.

Proposition 1. Questions to be asked in assessing the democratic anchorage in elected politicians

- To what extent are elected politicians aware of the presence, role, and character of the interactive governance arena in question, and to what extent do they have access to information about its processes, outputs, and outcomes?

- To what extent do they assume the role of metagovernors of that particular governance arena?

- To what extent have the politicians defined the objectives of their metagovernance, and are they combining different forms of metagovernance in ways that oblige an interactive governance arena to contribute to the realization of these objectives?

- To what extent do the politicians take an active part in and cooperate closely with public administrators in developing and pursuing a joint metagovernance strategy?

The degree to which politicians take on the role as metagovernors is, however, in the end an empirical question.

Reversing the arguments about metagovernance failure permits us to propose a list of questions that we should seek to answer in empirical studies of interactive governance networks. The proposed questions are summarized in proposition 1.

Anchorage in membership basis of participating groups and organizations

The rationale for anchoring interactive governance arenas in the membership basis of the participating groups and organizations takes its point of departure in pluralist and associative theories of democracy (Dahl, 1961; Hirst, 1994) that view intensely affected groups and organizations as "demoi" with a legitimate democratic right to be involved in decisions that affect them (Sørensen and Torfing, 2003: 617). Since interactive governance arenas bring together actors who implicitly or explicitly represent a plurality of groups and organizations, their democratic legitimacy depends on the degree to which these actors de facto represent the members of these different groups and organizations. If not, interactive governance arenas will probably be even more like organizations that turn into oligarchies (Michels, 1915).

But what does it mean to represent someone? The seminal work of Hannah Pitkin (1967, 2004) fully illuminates the complexity of the term. Does democratic representation call for representatives who bring the substantive views held by a certain group into the decision-making arena or should the representatives promote what they themselves view as in the best interest of those individuals? Recent critiques have been raised against the idea that the thing that is to be represented exists, that is, certain views or interests exist independently of the act of representation. Representatives play an active role in shaping what they represent (Saward, 2008).

The crucial role that political leaders play in shaping their political constituencies is among other things apparent in recent American politics where Bush's rhetoric established a deep divide within the American people between a "we" consisting of real Americans and a "them" who did not really belong, and one of the promises made by Obama in the 2008 election was to reunite the American people. In other words, the performative act of representation plays an active role in forming not only the preferences and views but also the political identities of the represented. Seen in this light, democratic representation is a dynamic relational act that is to be evaluated with reference to the degree to which decision-makers and those who are affected by the decisions they make have knowledge of and accept the relationship between them as an instance of democratic representation (Torfing, 1999: 183ff.).

The particular challenge pertaining to promoting the democratic representativeness of those who participate in interactive governance arenas concerns how to avoid tying down the hands and knees of representatives participating in interactive governance arenas through the issuing of detailed mandates. Although the tension between the democratic need to control representatives and the need representatives have for autonomy is also very much present in relation to acts of democratic representation in traditional government institutions it is spoken out in relation to interactive governance arenas. As majority control is not an option, the decision-making capacity of interactive governance arenas relies completely on the willingness and ability of the participating actors to change their position in the interactive processes. This ability is hampered by tight mandates.

Those who argue that interactive forms of governance as well as any other form of governance can be democratically tamed by tight mandates are mistaken. What can be done instead is to force those who participate in interactive governance arenas to take on the role as representatives and to gain acceptance as such by those they claim to represent. As pointed out by Robert Michels (1915), this is an uphill struggle. Participants in interactive forms of governance such as quasi-markets, partnerships, and governance networks are subelites and efforts to bind them to certain viewpoints held by their constituencies are bound to fail. The need to find alternative ways of establishing democratic ties between the participating subelites and relevant constituencies are imperative.

In representative democracies, this connection between the representative and the represented is institutionalized through general elections that grant all citizens a right to vote and thus to appoint or discard representatives. In comparison, the democratic legitimacy of interactive governance arenas depends on their capacity to represent affected groups and organizations. While a number of interactive governance arenas do appoint representatives for such groups and organizations through elections among those defined as affected stakeholders, other arenas rely on alternative ways of ensuring the democratic anchorage in affected groups and organizations. An effort to assess the degree to which they do so must, first, evaluate the degree to which participants in interactive governance arenas make claims to represent such groups or organizations (Saward, 2006: 191). The advancement of such claims must be perceived as crucial for the degree to which they are recognized as legitimate players by the other participants in the interactive governance arena. Second, the groups and organizations that the participants claim to represent must be aware of the claims to represent them that are made. Third, the status as representative must depend on the degree to which the represented have the capacities, information, and access to turn down representative claims. Finally, the degree of influence granted to the interactive governance arena must depend on the degree to which the representatives are responsive to the

---

Proposition 2. Questions to be asked in assessments of the democratic anchorage in participating groups and organizations

- To what extent is an interactive governance arena making claims to represent specific relevant or affected groups and organizations?
- To what extent are the represented groups and organizations aware of the fact that these claims are made and are they actively accepting them as legitimate?
- To what extent do the represented groups and organizations have the capacity and opportunity to critically evaluate the way that their interests and preferences are constructed and pursued by the representative(s)?
- To what extent does the influence of interactive governance arenas depend on responsiveness to criticisms, views, and interests of their constituencies?

---

criticisms, views, and ideas of their constituencies. To what extent they do so is in the end an empirical question.

In proposition 2 we list four research questions that must be asked in studies of the degree to which interactive governance arenas are anchored in the participating groups and organizations.

Anchorage in a territorially defined citizenry

The rationale for anchoring interactive governance arenas in a territorially defined citizenry takes its departure from the central role ascribed to the public sphere in theories of representative democracy. Hence, we shall claim that the democratic legitimacy of such arenas depends not only on the degree to which the participating actors represent directly affected groups and organizations but also on the degree to which interactive arenas are democratically account-able to a wider territorially defined constituency of citizens who are more indirectly affected by the decisions taken in the interactive governance arena. Hence, the citizens who live within the local, regional, national, or transnational territory in which an interactive governance arena is operating should be able to hold it accountable for the policies, policy outputs, and policy outcomes for which it is fully or partly responsible. Of course, the elected politicians help to anchor interactive governance arenas but the possi-bility of holding them to account is likely to increase if concerned publics can take a direct and active part in holding them to account for their actions.

As illustrated in the extensive literature on how to hold elected politicians and other public authorities to account, this is not a simple matter (Etzioni-Halevy, 1993; Behn, 2001; Bovens et al., 2008). One central problem has to do with the presence of complex causalities, which makes it difficult to determine who is accountable for certain outputs and outcomes. Is a financial crisis caused by the present government or by forces beyond its control? Another problem relates to the question of information asymmetries: What resources does it take to hold someone to account? While voters have the capacity to sanction politicians on election day, the complexity of governance issues makes it difficult for many to sanction wisely because they do not possess the necessary degree of knowledge. One way of dealing with this problem has been to combine vertical forms of accountability with horizontal forms of accountability through the institutionalization of a separation of powers among public authorities.

Holding interactive governance arenas to account calls for a similar mix of forms of accountability. First, they should be held to account by knowledgeable and resourceful public authorities through different forms of meta-governance such as naming and shaming and outcome assessments (Bovens et al., 2008). Second, they must be made subject to intense public contestation. Promoting democratic accountability through a high level of political contestation between interactive governance arenas and the affected public is paramount in order to avoid such arenas degenerating into closed and secret clubs that operate in the dark and without public approval (Fox and Miller, 1995; Newman, 2005; Dryzek, 2007; Bexell and Mörth, 2010). Public contestation basically involves public debate and critical scrutiny of the ways policy problems are defined; the listing and framing of feasible options; the procedures that lead to the choice of a particular policy; and the direct and indirect results of its implementation. As such, interactive governance arenas must provide public accounts of why, how, and with what result they do what they do, and they must engage in public dialogue with their opponents and be responsive to the criticisms that are raised. What we are talking about here is a new kind of narrative accountability whereby the interactive governance arenas' accounts are publicly contested by critical counter-accounts (March and Olsen, 1995: 141ff.).

The relevant counterpart of the interactive governance arena is the citizens within the territory bound by the decisions of the interactive governance arena, but we should not be under the illusion that all citizens will have their eyes tightly fastened on the decision-making, policy outputs, and policy outcomes of vast numbers of interactive governance arenas in order to criticize what they find problematic, wrong, or wanting. We will have to content ourselves with the critical engagement of concerned publics in terms of mass media, scientific and professional experts, interest organizations, social movements, competing interactive governance arenas, and politically interested and empowered individuals. Public audit and critical scrutiny of interactive governance arenas at multiple levels require a certain amount of resources, capacities, and political interest, which we cannot commonly expect to find among ordinary citizens, and least of all in unorganized groups of citizens with low education and income. The public contestation of the narrative accounts produced by an interactive governance arena is therefore often carried out by different kinds of subelites such as researchers and other experts, think tanks, and NGOs with specialized knowledge related to a certain policy field (Etzioni-Halevy, 1993).

There are three crucial requirements that must be fulfilled in order to facilitate a public contestation of the narrative accounts produced by interactive governance arenas. The first requirement is transparency. Interactive governance arenas and their tasks, remit, and composition should be fully visible to the general public, and they must produce regular public accounts for why and how they arrived at particular decisions, and what the results have been (Fung, 2004). As pointed out in Chapter 11, some level of secrecy and closure can be necessary in order to ensure democratic decision-making, but in those cases the need for secrecy must be explicitly explained and justified in the eyes of relevant publics through the formulation of narrative accounts. Second, the wider citizenry must be in ongoing dialogue with members of the interactive governance arenas through public hearings, press conferences, and mass media coverage. Finally, the interaction between interactive governance arenas and the citizens must be characterized by mutual responsiveness. One of the ways of promoting this kind of two-way responsiveness is to ensure that ongoing

---

Proposition 3. Questions to be asked in assessing the democratic anchorage in a territorially defined citizenry

- To what extent are the tasks, remit, and composition of an interactive governance arena transparent to relevant publics?

- To what extent are the goals and strategies, and audit of the outputs and outcomes of interactive governance processes publicly accessible?

- To what extent does an interactive governance arena produce narrative accounts that aim to justify its decisions, actions, and results in the eyes of the broader citizenry?

- To what extent do the participants of an interactive governance arena engage in an ongoing dialogue with citizens who contest their decisions, actions, and results, and show responsiveness to criticisms and alternative proposals raised in the public debate?

---

dialogue between citizens and interactive governance arenas is taken into account in the day-to-day procedures of interactive governance arenas.

With reference to the three above-mentioned requirements, we propose that an assessment of the democratic anchorage of interactive governance arenas must take the questions listed in proposition 3 into consideration.

Anchorage in democratic rules and norms

The rationale for anchoring interactive governance arenas in democratic rules and norms is found in participatory and deliberative theories of democracy. They argue that the legitimacy of political decisions depends not only on the extent to which decision-makers are linked to a series of external political constituencies but also on the degree to which the interaction between those participating in decision-making adheres to particular generally accepted norms and rules of conduct (Cohen, 1989; Mouffe, 1993). While there is a high degree of agreement about what democratic norms to apply, it is far more difficult to agree on how these norms are best translated into concrete behavioral rules and procedures. This is among other things witnessed by the variation of institutional forms we find in different representative democracies (Lijphart, 1999).

Just as we accept that there is not one but plural ways in which democratic norms can be translated into concrete rules of conduct in representative democracies, it must be accepted that there will exist different democratic rules of conduct in interactive governance arenas. Therefore, a measurement of the extent to which interactive governance arenas are anchored in democratic rules of conduct must focus on the extent to which they have formulated a set of concrete behavioral rules and procedures that can be said to realize generally accepted democratic norms for democratic participation and deliberation.

Three democratic norms appear to be of particular relevance in evaluating the degree to which interactive governance arenas are democratically anchored in democratic norms and rules. The three norms that must be translated into concrete rules of conduct relate to the formation, the functioning, and outcomes of interactive governance arenas, respectively. The first norm demands an equal inclusion of the affected and thus for the formulation of rules and procedures that institutionalize a continuous debate among the participants about who should be included with direct reference to the question of affectedness. The larger public should be informed about such rules and procedures (Young, 2000). The second norm concerns the demand for democratic deliberation based on an agonistic respect for the other participants' right to voice their opinions and their willingness to commit themselves to reaching a negotiated agreement despite differences in views and interests (Mouffe, 2005). The third norm demands for rules and procedures

Proposition 4. Questions to be asked in assessing the democratic anchorage in democratic rules and norms

- To what extent are inclusions in and exclusions from an interactive governance arena being justified with reference to explicit normative criteria and to what extent are these criteria subject to ongoing negotiations?
- To what extent are inclusions and exclusions made with reference to degrees of affectedness?
- To what extent are the deliberations taking place within an interactive governance arena based on agonistic respect and the participants' commitment to contribute to reaching negotiated agreements?
- To what extent do interactive governance arenas function in ways that promote democratic innovation and renewal?

ensuring that the interactive governance arenas are engaged in a constant effort to renew and improve the democratic functioning of interactive governance arenas through a self-reflexive search for ways to further democratize its way of governing. Democracy never reaches a final form, neither as a perfect set of institutions, nor as a regulative idea. Democracy must be constantly developed through a plurality of creative, partial, and experimental methods, and interactive governance arenas should be judged on their ability to facilitate such a development (Dewey, 1927; Dahl, 1989). The degree to which actual interactive governance arenas do live up to such norms is largely unknown. One might suspect that arenas such as quasi-markets and partnerships that tend to be involved in commercial enterprises do not live up to such norms. However, empirical studies are needed in order to obtain more knowledge about these issues.

The three general norms described in proposition 4 determine the questions that are to be asked in assessing the degree to which interactive governance arenas are democratically anchored in a democratic grammar of conduct that can be said to enact these rules in a concrete context.

Applying the model

The four sets of criteria outlined above aim to translate the key dimensions of the model of democratic anchorage into empirically assessable standards for evaluating the democratic quality of interactive governance arenas. As a general rule, the more politicized an interactive governance arena is, the more important it is that it performs well on all the different dimensions and norms. As such, the first step in contextualizing the anchorage model consists in assessing the degree to which a specific governance arena is operating in a highly politicized environment and is contributing to the making or implementation of controversial political decisions. A high level of democratic anchorage is comparably less important in case of interactive governance arenas operating in sedimented governance contexts with few disagreements and political conflicts. However, a democratic anchorage of interactive governance arenas is never unimportant because there are political issues at stake in all governance processes, and because a low level of politicization can sometimes be caused by a low level of transparency that hinders disputable issues from becoming politicized.

The next consideration concerns the question of whether all anchorage points are equally important and relevant in relation to different types of interactive arenas: Should the model be applied in the same way and to the same extent in studies of quasi-markets, partnerships, and networks? The general answer to this question is that it is impossible to make hard and fixed rules about the relevance of the different anchorage points. In the final instance, the relevance of the anchorage points depends on a concrete assessment of the form and character of the interactive governance arenas that are under scrutiny. In other words, the model cannot be applied in a mechanical way, but must be conceptualized so as to make sense in relation to what is being studied.

Nevertheless, it is possible to set up some general guidelines for how the model could be applied in relation to different types of interactive governance arenas such as quasi-markets, partnerships, and networks. Table 10.1 suggests ways to operationalize the model in relation to these three kinds of interactive governance arenas.

Table 10.1 illustrates that different interactive governance arenas are democratically anchored in slightly different ways. The most significant difference is to be found in how quasi-markets, partnerships, and networks are anchored in elected politicians. While quasi-markets require a relatively tight top-down metagovernance where goals and economic conditions are clearly defined in advance and outcomes are evaluated with reference to pregiven standards, partnerships and networks entail more horizontal forms of metagovernance. Partnerships are metagoverned in ways that leave considerable space for them to set and pursue their own more detailed and situated goals while networks bring public authorities and other network actors together in a shared effort to define and implement policies. As such it could be argued that although all four anchorage points are important for quasi-markets, partnerships, and networks, they are more so in the case of the two latter than in the case of the former.

Table 10.1. Assessing the democratic anchorage of quasi-markets, partnerships, and networks

	Anchorage in elected politicians	Anchorage in participating groups and organizations	Anchorage in territorially defined citizenry	Anchorage in democratic rules and norms
Quasi-markets	Clear and detailed political goals, contracted budget, and frequent performance assessments	Voice options promoting dialogue between a producer and those claiming to represent the consumers and exit options allowing consumers to go elsewhere	Public scrutiny of the goals, procedures, and outcomes of market arrangements	Relational contracts that rely on democratic rules and norms
Partnerships	Clear but general political goals, and funding schemes that give partnerships incentives to pursue these goals	Voice options that encourage dialogue between partnerships and those claiming to represent affected stakeholders, and exit options that allow stakeholders to reject partnership arrangements	Public scrutiny of the goals, procedures, and outcomes of partnership projects	Partnership agreements that rely on democratic rules and norms
Networks	Intense, ongoing dialogue between politicians and network actors	Voice options that grant the affected access to be represented and to reject representative claims, and exit options that allow them to reject network arrangements	Public scrutiny of the goals, procedures, and outcomes of networks	Network constitutions that rely on democratic rules and norms

Improving the democratic anchorage through metagovernance

The model for assessing the democratic anchorage of interactive governance arenas is important because it paves the way for obtaining new and more detailed knowledge about the relationship between interactive governance and democracy. First, the model encourages comparative studies of interactive governance arenas that can provide important knowledge about the impact of institutional and contextual factors on the democratic quality of interactive governance. Second, the model makes it possible to draw democratic profiles of particular interactive governance arenas and thus to develop tailor-made strategies for increasing their democratic anchorage through different forms of metagovernance. Hence, it should be stressed that metagovernance can not only be used to enhance the effectiveness of interactive governance processes (Koppenjan and Klijn, 2004; Sørensen and Torfing, 2009) but can also strengthen their democratic anchorage. Although metagovernance of interactive governance arenas can in principle be exercised by many different actors, the main responsibility for promoting the democratic quality of such arenas rests on the shoulders of the politicians who have the democratic legitimacy to do so. As such, politicians have a double task of metagoverning the policies as well as the processes through which these policies are formulated in and around the interactive governance arenas.

As mentioned above, the metagovernance of quasi-markets relies heavily on top-down hands-off forms of metagovernance that operate through an institutional design and political and economic framing of public service providers. These forms of metagovernance, however, can not only be applied in ways that ensure that quasi-markets act in accordance with predefined political goals and objectives but can also enhance the democratic anchorage of quasi-markets. One of the means to do so is the contract. Politicians could insist on including in the contract that no restrictions must be made that delimit the consumers' exit options or exclude particular groups from requiring a service; that user boards or other interactive arenas are established, which facilitate an ongoing dialogue between service providers and consumers; and that the content of the assignment given to the service provider and evaluations of performance are publicly accessible on a homepage or otherwise. Moreover, politicians can design a competitive context that gives service providers an incentive to be responsive to customer demands. However, hands-on forms of metagovernance can also contribute to enhancing the democratic anchorage of quasi-markets. Relational contracts can institutionalize regular evaluations of the democratic performance of the service providers and public or semi-public naming and shaming events that make it prestigious to do well in terms of democratic anchorage.

In the case of partnerships, metagoverning politicians can set up as an explicit goal that partnership arrangements add to the democratic anchorage of public policymaking. This goal formulation can be supported by the design of incentive structures that motivate public actors to form partnerships not only in light of the resources that potential partners possess but also with reference to whether these partners can be said to represent affected stakeholders. In addition, a requirement for obtaining funding could be that partnerships present an elaborate strategy for how they intend to make their activities transparent to the affected stakeholders as well as to the wider public. Finally, metagoverning politicians could develop a set of norms and guidelines for how public authorities who participate in partnerships are to manage or otherwise influence partnership activities in ways that enhance their democratic anchorage.

Finally, in the case of networks metagovernance by means of institutional design, network management, and network participation seems promising in enhancing their democratic anchorage. As political framing becomes more negotiated, hands-on forms of metagovernance must take over. Skillful network management and strategic network participation become central tools for promoting the formation and realization of democratic norms, standards, and procedures within the network as well as between a network and the constituencies it claims to represent. These hands-on metagovernance activities can be supported and enforced through institutional designs and economic incentives that construct interdependencies between network actors in ways that promote the democratic inclusion of representatives for affected stakeholder groups in the formation of new networks as well as in the activities of well-established networks.

Democratic anchorage in the light of globalization

Although the model for the democratic anchorage of interactive governance arenas is helpful in pointing out how to assess the democratic anchorage of interactive governance arenas and indicate how it can be improved, it leaves us with unfinished business. Hence, the model relies on the assumption that it is possible to identify a body of politicians that has the undisputed legitimacy and authority to metagovern interactive governance arenas. However, this assumption is challenged by the fact that not all societies have political authorities that are strong enough to take on the role of metagovernor. This counts for a number of Western democracies but in particular it is the reality in many third world countries (Migdal, 1988; Atkinson and Coleman, 1989; Milliken and Krause, 2002; Lauridsen, 2004; Lund, 2007).

The idea that it is possible to identify authoritative metagovernors is, furthermore, challenged by the increasing political globalization that has led to the establishment of a plurality of multilevel governance arrangements (see Chapter 5) and transnational governance arenas (Ansell, 2000; Bohman, 2005; Keane, 2009) that operate above the nation state. Among these more or less formalized and politically authorized governance arenas, courts, media arenas, and NGOs count the UN, WTO, G20, EU, Mercosur, the World Bank, the International Court of Law, and a series of human rights associations. While a few of these transnational institutions have been in existence for a considerable number of years, many have recently been established and/or have gained prominence and influence. As transnational governance arenas grow in numbers and influence, it becomes ever more difficult to determine who has the responsibility, legitimacy, and capacity to take on the role as metagovernor.

The question that needs to be addressed in this context is *to what extent and how the democratic anchorage of interactive governance arenas in metagoverning politicians can take place in the case of either one weak metagovernor as in the case of failed states or many competing metagovernors as is the case on the global political scene.* In line with Jan Kooiman's famous statement, that no one actor has the capacity to govern on their own (Kooiman, 1993a: 4), we shall argue that in today's globalized system of governance there are few situations in which individual political authorities—local, national, or transnational—have the capacity to metagovern interactive governance processes effectively on their own. In order to be effective, metagovernance initiatives aiming to direct interactive policymaking and policy implementation as well as enhancing the democratic anchorage of such processes must in most cases be exercised by intergovernmental networks consisting of two or more political authorities.

Currently, there is an urgent need to conduct studies of to what extent and how the many intergovernmental networks at play on the global political scene are seeking to metagovern interactive governance arenas in ways that promote their democratic anchorage. Such studies can gain inspiration from the rapidly progressing theoretical debate about what a transnational or global democracy might look like. While some push for the establishment of a world government capable of metagoverning interactive governance processes (Held, 2006), others put their faith in the establishment of a complex plurality of public authorities and network-based forms of intergovernmental governance capable of monitoring interactive governance arenas (Bohman, 2005; Keane, 2009).

Although the model for the democratic anchorage of interactive governance arenas does not address this issue head on, it highlights the need to institutionalize points from which elected politicians—be they elected by the same or different political constituencies—are capable of metagoverning interactive governance arenas in ways that promote their democratic anchorage. The danger of globalization does not so much spring from the growth in interactive governance arenas at the transnational level as from the lack of intergovernmental institutions or networks capable of metagoverning them.

Conclusion

The relationship between democracy and interactive governance is full of tensions. In this chapter, we have argued that interactive governance arenas are neither intrinsically democratic nor intrinsically undemocratic. They definitely challenge traditional ways of understanding and institutionalizing well-established democratic norms such as political equality, political competition, democratic accountability, and individual liberty. However, at the same time, interactive governance arenas provide new mechanisms for exploiting the democratic potentials not only on the input side of the political system but also on its output side, for distributing political influence equally with reference to territorially as well as functionally defined patterns of affectedness, for instating a level of active and well-informed subelites who have the capacity to contest accounts given by political elites, and for developing democratic political identities capable of taking part in collective decision-making in contexts characterized by diversity and difference.

The complex relationship between democracy and interactive governance highlights the need to stop discussing whether or not interactive governance arenas are democratic at a general level and begin to study the extent to which concrete governance networks function in a democratic way. In support of such studies, we have proposed a model for assessing the democratic anchorage of interactive governance arenas. The model points out four anchorage points that must be in place if an integrative governance arena is to qualify as democratic. In addition, we have proposed a set of research questions to be asked in assessments of the extent to which the four anchorage points can be said to be in place. Moreover, it has been considered how the model can be applied in studies of different kinds of interactive governance arenas, for example, quasi-markets, partnerships, and governance networks and how their democratic anchorage can be advanced through different forms of metagovernance. Finally, we have pointed out that a shortcoming of the proposed democratic model is that it takes departure from the assumption that interactive governance arenas operate in a context in which it is possible to identify a body of elected politicians who can take on the task of metagovernors although this is not always the case and is less and less so in an increasingly globalized world.

As such, the model does not solve all problems in clarifying the relationship between democracy and interactive governance. However, by proposing a set of concrete standards for assessing the impact of interactive governance arenas on democracy, the proposed model highlights the need to find ways to exploit the democratic potentials that are to be found both on the input side and on the output side of the political system, and to form networks of those elected politicians who are relevant for metagoverning a concrete interactive governance arena. One of the ways ahead in dealing with these challenges is to do more empirical studies. Such studies will hopefully, as is often the case, show avenues to take in developing new forms of democracy that can assist the institutions of representative democracy in carrying out the difficult task of ensuring the democratic quality of current governance processes.

11

Transparency and governance

In 2010, Wikileaks disclosed hundreds of thousands of classified government documents and diplomatic reports, causing embarrassment to political leaders around the world. To Wikileaks, the disclosure served to reveal to the public the consequences of an opaque government, as manifested in the rather significant differences between the public rhetoric and the candor that characterized the classified documents. Political leaders, in their defense, maintained that much of the jargon in diplomatic reports should not be taken too seriously and, more importantly, that some degree of seclusion is a prerequisite for complex problem-solving and ultimately necessary to democratic governance.

The Wikileaks disclosures highlight one of the perennial problems in almost all forms of democratic governance: the balance between efficient governance on the one hand and the need for democratic transparency and accountability on the other. Those values tend for the most part to be tied to traditional government institutions that can be regulated to uphold those values. Interactive governance makes the call for transparency more challenging to meet due to the lower degree of institutionalization of procedure, and there are arguably better opportunities than in conventional government processes for avoiding disclosure and public accountability. However, interactive governance processes that are secluded from the public do not rhyme very well with core democratic values. In much of democratic theory, it is considered a fundamental Rosseauian right of the people to have access to information about government's decisions and actions (Hood, 2006a). Indeed, it is difficult to see how transparency and the sharing of information could have any other than positive values for governance and society.

At the same time, however, history is replete with examples of opaque forms of governance where seclusion appears to have been integral to a positive outcome. This has been the case not least in relation to sensitive negotiations aiming to settle conflicts. The Oslo negotiations to start up the Middle East peace process and the Good Friday agreement in Northern Ireland are two good examples of extremely sensitive negotiations, which quite likely would have failed had the negotiations been continuously reported in the media. Transparency forces negotiators to speak their organization's line in public, which significantly complicates the search for compromise and common ground (Fung et al., 2007). This counts for governments as well as for interactive governance arenas.

The need for secrecy and seclusion occurs not only in such historically defining moments but is present also in the day-to-day mundane political process. For governments, some degree of seclusion is needed in bargaining processes in foreign policy or defense policy, and in negotiations among political parties in a coalition government. In interactive governance processes, the same can be said about the negotiations that take place between public and private actors in quasi-markets, partnerships, and governance networks (Stone, 1989; Naurin, 2007) or among politicians and senior civil servants in the government office, and so on. Thus, as much as democratic discourse heralds openness, information, and involvement, there are stages in the process of governing where such transparency would be dysfunctional or even detrimental to governance. Indeed, too much transparency at sensitive stages of the governance process harbors an explanation of governance failure, particularly if such openness was insisted upon in the early stages of the policy process.

In order to escape this dilemma, we will argue that there is an important difference between transparency in process and transparency in outcomes. It may be acceptable, from a democratic theory point of view, to have transparency in outcomes while certain details of the policy process are withheld from the public. If the public, elected officials, and affected parties can assess the final outcome of a governance process and even reverse the policy decisions if they are deemed unacceptable, such an arrangement would at least to some extent allow for an opaque process. Furthermore, it is important to understand the differences between secrecy that is implemented to protect an autocratic government on the one hand and secrecy that indirectly serves to promote efficiency or democracy in the interactive governance processes, on the other.

Interactive governance draws to a significant degree on the availability of information. In order for actors to become involved in a meaningful way in the governance process, they must possess some knowledge about the plans and intentions of the major players, and not least in the involved public authorities. In interactive governance settings where participation, and subsequently influence, is not a given condition but is contextually defined and subject to ongoing power struggles, the policy process could be seen as a series of opportunity structures for societal actors. In that perspective, transparency becomes a prerequisite for interactive governance. At the same time, governance processes that are fully transparent in terms of policy objectives and the scope of financial and other resources easily become overloaded by actors with a stake in the policy issues or the resources to be allocated. Here, strategically structured seclusion becomes a powerful instrument for shaping policies and for the distribution of funds. Thus, in interactive governance processes, knowledge is a powerful resource and actors have an interest in holding on to important pieces of information. Indeed, information is a commodity that can be traded for access or influence.

Transparency is an idea in vogue and it is integral to the information society. There is an assumption in this line of reasoning about the blessings of transparency in governance arrangements that need to be tested empirically. There has been some interesting work in this respect reported lately. Naurin (2007), in a study on lobbyists in Stockholm and Brussels, concludes that the positive aspects of publicity and transparency on democratic governance could well be exaggerated. The key point to understanding lobbyism is not the difference between publicity and seclusion, he argues. Instead, lobbyists must learn to accept and subscribe to the rules, norms, and practices pertaining to public deliberation as opposed to those pertaining to secluded negotiation and bargaining. Hood and Heald and their associates give a broad assessment of different aspects of transparency and find that as much as transparency is central to democratic governance, it is not without problems or contradictions (Hood and Heald, 2006). Interestingly, although transparency is often believed to be essential to restoring the public's trust in politicians and the political process, the empirical evidence of the linkage between trust and transparency is surprisingly weak (O'Neill, 2006).

Perhaps the key value of transparency is that it is a prerequisite for accountability. Advocates of transparent governance will emphasize that without transparency there cannot be accountability. Furthermore, transparency is believed to contribute to other positive aspects of government. It is common today to use indicators on government transparency as key indicators of "good governance" and the overall quality of government and democracy, as is done by Transparency International. Transparency is believed to curb corruption, promote democracy and accountability, and to foster good relations between the state and the citizens although the empirical evidence suggests that transparency alone does not reduce corruption (Lindstedt and Naurin, 2006; Kolstad and Wiig, 2009).

By ensuring transparency, actors are assumed to choose, democratically speaking, a better course of action than they would otherwise have done. Only very few observers put forward the proposition that transparency can impede governance, or even democracy, and be detrimental to good governance. To some extent, this pattern could be explained by different notions about where in the policy process, and why, transparency can be dysfunctional. As this chapter will suggest, most observers would probably agree that transparency as a rule is desirable but also that there are instances and specific contexts where transparency can in fact work against the very objectives it is said to promote.

The chapter thus explores the argument that some degree of seclusion, perhaps even secrecy, in particular stages of the policy process or in particular political contexts may not only be functional to democratic governance but, in fact, a prerequisite for such governance. Interactive governance is in many ways a more efficient model of governance in this respect as it represents a less formalized model of governance. The chapter also argues that the recent tendency to measure public sector performance, while central to public management, is a type of transparency that not only facilitates choice among service producers but also potentially undermines institutional trust. In order to elaborate these arguments, the chapter first discusses transparency and seclusion in a democratic theoretic perspective and the special features of secluded governance as compared to more traditional models of governance. Following that discussion, the chapter assesses the political and democratic significance of the differences between transparent and secluded governance. As is the case throughout this book, the analytical focus is on interactive governance and the particular issues this form of governance raises as opposed to other forms of governance.

More specifically, we raise five questions related to transparency and secrecy. First, is transparency always a blessing for democracy? Second, how valid is the argument that there is a trade-off between democracy depending on transparency and efficiency depending on seclusion? Third, given the stakes and power games that characterize politics, is transparency a realistic possibility? Fourth, given the contextual incentives for actors to mobilize external actors and the growing importance of new social media, is seclusion a realistic possibility? And, finally, what can be done to balance transparency and secrecy in realistic and democratically desirable ways?

The blessings and perils of transparency

Democratic theorists, the media, concerned citizens, and participants in Canadian citizen's panels all seem to agree that democratic governance requires transparency and information on all aspects of government activities. Such openness serves several core democratic objectives. First of all, citizens and voters will be in a better position to hold elected officials to account if they have detailed knowledge about their bargaining, decision-making, and actions. Recent empirical evidence suggests that countries with "attentive" citizens, that is, where social norms dictate that citizens should pay close attention to government action, are characterized by more effective government and higher-quality governance compared to other countries (Geissel, 2008). Knowing what goes on within government is also believed to foster societal trust in those institutions. To some extent, the recent campaign for increased transparency is a sign of lack of societal trust in traditional mechanisms of accountability. Concerned citizens do not seem to trust political parties or judicial institutions to monitor and evaluate the behavior of politicians or bureaucrats; instead they want to be able to collect information about their performance themselves and assess to what extent that performance is acceptable.

Furthermore, there seems to be a theory that transparency leads to anticipatory behavior among politicians; if elected officials know that they are being closely monitored, they will not abuse public office. By allowing the public to closely scrutinize politicians' behavior, the risk of politicians being corrupted by political power is minimized. The politicians' knowledge that citizens and the media observe their behavior becomes a safeguard against abuse of public office. Similarly, it becomes politically difficult to advocate seclusion because it suggests that government is contemplating action that it does not want its people to know about, presumably because had they known, they would have disapproved of it and tried to prevent it from happening. Again, information is a valuable asset in the governance process; we need only think of politicians or bureaucrats "leaking" information to the media in order to change the direction of a policy process.

The position that transparency is inherently good for democracy and that secrecy is inconsistent with democratic governance would not be an issue had it not been for two intriguing problems. One issue that complicates the matter is that transparency is not always conducive to democratic governance; in some ways, there appears to be a trade-off between transparency and effective governance (Scharpf, 1999). This is particularly the case at sensitive stages of the policy process. Negotiating and bargaining in public is an obvious example of how transparency can distort the political process; making concessions and reaching compromises is far more difficult when conducted with the media watching and reporting. An opaque decision-making process is consistent with democracy as long as citizens have constitutionally sanctioned that certain phases of the governance process take place in seclusion and that they have the information necessary to be able to assess the outcome of that process and hold politicians to account. Interestingly, studies of intraparty negotiation and bargaining during politically sensitive time periods suggest that there are only very few instances where the party leadership has argued one thing *in camera* and another thing in public. Although deliberation within the party leadership does not fall under what constitutionally speaking should be public discourse, there was a high degree of correspondence between what the party leadership discussed among themselves and what they told in public (von Sydow, 1978). Later, we will return to this issue in more detail.

The other issue related to transparency is that it can be downright dysfunctional; it may create a behavior among those involved in governance processes that is not in the interest of either the observers or the observed. This problem is more common in relation to public service delivery than when it comes to controlling elected officials although to some extent the basic problem applies to both contexts. A case in point is the proposal put forward by the British National Health Service (NHS) in 1995 to install closed-circuit TV cameras in operating theaters. *The Sunday Times* (March 19, 1995; quoted in Tsoukas, 1997: 835) was critical toward the idea, suggesting that "some doctors fear that faith in their work would be undermined if people discovered that operating theatres were in reality relatively relaxed places, often full of laughter and joking—some of which were at the expense of the patient—and that intricate life-threatening surgery is being performed to the accompaniment of heavy rock music or streams of oaths at every unexpected gush of blood." Thus, public monitoring of experts in action may be counterproductive, if not downright detrimental, both to public trust in the service and to the execution of the service.

The idea that human performance improves when being subjected to monitoring is not new. It is the basic meaning of the Hawthorne effect observed in the late 1920s. The effects of monitoring on trust in a particular service, however, is more novel and takes on a special meaning in the information society. Tsoukas argues that "not only is [transparency] illusory, but... the very process for allegedly reaching it undermines the trust that is necessary for an expert system to function effectively... the paradox is that the more information on the inner workings of an expert system observers seek to have, the less they will be inclined to trust its practitioners; the less practitioners are trusted, the less likely it is for the benefits of specialized expertise to be realized" (Tsoukas, 1997: 835).

How does this apply to political life? Except for politicians' memoirs and the odd in-depth study of political leadership, we do not know very much about the inner life of political elites. Former US President Nixon's tapes of informal discussions in the White House could have been a source for such analysis had it not been that they became a political weapon, ironically used against Nixon himself in the Watergate affair. However, there is good reason to expect that closer and more continuous scrutiny of elected officials would have an impact on their behavior, but it might not be to the intended effect. As there is always need for candid and unrestricted conversations in small closed circles of participants, it is likely that if a system of more continuous transparency were to be set in place, essential discussions and de facto decisions would find a venue secluded from that scrutiny as well.

Thus, for all the values that we accord open, transparent, and accountable government, it is only logical to acknowledge that some elements of the political process are better performed *in camera*. Such seclusion is not harmful in the larger scheme of holding politicians to account; rather it is a precondition for efficient policy bargaining and collective decision-making. These issues, in turn, speak not only to the degree to which governance is democratic but also to its efficiency (Scharpf, 1999). To quote a phrase, to govern is to choose, and choosing is for the most part easier to do protected from scrutiny, which can serve as a catalyst for political pressures. Also, to govern is to execute and implement decisions and, again, while transparency is a prerequisite for accountability that transparency need not involve all stages of policy implementation as we will see later.

Understanding secluded governance

The tension between transparency and seclusion is to some extent one between the democratic and the executive dimensions of the political process. In conventional models of governance, institutional control mechanisms seek to ensure that the executive branch of government is held to democratic account. Thus, although the executive exercises some degree of discretion and integrity in relationship to other branches of government, some degree of accountability is still built into the system. In reality, however, such democratic control can be difficult to exercise. Ascertaining what the government is responsible and not responsible for is often itself a task worthy of a political science research program, yet the traditional accountability mechanisms expect the electors to be able to clarify that. Transparency, publicity, and access to information are important instruments in that process but even with public records and free media executive institutions can, and have incentives to, conduct governance with only limited outside control. In order to address these issues, some countries, not least in Scandinavia, appoint ombudsmen or similar institutions to support citizens' claims against government, including the provision of information.

In interactive governance processes, accountability occurs among the participants as an informal and internal form of checks and balances that are more oriented toward the evaluation of relationships and performance outcomes than toward matters of formal procedure. In these often relatively informal settings, secrecy is easier to achieve compared to that in strictly formalized governance arenas and "going public" becomes a bargaining chip in negotiations within interactive governance structures such as quasi-markets, partnerships, and governance networks.

The systemic requirements for transparency are obstructed by incentives for those participating in interactive governance processes to avoid publicity. As mentioned earlier, some governance issues may be extremely sensitive and publicity can jeopardize efforts to deal with them. Other matters require seclusion because they include mobilization of external resources with potential political consequence and while the final outcome of such resource mobilization can be made public, the process of mobilization itself must be secret. Emerging interactive governance arrangements—quasi-markets, partnerships, and networks—aiming to enhance the executive capacity of political institutions draw to some extent on at least partially secluded governance. They accord the political executive significant degrees of freedom vis-à-vis elected assemblies and therefore tend to entail democratic deficits. In return for pooling resources, NGOs and private businesses will want some input on the policy, something that would give them a privileged position in the governance process. Finally, policies that are believed to be unpopular, at least in the short term, are likely to be treated with as little publicity as possible (Pierson, 1995; Ross, 1997). As pointed out in Chapters 7 and 10, ensuring some degree of transparency in these interactive governance processes can only be attained through metagovernance rulings to that effect.

Whether an interactive governance process is conducted in public or *in camera* affects the role of the institution(s) within which the interaction takes place. This is true for government institutions as well as for interactive governance arenas. The party congresses of the Swedish Social Democratic Party were closed meetings from the creation of the party and well into the 1960s when frequent leaks from negotiations called the secluded nature of the congresses into question. In 1964, a new policy was adopted according to which the media should have full access to the congresses. This new policy changed in many ways the role of the congress internally and, obviously externally, from having been loci of candid debate on party policy to media-driven manifestations of party unity and strength (Pierre, 1986). In the same vein, efforts to make contract negotiations in quasi-markets or negotiations in partnerships and governance networks more transparent would push sensitive debates to other arenas. The conclusion of this analysis speaks to different governance arrangements; insisting on transparency may remove sensitive elements of political discourse from those arrangements to more secluded settings.

In a democracy, the issue of whether different stages of the policy process should be transparent or secluded from the public is not entirely in the hands of the politicians. Given the overarching value of transparency in government, exceptions from that rule need to be specifically justified in the eyes of the public. Furthermore, the logic of the media is that the more secluded the process, the stronger are the incentives for each individual media to extract information about what goes on behind closed doors, since that would give that particular media a unique scoop. Interestingly, those incentives coincide

215

with the incentives of potential losers in secluded negotiations to provide that very information to the media, as we will see below.

Thus, the issue of whether the policy process should be transparent or secluded is not just a matter of normative democratic discourse. It also has a significant influence on the capacity and integrity of involved actors and interactive governance arenas where deliberations and decision-making take place. The capacity of government institutions to implement policy or to steer society depends to some extent on the integrity of those institutions vis-à-vis the policy targets (Rockman and Weaver, 1993). If that integrity is compromised during the bargaining phase, it will be difficult for the institution to reclaim that integrity during the implementation phase. This pattern applies to essentially all governance instruments, ranging from obtrusive regulation to quasi-markets, partnerships, and governance networks.

That having been said, the linkage between transparent policy deliberation and institutional capacity plays out somewhat differently in different political settings. The corporatist model of governance assumes that societal involvement in policy deliberation enhances compliance with policy in the implementation phase (Schmitter, 1974; Pierre and Peters, 2005). However, this pattern is consistent with the notion of a negative relationship between transparent policy deliberation and institutional capacity. In the corporatist model, corporatist organizations' acceptance of policy is purchased at the price of political and institutional integrity since those organizations are given influence on the policies they will later be subjected to in the implementation of policy.

Transparency and seclusion in the policy process

Let us now look more closely at how these issues play out in different stages of the policy process. The stages model is not intended to suggest that policy necessarily evolves through these stages or in this order. As other chapters in this book have shown, in interactive governance policymaking and implementation processes can be more or less parallel or integrated. We will briefly comment on participation, resource mobilization, deliberation and decision-making, implementation and service delivery, and accountability and legitimacy as different aspects of the policy process in order to provide a somewhat more detailed account of how the purported tension between transparency and secrecy manifests itself there.

Participation

Some governance actors can be quite informal and prefer to operate behind the scenes—the *esse non videre* of governance—whereas others work hard to market their existence in order to engage other actors and interests. The influence of actors may be tied to their strategy with regard to how they use the transparency–seclusion issue. If interactive governance is a process that occurs "in the shadow of hierarchy" (Scharpf, 1997), there could be actors in that shadow who might not wish to have their involvement disclosed to outside actors. Partnerships between political officials and senior corporate players could be one example of governance arrangements that can remain unofficial, perhaps in the interests of both parties.

Deciding who should participate is a key dimension of secluded governance. Formal political decision-making regulates participation in some detail in order to ensure that only accountable actors are involved and that those actors have an equal say. In more secluded and informal settings, participation is determined mainly by resources, which is an arrangement that entails a greater risk of political inequality that relates to the actors' strength, centrality, and resources (Peters and Pierre, 2004).

In interactive governance, the demarcation of the participating actors tends to be less formalized and the boundaries that are drawn between players and spectators more blurred. That circumstance makes it difficult to arrange and sustain a pact of silence where all actors in a governance process agree not to go public until the final decisions have been made. That, however, does not necessarily mean that interactive governance is more transparent than conventional governance arrangements.

Resource mobilization

The mobilization of external resources tends to be a cause, not an effect, of secluded governance. Resource mobilization increasingly involves market actors who control financial resources and can manage those resources under less scrutiny than public actors. Hence, coalitions of different types are forged between public and private actors with a primary view of mobilizing resources for joint projects. Again, public–private partnerships often revolve around the idea of joint mobilization of political and economic resources and there are incentives not to be too public about such transactions as they might call the integrity of political officials into question. Also, the process of mobilizing such resources itself would probably be significantly impaired if conducted under media scrutiny. Interactive governance arrangements are less constrained by regulations in resources mobilization compared to more conventional arrangements, and financial and other resources brought to the table by public and private actors can therefore be pooled more easily.

Deliberation and decision-making

Conducting political deliberation and decision-making in an accessible and transparent process does not only feed the public with information about the process but also opens the process to external information. Seclusion can be seen as a gate-keeping safeguard against excessive, unintelligible, and inconsistent information. As Hood (2006b: 223) puts it, "since the quantity of data generated can easily drive out the quality and intelligibility of that data . . . the pursuit of transparency can indeed become self-defeating for the goal of advancing democracy through demystifying government." Furthermore, if we think of policy negotiation and decision-making as a process through which competing options are eliminated, that process is easily disturbed if conducted "in the open," as all options have some constituency that will scramble to make sure it stays alive. Thus, seclusion is essentially a strategy to simplify decision-making. This is more relevant to conventional governance arrangements than it is to interactive governance where there is less regulatory pressure for transparency. In interactive governance, since there are few rules dictating a certain degree of transparency, deliberation and decision-making are as transparent or secluded as the actors involved in governance want them to be.

There are, of course, many other reasons why political decision-makers in traditional forms of government as well as in interactive governance arrangements would want to avoid publicity. Transparency complicates the search for compromise; the process of finding tit-for-tat accommodation and saving political face is infinitely easier if not continuously covered by the media, and so are implementation processes that involve a concrete downsizing of particular tasks. Opaque models of governance also allow political actors to discuss more freely and develop shares, ideas, and strategies. It is also easier to hide that some are winners and others are losers, and sell a decision as a win-win situation to different constituencies.

That having been said, the deliberation of policy is a process where there are considerable tensions between collective interests and individual actors. On the one hand, there is a collective interest and also an institutional interest in keeping negotiations and discussions during this stage of the policy process protected from the public, since seclusion probably is conducive to formulating coherent policies that are able to address the problem at hand. On the other hand, however, negotiating parties may sometimes have an interest in promoting their objectives by mobilizing voters, or, alternatively to discredit opponents by "leaking" information to the media. The tighter the lid on negotiations, the stronger the incentives for potential losers in the negotiations become to score political points by mobilizing external opinion.

Implementation and service delivery

We will discuss below the ways in which public management reform that introduces interactive forms of governance has entailed greater transparency. Here, we look more closely at policy implementation and public service delivery. Implementation is an interorganizational process that requires transparency. Interestingly, the introduction of quasi-markets that make use of market-like mechanisms for customer choice in public service delivery appears to have both increased and decreased transparency. On the one hand, as a result of management reforms the degree of transparency in policy implementation and public service delivery is today higher compared to that a few decades ago in terms of the general knowledge about the performance, quality, and costs of the services provided by competing service providers. Decision-makers evaluate their performance and potential consumers have access to data of this performance on websites and elsewhere in ways that help them make informed choices. On the other hand, however, much of that service is delivered by market actors who are not obliged to conduct their business in a transparent fashion. This has created a new type of problem in terms of safeguarding the rights of whistle blowers or in terms of assessing the quality of market-delivered services. Thus, while transparency and market solutions are both popular ideas, there is to some extent an inverse relationship between those two objectives.

Accountability and legitimacy

Are public and transparent governance models better at generating legitimacy for their actions compared to more spontaneous, informal, and less transparent arrangements? To what extent are interactive arrangements of governance that tend to be more informal such as, for instance, the proverbial smoke-filled rooms more suited for efficient capacity building and action than traditional governance arrangements in which the call for transparency is formally ensured? Are public governance arrangements impaired by having to deal with the media and political actors outside the arrangement?

In some ways, the perceived need for transparency is derived from traditional models of representative democracy and input legitimacy, that is, it is a model of democracy where elected politicians are held to political account. However, there is much to suggest that output-based legitimacy is becoming at least as important as input-based legitimacy. Increasingly complex governance processes, not least in the EU, challenge the prospect of holding political actors to account in terms of programs and decisions (Scharpf, 1999; Papadopoulos, 2003). Outcomes are more easily assessed and granted with the same degree of complexity in terms of assigning credit or blame as is the case

219

with input-based models of legitimacy. There is, of course, an important distinction to be made between process and outcomes in this respect, but the transparency advocates are not content with only assessing outcomes. Thus, traditional transparency rests on the assumption that elected officials have sufficient control over executive institutions to also assume responsibility for their actions. With recent administrative reform, however, that control has been largely surrendered to autonomous managers. Also, models of customer choice and other market-based models of public service delivery have to a considerable extent shifted the channels of accountability from the input-side to the output-side of the political system.

If this pattern persists, we need to know more about how issues of transparency, seclusion, and accountability play out on the output-side of the system. Let us now turn to that discussion.

Transparency and public management

A keystone element of New Public Management (NPM) reform is to measure outputs and make data available both to managers and decision-makers and also to the public. The "naming and shaming" model of identifying and publishing underperforming public service facilities as a means of making consumer choice more informed is a strategy that epitomizes the idea of bringing in transparency as a means of enhancing the quality of public services. More broadly, market-like models of public service delivery have powerful incentives for presenting performance data on websites and to the media, so much so that there have been several instances where schools present grade averages that exaggerate student performance. Performance measurement and management are key elements of current public management models. While knowledge about public sector productivity is essential to public management, performance measurement has been severely criticized on several accounts, including the use and abuse of productivity statistics and focusing public services on what can be measured and "naming and shaming" service providers rather than responsible politicians and bureaucrats (Radin, 2006).

The new type of disclosure that comes with public management reform is important because it turns transparency and information into instruments of governance (Fung et al., 2007). In a governing context where participation is contextually defined, information becomes hard currency. Therefore, claims for increased transparency somewhat paradoxically lead to stronger incentives for public officials to control the flow of information and to "spin" that information to ensure that it is interpreted in certain ways. We should also reflect on Marilyn Strathern's intriguing question: "What does visibility

Table 11.1. The contributions of transparency and secrecy in enhancing democracy and efficiency

	Input	Throughput	Output
Democracy			
Secrecy	Gate-keeper	Efficient decision-making	Prioritize
Transparency	Legitimacy	Deliberation	Accountability
Efficiency			
Secrecy	Reduced pressure	Creative and dynamic bargaining	Shared responsibility
Transparency	Social knowledge	Public understanding	Informed implementation

conceal?" (Strathern, 2000: 310). All measurements, and, indeed, all information made available by government institutions, highlight certain features of the public sector at the same time as they conceal others. Performance measurement and management have shown us that measurement is a powerful steering instrument since those being measured will prioritize that which is being measured. Moreover, the selection of those measurements, criteria, and assessments serves as a powerful steering signal for public sector institutions. Thus, controlling measurement and the management of information is essentially a way to control them.

Table 11.1 summarizes the different ways in which democracy and efficiency are being promoted by transparency and secrecy in different steps of the policy process.

Transparency can promote democracy in a number of ways. By making decision-making processes transparent, policymakers can ensure legitimacy, deliberation, and accountability. However, secrecy also plays an important, albeit less expected, role in the context of democracy. An opaque process provides for gate-keeping and more efficient decision-making and enables government to formulate and implement policies that balance between views and interests carried by different political and social constituencies.

Transparency promotes efficiency by raising the level of social knowledge about the problems facing the political system and popular understanding of and respect for the complex challenges facing politicians, and commits public employees and citizens to policy implementation. Secrecy, too, can enhance efficiency in the policy process, for instance, by reducing pressure on the input-side and ensuring that social demand for a given program is low because few know about it. Secrecy also paves the way for creative and dynamic bargaining and shared responsibility.

Transparency and secrecy in different governance arrangements

The tension between transparency and seclusion confronts all governance arrangements but the issue plays out somewhat differently in different models of governance. This depends in part on the cast of actors, which is typical to each of those arrangements. It also in part depends on the degree to which political institutions are the *primus inter pares* of governance, or merely one type of actor among many other types, or not at all involved in a particular governance context. Furthermore, the manifestation of the tension between transparency and seclusion is related to the extent to which the issues to be coordinated relate to more formal, political issues or whether they are of a more self-regulatory nature. If there are significant amounts of public funding being allocated by the governance structure, there are likely to be pressures for public control in some form. Similarly, governance arrangements operating as delegated authority tend to be required to be transparent in terms of their actions.

We mentioned earlier that public management reform in some ways has indirectly promoted transparency by focusing on performance and quality. However, other elements of the NPM model of administration seem to pull in the opposite direction. The separation of policy formulation and policy implementation and the creation of operative structures have created problems of ensuring transparency in these new devolved, executive structures. This problem becomes most obvious in those cases where executive agencies interact with private business, for instance in the research and development or economic development areas. Many private businesses will only engage with public institutions if they have some form of assurance that corporate secrecy and intellectual property are safeguarded. In these sectors, insisting on transparency becomes an obstacle to public–private joint ventures. The same basic problem emerges in collaborative projects between public authorities and NGOs who do not want to subordinate themselves to the same transparency requirement that most public institutions are subjected to. Autonomous organizations are formed precisely in order to avoid transparency (Peters, 1998).

Insisting on transparent governance means that private actors must be willing to accept that some of their privacy becomes compromised. Since governance arrangements typically seek to bridge the public–private border in society, valued rules of conduct that are rooted in these spheres tend to be transmitted across that border. It is extremely difficult to think of a governance arrangement where some of the participating actors subscribe to principles of transparency while other actors do not. Thus, the quest for transparency, which is common today, not only opens up government to society but also makes society more transparent to government.

In state-centric governance models, with their tight institutional control of the policy process, one would predict that both transparency and secrecy are easily achieved; if anything, secrecy is almost too easily achieved. In authoritarian countries, secrecy is treated rather arbitrarily such as in the Chinese secrecy laws, where the government lists all the specific items that are to be classified and, in addition, "anything else that ought to be secret" (Burns, 2010). There is no risk of leakage from private governance partners because interactive governance is orchestrated by political institutions. If, on the other hand, it is politically desired that as much as possible of government matters should be made available to the public, there is very little chance of obstructing such transparency. Thus, the degree of transparency of state-centric governance is very much controlled by the government itself. The most prominent exception to this rule is Wikileaks, which circulated classified government documents to the media. Such disclosure is, however, not related to the governance model per se but could happen in any governance arrangement.

In pluralist or corporatist governance arrangements (Pierre and Peters, 2005) where political institutions blend with organized interests, however, questions about the relationship between and the role of transparency and secrecy, are far from self-evident. Institutional actors are required to uphold values of transparency and accountability but as this chapter argues that requirement may sometimes be neither productive nor feasible. The history of corporatist governance is one of peak-level negotiations in which the state is either an actor in tri-partite arrangements of interest mediation or a more passive actor mediating conflict among societal actors. Thus, this is a model of governance that draws on negotiation, bargaining, and accommodation, something that would suggest that important processes are secluded from the public. The participating organizations' rank-and-file membership can only hold their leaders to account after the bargaining process is concluded and outcomes are presented to the public. Accountability in a broader, electoral perspective is more complex, something that has been a source of continuing critique against this form of governance.

In interactive governance models, finally, those involved in partnerships and networks are linked together by a shared purpose or objective. If it is believed to be disadvantageous to the collective pursuit to go public, there is every chance to keep the activities of the network secluded from public scrutiny. However, as we have argued earlier, bringing societal actors into the public policy process greatly complicates the quest for secrecy or seclusion. The actors involved in these governance arrangements may either obstruct transparency demands, or, conversely, seek to use publicity when that is assumed to promote their interests. Unlike most public actors, private actors have a choice regarding transparency; they can open up to the media or other external actors if they so choose or they can stick to a more opaque strategy if they believe that to be in their interest. This means that governance arrangements that blend public and private actors, paradoxically, can be both more and less transparent than a constellation of purely public actors all depending on context and the strategies selected by the involved actors. It is difficult for metagovernors to impose transparency on cohesive partnerships and networks if all participants agree to keep their deliberation and decisions to themselves.

Thus, the three governance arrangements differ in terms of how they safeguard transparency and in what might jeopardize openness. Interactive governance arrangements have the option to avoid transparency if they believe it to be in their interest to do so and if the arrangement is sufficiently cohesive to ensure collective action. However, both more or less formal and informal governance arrangements can prevent disclosure. Formal arrangements can do so by relying on what could be called legitimate procedural secrecy—that is, allowing for opaque political or administrative behavior during sensitive stages of the policy process but where there is accountability at the final stages of the process. Informal governance arrangements can allow joint interest within the network to obstruct transparency. Thus, the decisive factor supporting or obstructing transparency is not so much the degree of formality of the governance arrangement. It seems to be more a matter of the extent to which actors can use transparency as a bargaining chip, whether there are strong collective pressures to either promote or obstruct transparency, or whether governance arrangements are under democratic pressure to open up to society.

To sum up this brief discussion of the relationship between forms of governance and the role of transparency and secrecy in them, it seems clear that both have their virtues and pitfalls and both relate to efficiency and democracy objectives in governance (see Table 11.2).

The efficiency dimension of governance can be sustained by both transparency and secrecy. Policy implementation requires a great deal of transparency; if we think of implementation as a case of interactive governance, we understand that withholding information is detrimental to efficient implementation. Bargaining in the policy process benefits from seclusion, as we previously discussed; conducting negotiations in the open makes compromise much more difficult to attain. With regards to democratic objectives, accountability is conditioned on transparency while complex negotiations benefit from some

Table 11.2. Transparency and secrecy related to efficiency and democracy objectives

	Transparency	Secrecy
Efficiency	Implementation	Bargaining
Democracy	Accountability	Deliberation

degree of seclusion. If we bring in the analysis of transparency and seclusion in different stages of the policy process, we find that seclusion in certain stages of the process and transparency in outcomes seem to be the most effective arrangement, which serves both the public's right and need to be informed as well as the political leadership's need to deliberate and bargain in opaque contexts.

A key aspect of the issue of transparency and secrecy—and a very common argument in the political debate on these issues—is the instrumental aspect of transparency; as voters we need information about who is responsible for what. While accountability is a very complex process of assigning responsibility to agency, that process becomes even more difficult without transparency. In state-centric models of governance, accountability is de jure tied to hierarchical political leadership and voters can vote out leaders who they believe have not done a proper job in office. In interactive governance, the level of institutionalization is less distinct and stable. Accountability becomes a process involving stakeholders and other participants in the governance arrangement but no one outside the governance structure. Even where transparency can help uncover malfeasance, assigning that malfeasance unambiguously to agency remains difficult. Transparency requires metagovernance that uncovers the role of interactive governance arrangements and makes support and funding contingent on the degree to which the public is informed about decisions and outcomes.

Conclusion

The chapter departed from what appeared to be a complex, possibly zero-sum relationship between the democratic claim that the public should be informed about what transpires in governance processes on the one hand and the decision-makers' need for some degree of secrecy in order to do the job they are expected to do in an efficient way on the other. A closer inspection shows that there is not necessarily a trade-off between democracy's call for transparency and an efficiency call for secrecy. Transparency can in fact enhance efficiency just as secrecy can advance the democratic quality of governance. Democratic governance requires secluded spaces to accommodate collective decision-making in light of conflicts, and secrecy during some stages of the policy process does not necessarily become a democratic problem as long as voters, clients, and stakeholders accept the existence of those moments of secrecy, and have the opportunity to assess the final outcomes and means to sanction those who are responsible for those outcomes. As several of the previous chapters show, such sanctions can take a variety of different forms in relation to different governance arrangements.

Let us return to the specific questions about transparency and secrecy in governance raised in the beginning of this chapter. We asked if transparency is always a blessing for democracy and we have found that it is generally a good thing but that seclusion is also needed in certain phases for democracy to function well. Second, we pointed out that the debate has stipulated a trade-off between democracy depending on transparency and efficiency depending on seclusion. We answer now that such a trade-off does not exist as both democracy and efficiency demand a balancing of the two. Third, we asked whether transparency is a realistic possibility and answered that it is not realistic in any comprehensive meaning as those involved in governance—be it in traditional state-centric, corporatist, or new interactive forms of governance—are in need of some level of secrecy in order to be able to govern. Fourth, we asked if secrecy is a realistic possibility and answered that this is just as unrealistic as, and more and more so, in political systems in which interactive governance arrangements play a more considerable role than in monolithic state-centered regimes. Fouth, we asked if secrecy is a realistic possibility and answered that it is just as unrealistic in interactive governance arrangements as it is in state-centric models of governance.

These five general conclusions need to be elaborated somewhat and placed in the context of different reform campaigns in the public sector. The growing interest in transparency is linked to two waves of reform in the public sector, which have both promoted interactive forms of governance. One wave consists of market-based reforms that are predicated on providing the public with information about the performance of competing service providers. If clients, or "customers," are to make informed choices among different providers of medical care or education, it is essential that they are provided with relevant information. This information is usually not provided independently but by the service producers themselves and, like a private market, competing providers of public goods and services have strong incentives to boost their data.

The other waves of governance reforms are related to modernizing democratic processes, opening new avenues for popular involvement, and increasing transparency and accountability. Transparency is heralded in all sorts of assessments of governmental performance and is frequently used as a key variable in research on good governance or democratic consolidation. Countries that score low on Transparency International's indices are not considered to be fully democratic.

The general expectation is that governance processes should be transparent and that exceptions to that rule are allowed only when they clearly serve political purposes and where there will be some form of accountability at a later stage in the process. Another way of formulating this would be to suggest that outcomes, not process, should be the main consideration when assessing transparency in governance. There are, however, several problems with that position. It is hardly tenable in a strictly democratic perspective that pays attention to process and the people's right to know how that process evolves and what is happening at various stages; nor is it acceptable from an efficiency perspective since it focuses only on what can be measured and not on broader aspects of the quality of public policies and services. Thus, although opaque behavior often—but not always—serves benign political projects, ex post accountability is not an entirely satisfactory arrangement. Alternatively, political elites acting *in camera* in the pursuit of collective goals may claim that they are acting under delegated authority in which case delegation, not the exercise of political power, becomes the key criterion for assessment and accountability.

A secluded process becomes difficult to sustain when societal actors are present at several key stages. NGOs and private companies participate under quite different circumstances compared to ex officio, public sector participants who are professionally obliged not to circulate information. Indeed, the whole idea of lowering the threshold between the public sector and the surrounding society makes the distinction between public and secret information difficult to sustain.

Political actors have a collective interest in ensuring that deliberation and negotiation are conducted *in camera*. However, individual actors can also have incentives to "leak" information if they believe that to be in their interest. Also, there are, as we have seen, systemic aspects that seem to justify and necessitate informal and secluded models of governance. That having been said, however, it is difficult to conceive of truly democratic governance without a considerable degree of transparency in governance. If political processes benefit from some degree of seclusion from the public and the media, there will have to be opportunity for the public to evaluate the outcome of those processes and hold decision-makers to account.

The Rousseauian model of governance caters to core democratic objectives such as participation, debate, and legitimacy. It is not, however, a model of governance that performs well when it comes to efficiency and governance capacity. Thus, essentially, all systems of government search for a point of balance between seclusion and transparency. The current political trend—also reflected in much of contemporary administrative reform—to maximize transparency is thus likely to have a negative effect on the capacity to govern. Measurement not only reflects behavior but also steers behavior and the gathering of information necessary to manage the system or to inform the public might not be the appropriate signal for the steering of the system. Public schools in a competitive market have incentives to present good grades for their pupils, something that becomes a signal to the staff to allow high grades.

227

Again, this is not to suggest that secluded governance is entirely functional or dysfunctional. It clearly serves some systemic needs; at the same time it will, if taken too far, be detrimental to the democratic foundation of governance. Should those values collapse, it is little help that the political system is efficient and of high capacity. Democratic governance is built on transparency and accountability as well as on some institutional capacity of governance institutions (March and Olsen, 1995). Short of such capacity, governance arrangements cannot deliver services or implement public policy, something that is also fatal to democratic governance. Thus, the diffusion of information, either from decision-making processes in government or from public service institutions, becomes essential to democratic governance at the same time as it significantly complicates that governance.

The increasing emphasis on output legitimacy in democratic governance speaks directly to these issues. If citizens and voters are less concerned with trusting elected officials or political parties and more interested in assessing the specific services they receive at the output end of the political system, politicians would be under less pressure to conduct transparent deliberation. It would, however, mean increased scrutiny of public service quality, something that presents a different set of problems. Again, governing becomes a challenge of balancing efficiency against democracy. Finally, as pointed out by Almond and Verba in their huge study of the linkages between institutional setups and political culture, a one-sided reliance on output-side forms of accountability would transform the political culture in Western democracies in ways that are likely to reduce their long-term stability and legitimacy (Almond and Verba, 1963).

Most important, perhaps, is the issue of how new or emergent forms of interactive governance relate to the issue of government transparency. The value of transparency as a means of ensuring accountability is almost exclusively tied to the public sector. Interactive forms of governance seeking to bring together public and private actors in a joint effort to solve pertinent governance tasks become to some degree vehicles for spreading the need for transparency. In public–private partnerships, it is difficult for the public part to insist on transparency while the private part opposes it. Interactive governance thus not only tends to promote transparency—regardless of its costs and benefits—but also forces private actors to embrace similar values.

12

Conclusions

Fiscal pressures emanating from the economic repercussions of the credit crunch, the changing demographics in the aging Western societies, and the rising cost of state-of-the-art public services in health, education, and transport put a significant strain on the public sector in advanced industrial societies. However, the challenge to practitioners and researchers in the field of public policy and public administration appears much larger than the current fiscal constraints. Many central decision-makers and academic scholars feel that they have lost the ability to navigate in, and make sense of, public policymaking. There is a deep and growing frustration summarized in persistent complaints about how complex and complicated it is to govern society and the economy. The frustration is largely caused by the multiplication of relevant actors, sectors, levels, sites, arenas, governance modes, policy tools, target groups, and publics. In addition, there are a growing number of "wicked problems" (Koppenjan and Klijn, 2004), cumulative feedback mechanisms, and perceived risks that make it difficult to narrow down the range of feasible policy options. Last but not least, we have seen a gradual widening of the temporal and spatial horizons for strategic action in the field of public policymaking. As such, it is becoming increasingly clear that many policy problems are ill-defined and that public problem-solving involves a growing number of choices about who to involve, when, where, and how. In those cases, when agreement about the nature and character of policy problems is reached and decision-making processes are properly structured, the problem is that the impacts of many policy solutions are either delayed and uncertain (global warming) or have complex global and regional repercussions (agricultural subsidies).

In the face of this predicament, the traditional model based on political decision-making in governments and parliaments and bureaucratic implementation through command and control seems neither to provide an all-inclusive way of governing society and the economy nor to offer a comprehensive understanding of how such a governing might be facilitated in our increasingly fragmented, complex, and multilayered societies. Relying only on formal political and administrative steering will not suffice for government in its efforts to solve governance problems and, by the same token, only looking at formal governance arrangements will not allow the observer to capture the full picture of contemporary governance.

The new focus on governance, which is supported and informed by the emergence of a broad and multidisciplinary governance research in the social sciences, aims to address the growing frustration and the sense of dislocation among academics and practitioners by urging us to focus on *processes* rather than *institutions*. Instead of beginning the analysis of public policymaking with an account of the actual and prescribed role of the formal institutions of government, we can benefit from envisioning the more or less institutionalized processes through which different actors from different sectors and levels come together at different sites and in different arenas where they combine governance modes and policy tools in ways that target a variety of groups and communicate with different publics. The process perspective implicit to the governance paradigm brings forth the complementary, iterative, and sometimes integrated practices of problem definition, goal setting, policy formulation, implementation, and evaluation and connects these practices with different constellations of actors and particular institutional sites and arenas. The process perspective also draws attention to the structural and institutional factors that influence the policy process as well as the reflexivity of the actors. Finally, the process perspective emphasizes the search for and creation of context-specific solutions rather than the dissemination of generic policies in terms of best practice. These different focus points all seem helpful in mapping the non-linear trajectories of public policymaking.

While hierarchies and markets continue to play a crucial role in public governance processes, both as an overall framing of governance and as specific policy tools, interactive forms of governance based on sustained negotiation between public and private actors have received growing attention. They have been considered not only as practical alternatives to hierarchical and market-based forms of governance but also as a cognitive and scientific model for understanding multilateral action that blurs the distinction between the public and the private and connects different levels and separate localities. Despite the growth of the research on interactive governance, it is still a new paradigm in need of further consolidation and development. This need for clarification and bolstering of the paradigm explains why we have devoted this entire book to the study of key aspects of interactive governance, rather than adding to the well-established literature on the role of governments and public bureaucracies or the experiences with the introduction of market forms of governance in the public sector.

The interactive governance paradigm helps us to understand the prospects for collective action in areas where more formal institutions of governance either fail, or do not provide an adequate framework for collective action and where the nature and character of the policy tasks make reliance on the market forces inappropriate or misguided. However, different forms of governance frequently coexist. Interactive forms of governance do not necessarily have to evolve as substitutes for more traditional forms of governance but will often rather provide a complement to those governance forms. Indeed, there are numerous examples of interactive governance arrangements being promoted by traditional hierarchical organizations in order to meet specific governance requirements. Nevertheless, interactive governance adds to our general thinking about governance by showing how multilateral action is organized either in the shadow of hierarchy or out of sight from hierarchy. At the same time, it raises important questions about the degree to which governance arrangements operating at some distance from elected officials can provide effective, democratic, and transparent governance. Previous chapters have addressed these issues in detail.

Advancing the interactive governance paradigm

The chief aim of this book has been to advance the interactive governance paradigm that has emerged as a subset of the broader research on governance. We have pursued this ambition by identifying a number of gaps and lacunae in the interactive governance paradigm and by attempting to fill these gaps with theoretical reflections combined with empirical examples and references. Throughout our discussions, we have used governance networks, public–private partnerships, and quasi-markets as ideal-typical examples of interactive governance arrangements. We use them as shorthand for instruments and arenas for collective action, which tend to be more temporary and more aimed at specific problems of policy and governance than traditional governmental structures.

We shall not reiterate all the arguments and conclusions from the previous chapters, but merely highlight some of the ways that we have attempted to fill the gaps in the emerging interactive governance paradigm. In response to the lack of conceptual clarity, the incomplete understanding of the societal and intellectual background, and the Eurocentric bias of the governance debate, *Chapter 1* has defined governance and interactive governance, reconstructed the genealogy and theoretical roots of the interactive governance paradigm, and provided a global perspective on the governance debate that reveals the different ways that governance and interactive governance are discussed in different parts of the world.

Chapter 2 aimed to provide a much needed overview of the cross-disciplinary debate on governance in the social sciences. It shows that political science and public administration are far from the only strands of the social sciences that are doing research on governance, but it also revealed that governance is defined in many different ways across the social science disciplines. As such, the chapter clearly demonstrates that the governance debate is truly a cross-disciplinary venture and that there is a good prospect for cross-fertilization. Hence, despite notable problems in some of the other social science disciplines, political science and public administration can learn from the insights they convey and the questions they are asking.

The role and impact of politics and power in interactive governance are often neglected both in the managerial discourses on governance and in some strands of the scholarly debate on interactive governance. *Chapter 3* has aimed to compensate this neglect by offering a multifaceted approach to the analysis of the intrinsic link between power and interactive governance. The analysis calls for a broad analysis of the power relations *in* interactive governance arenas, the power effects *of* interactive governance, the endeavor to exercise power *over* interactive governance, and the attempt to see interactive governance *as* a new form of power. The analysis shows not only how interactive governance is pervaded by politics and power but also how our understanding of power is transformed by the study of interactive forms of governance.

Although there are many attempts to measure the outputs and outcomes of different forms of governance, there have been few endeavors to measure governance and interactive governance as a process of collective decision-making. *Chapter 4* fills this gap in the existing literature by means of discussing, first, the problems relating to the measurement of traditional forms of governance, and second, the even greater problems related to the measurement of interactive forms of governance. The analysis of measurement concludes that process analysis and comparative case studies based on qualitative methods that defy interval scale measurement seem to be the only way forward in measuring interactive governance.

The research on interactive governance has paid a lot of attention to the collaboration between public and private actors. As such, interactive governance is claimed to invoke a blurring of the public–private divide. Interactive governance also cuts across different levels and jurisdictions, but this spatial dimension of interactive governance has received only scant attention. *Chapter 5* attempts to compensate this neglect by analyzing interactive governance along the vertical and horizontal axes. This analysis has demonstrated the need for recasting of our previous conception of governance in terms of a well-ordered system of hierarchical levels and clearly defined and separated domains and jurisdictions.

Despite the fact that most governance theories draw on some version of the new institutionalism, there have been few attempts to analyze the institutionalization of different forms of governance. Perhaps the problem is most pronounced in relation to interactive forms of governance, where some scholars have suggested that governance processes take place in an institutional void (Hajer, 2003). Although it might be true that interactive forms of governance initially lack a common constitution and seldom take the form of formalized institutions, we believe that both government and interactive forms of governance must be institutionalized in order to provide stable and well-functioning governance. In order to address the issue of institutionalization head on, *Chapter 6* discusses what institutionalization can mean from the point of view of a process-oriented governance perspective and analyzes the institutionalization of government, interactive governance, and their mutual linkages. Among other things, the analysis highlights the problems associated with under-institutionalization and over-institutionalization of both government and interactive governance.

The research on interactive governance has emphasized the need for network management, institutional design, and metagovernance, but the debate has been somewhat fragmented and has mainly focused on the tools for metagoverning interactive governance arenas. *Chapter 7* aims to bring together the different bodies of literature and to refocus the debate on metagovernance. In doing so the chapter has demonstrated how metagovernance connects governments at different levels with interactive forms of governance. It also discusses and compares different theoretical approaches to metagovernance and provides an overview of the different objectives, means, and forms of metagovernance. The main claim is that metagovernance is a new assignment that governments cannot afford to pass over if they want to be able to take advantage of and direct the new forms of interactive governance.

We all have an idea of what it means to be a politician, an administrator, a citizen, or a private actor, and these ideas are to a large extent inspired by role images associated with liberal-democratic government. However, these highly institutionalized role images are challenged and likely to change as the use of interactive forms of governance increases and interactive governance is becoming a part of the standard repertoire of governance modes. *Chapter 8* advances our understanding of the new role images that are relevant in relation to interactive forms of governance and provides a much needed discussion of the role dilemmas that are facing the actors in interactive governance settings and the coping strategies that they might apply. The chapter has shown that all the different groups of actors are confronted with a number of challenges when operating in interactive governance arenas, but it has also shown that new role images and coping strategies are in the making.

The first of three chapters discussing the normative assessment of interactive governance focused on the contribution of interactive governance to effective governance. Although effective governance has been intensely discussed in relation to more traditional governance forms such as hierarchies and markets, this is not the case for interactive governance. *Chapter 9* compensates for this neglect by discussing how the effectiveness of governance networks and other interactive policy arenas can be measured and improved through metagovernance. The chapter has provided a multidimensional measure of the effectiveness of interactive forms of governance and shown how different metagovernance tools can enhance it.

Democracy is the Achilles' heel of interactive governance. Although interactive governance has a democratizing effect, it also fails to live up to some of the democratic values and principles cherished by liberal democracy. While this dilemma has been widely debated in the literature, there has been little discussion of how to measure the democratic performance and quality of interactive forms of governance. *Chapter 10* attempts to close this gap by offering a detailed discussion of how to assess the democratic anchorage of governance networks, partnerships, and quasi-markets. The further elaboration of the concept of democratic anchorage is helpful in guiding empirical analysis of democratic network governance.

Transparency is a core value of liberal democracy and it applies both to government and new forms of interactive governance. Whereas most discussions of transparency have hitherto focused on transparent government and readily assumed that full transparency is a goal that should never be compromised, *Chapter 11* draws a much more complicated picture of the relationship between seclusion and transparency in hierarchical government and interactive forms of governance. The chapter shows that there are always limits to the quest for transparency, and that seclusion, under certain circumstances, can enhance effective governance and may even serve democratic purposes in government as well as in interactive forms of governance.

The analytical reflections, conceptualizations, and arguments advanced in the previous chapters are not meant to provide conclusive answers to the yet unanswered questions within the interactive governance paradigm. Rather, it has been our goal to open up new scholarly debates and take some further steps in advancing our current thinking about interactive governance. There are loose ends and unexplored avenues in our attempt to fill the gaps in the rapidly expanding field of interactive governance, but at least we hope that this book will provide a platform for further research on interactive governance.

Interactive governance and the role of the State

One of the most controversial questions in the debate on interactive governance is how to perceive the role and character of the State. As we have argued throughout this book, we are convinced that the role of the State has changed. Local, regional, and transnational agencies and organizations have become increasingly powerful and nongovernmental actors are challenging government authority at all levels. At the same time, the historical contingent "territorial synchrony" of political institutions, cultural adherence, and economic development has been dislocated (Hajer, 2009). As such, the culturally defined communities that are the source of legitimacy and the regions of socioeconomic growth and development are no longer congruent with the regulatory space of the nation state. This development poses a tremendous challenge to the State, which on top of its usual functions and tasks is forced to take on the task of metagoverning and of participating in vertical, horizontal, and diagonal arenas of interactive governance. It is not easy for government officials to cope with these new tasks since they are used to possessing all the political and administrative power and all the responsibility for societal governance. To share power and responsibility with other actors in a constructive way requires a different mindset. Furthermore, managing interaction among internal as well as external actors calls for the development of new competences and capacities of public officials. Devolution of power to lower level managers who are both participating in and metagoverning interactive governance arenas is also necessary, and might trigger a turn toward more centralized control systems that can monitor and coordinate the many arenas of decentered, empowered, and interactive governance (Dahlstrom et al., 2011).

The State is changing in the face of the rise of new and more interactive forms of governance, but we do not like to think of this change as a "shift from government to governance" as government remains an essential player in public governance and even in interactive forms of governance. That having been said, there is considerable distance between Stephen Bell and Andrew Hindmoor's account (2009) of contemporary governance as still firmly in the hands of government and Rhodes' image (1996) of the "new governance" that seems to involve "governing without government." We have in this book distanced ourselves from both of these polar extremes and insisted that the relation between government and interactive forms of governance is not a zero-sum game where one of the two sides must necessarily diminish for the other side to expand. The role and impact of interactive governance arenas is growing either because such arenas are promoted by traditional hierarchical organizations or because other actors see a need for coordination that is not satisfied by the formal institutional of government. However, the surge of interactive governance is both supplementing and supplanting government action and in both instances government agencies tend to play a vital role in terms of facilitating, managing, and participating in interactive policy arenas. Government and interactive forms of governance tend to coexist, and even to presuppose each other. On the one hand, there are things that governments can do better, or that they appreciate is being done, through interactive forms of governance. On the other hand, interactive forms of governance are empowered, stabilized, and coordinated by government agencies. That being said, we recognize that there also many cases of conflict and rivalry between government and interactive forms of governance, but that does not imply that there is a zero-sum game.

It is the coexistence and coevolution of government and interactive governance that force the State to change along the lines described above. As such, the result of the surge of interactive governance is an increasingly circumscribed State that is rapidly developing new competences, capacities, organizational forms, role images, and mechanisms for centralized and decentralized coordination. Through these transformations, the State is not only regaining some of its lost power but also developing new powers through the deployment of new ways of governing that might be described as "regulation of self-regulation" (Sørensen and Triantafillou, 2009).

Likely scenarios for the future development of governance

The State will continue to play a pivotal role in governing society and the economy, but the combination of governance modes has been changing over the past couple of decades, and there is hardly any reason to suspect that the current combination of governance modes represents the end of that development. Social complexity and globalization, often considered the two main drivers of changes in governance, are not likely to play any lesser role in the future governing of states, regions, and cities.

Perhaps the most important issue in the future development of governance modes is what we should expect in terms of the relationship between the formal institutions of government and the interactive forms of governance discussed in this book. Here, we can identify several scenarios that will have different consequences for our ability to govern society and the economy.

One future scenario would be a growing skepticism toward interactive governance. The displacement of accountability, opaque decision-making, and the sheer messiness of interactive governance processes might drive citizens and political parties to demand a reaffirmation of the role of representative institutions and public bureaucracy. To some degree, this would mean strengthening the role and position of formal institutions and actors whose capacity to provide governance in a complex society and a global economy has previously been called into question. Such concerns might be considered as secondary to the broader objective of reinstating traditional forms of government, but the result of such a "re-formalization" of governance might well be a lack of flexibility, innovation, resource exchange, and program ownership in public governance.

An alternative scenario would be a development driven by an overenthusiastic embrace of interactive forms of governance, potentially leading to policy failure and democratic deficit. Interactive governance would in many cases provide more efficient problem-solving than the formal institutions of government and would help work across sectors and jurisdictions, thus offering more coordinated efforts to govern policy problems. However, there would also be a risk that problems that are not amenable to interactive governance are becoming subject to networking and the formation of partnerships; that the same few policy actors are overwhelmed by the burden of participating in an endless number of interactive governance processes; that the responsibility for fundamental tasks and services ends up falling between many different chairs; and that key actors are excluded from the elusive and secluded arenas of interactive policymaking. In such a situation, traditional institutions of government would seek to maintain a supervisory role and act as a hierarchical "shadow," but such a position would over time prove increasingly difficult to sustain as hierarchical rule will be conceived as "ineffective" and "obsolete." As a result, there will be frequent interactive governance failures, and a growing disparity between the formal roles of government institutions and their de facto governing role, as governance is moved to interactive, contextualized, and temporary arenas.

In the third and final scenario, we see a cautious expansion of interactive forms of governance based on reflexive and pragmatic choices between different governance modes in relation to particular policy problems and policy tasks. Even a cautious expansion of interactive governance would entail some redefinition of the role and function of the representative and executive institutions of government. However, there would continue to be much formal power vested in the traditional institutions of government that will not be surrendered to interactive governance arenas without opposition. The point here is that interactive governance would not assume all the roles we today accord representative institutions and public bureaucracies at different institutional levels. Rather, this scenario would suggest that interactive governance instruments come to play a more prominent role alongside those traditional government institutions. The vain hope might be that a balancing of formal government and interactive governance will make it possible to reap the fruits of both of these modes of governance while mitigating the problems associated with a one-sided reliance on one of them.

Today, we see scattered evidence of all three scenarios. Struggles between different storylines, institutional interests, and political projects will determine which of the scenarios will win out in the long run. Hence, a preference for the last of the three scenarios is no guarantee that it will be realized.

Unfinished business and future challenges

The aim of this book has been to consolidate and advance the interactive governance paradigm that will continue to be an important tool for understanding governance in the future, no matter which of the three above-mentioned scenarios will be realized. Although we believe that we have come some way in advancing the interactive governance paradigm, there is still a good deal of unfinished business and some crucial analytical challenges that will need attention in the years to come.

First, since we have not been able to fill all the gaps in a single volume, there is some unfinished business in relation to a number of classical political science themes that need to be addressed and possibly rethought from the perspective of interactive governance. One such theme is authority and how it relates to power (a subject we have examined). What happens to authority when it is not only exercised de jure but also exercised de jure in a multi-actor arena? Maarten Hajer (2009) offers some helpful reflections on this topic that could serve as a starting point for further investigations. Another theme is the rule of law and the whole question of the role and character of law in relation to interactive forms of governance. As mentioned in Chapter 3, the new ideas of procedural, or reflexive, law are interesting in this respect (Teubner, 1986), but they need to be linked to theories of interactive policymaking. A last theme concerns the question of political change and policy reform that will have to be reconsidered since the whole debate on path-dependence and path-shaping might look slightly different in an interactive governance perspective since the degree of institutionalization is lower and the possibility of forging alliances supporting change, or aiming to revive old and rejected policy paths, might be bigger. Mark Considine and Sylvain Giguére (2008) have reflected on this issue, but much more work is required to fully grasp the prospect for political reform in a context of multilateral action.

Practical experiences with policymaking in interactive governance arenas have also highlighted some urgent topics that are not covered in this book. Some people have noted the huge influence of mass media in interactive governance processes (Bennett and Entman, 2001; Cook, 2005; Crozier, 2007). Others have begun to explore the impact of negotiated interaction and governance networks on public innovation (Hartley, 2005; Considine et al., 2009; Eggers and Singh, 2009). Questions have also been raised about the nature and character of policy interaction and how to make collaboration work (Straus, 2002). Finally, there seems to be a growing need to explore the gray zones where interactive governance overlaps with hierarchy and market (Meuleman, 2008).

There are also some crucial theoretical, methodological, and empirical challenges to the advancement of the interactive governance paradigm. The first challenge is that the research on interactive governance continues to be undertheorized. Recent attempts to provide an overview of different theories and schools of thought (Sørensen and Torfing, 2007) cannot hide the fact that there is a profound lack of scholarly discussions about suitable theories and their problems and merits. In future debates it might be timely to add new theories such as systems theory and complexity theory to the present theoretical toolbox that mostly consists of theories subscribing to different strands of the new institutionalism. We might also explore how theories of learning, innovation, and communication can help us to illuminate what goes on in interactive policy arenas.

Another challenge is found at the methodological level. There is a persistent need for critical reflection on how different qualitative, and perhaps quantitative, methods can be used in studying interactive governance and how new methods can be developed (Bogason and Zølner, 2007). There is also an urgent need to bridge the gulf between qualitative policy network analysis and quantitative social network analysis. A few studies have aimed to cross the bridge, but a huge unexplored potential remains.

Last but not least, we need empirical studies that go beyond single-case and single-country studies and permit concept development, hypothesis testing, and theory building through multiple and comparative case studies of interactive governance. Reflecting on the impact and variability of political and institutional contexts will be crucial when comparing cases across countries and policy areas, but comparative case studies are important in order to generate a deeper understanding of interactive governance and its conditions, development, and impact.

With growing interest in interactive forms of governance, we are confident that these theoretical, methodological, and empirical challenges will be met in the near future. Interactive governance is here to stay and so is the research on interactive governance that seems to grow stronger and stronger as new challenges are taken on and the conceptual and argumentative framework is refined and supported by solid empirical analysis. We hope this book will prove helpful in this collective endeavor.

References

Agere, S. (2000), *Promoting Good Governance: Principles, Practices and Perspectives*, London: Commonwealth Secretariat.

Agranoff, R. I. (2003), *Leveraging Networks: A Guide for Public Managers Working across Organisations*, Washington D.C.: IBM Endowment for The Business of Government.

—— (2006), "Inside collaborative networks: Ten lessons for public managers," *Public Administration Review*, 66(6), pp. 56–65.

—— McGuire, M. (2003), *Collaborative Public Management: New Strategies for Local Government*, Washington D.C.: Georgetown University Press.

Agyris, C., and Schön, D. (1978), *Organizational Learning*, Reading: Addison-Wesley.

Aldrich, H. E. (1979), *Organizations and Environments*, Englewood Cliffs: Prentice Hall.

Almond, G., and Verba, S. (1963), *The Civic Culture: Political Attitudes and Democracy in Five Nations*, Princeton: Princeton University Press.

Alvarez, S. E., Dagnino, E., and Escobar, A. (Eds) (1998), *Culture of Politics/Politics of Cultures: Re-visioning Latin American Social Movements*, Boulder: Westview Press.

Andersen, I. E., and Jæger, B. (1999), "Scenario workshops and consensus conferences: Towards more democratic decision-making," *Science and Public Policy*, 26(5), pp. 331–40.

Andersen, J., and Torfing, J. (2004), *Netværksstyring af kommunernes arbejdsmarkedsrettede indsats*, Aalborg: Aalborg University Press.

Andersen, N. Å. (2000), "Public market – Political firms," *Acta Sociologica*, 43(1), pp. 43–61.

—— (2008), *Partnerships: Machines of Possibility*, Bristol: Policy Press.

Ansell, C. (2000), "The networked polity: Regional development in Western Europe," *Governance*, 13(3), pp. 303–33.

Atkinson, M. M., and Coleman, W. D. (1989), "Strong and weak states: Sectoral policy networks in advanced capitalist economies," *British Journal of Political Science*, 19(1), pp. 47–67.

Bache, I., and Flinders, M. (Eds) (2004), *Multi-Level Governance*, Oxford: Oxford University Press.

Bachrach, P., and Baratz, M. S. (1970), *Power and Poverty: Theory and Practice*, Oxford: Oxford University Press.

Baker, K., Justice, J. B., and Skelcher, C. (2009), "The institutional design of self-governance: Insights from public–private partnerships," in E. Sørensen and P. Triantafillou (Eds), *The Politics of Self-Governance*, London: Ashgate, pp. 77–95.

Bang, H. P. (Ed.) (2003), *Governance as Social and Political Communication*, Manchester: Manchester University Press.

—— (2007), "Critical theory in a swing: Political consumerism between politics and policy," in M. Bevir and F. Trentman (Eds), *Governance, Consumers and Citizens: Agency and Resistance in Contemporary Politics*, London: Palgrave Macmillan, pp. 191–230.

—— Sørensen, E. (1998), "The everyday maker: A new challenge to democratic governance," *Administrative Theory & Praxis*, 21(3), pp. 325–42.

Banthien, H., Jaspers, M., and Renner, A. (2003), *Governance of the European Research Area: The Role of Civil Society*, Brussels: The EU Commission.

Barber, B. (1984), *Strong Democracy: Participatory Politics for a New Age*, Berkeley: University of California Press.

Bartlett, W., and Le Grand, J. (Eds) (1993), *Quasi-Markets and Social Policy*, London: Macmillan.

Beauregard, R. A. (1995), "Theorizing the global–local connection," in P. L. Knox and P. J. Taylor (Eds), *World Cities in a World-System*, Cambridge: Cambridge University Press, pp. 232–48.

Beck, U. (1994), "The reinvention of politics: Towards a theory of reflexive modernity," in U. Beck, A. Giddens, and S. Lash (Eds), *Reflexive Modernity*, Cambridge: Polity Press, pp. 1–55.

—— (1997), *The Reinvention of Politics: Rethinking Modernity in the Global Social Order*, Cambridge: Polity Press.

Behn, R. D. (2001), *Rethinking Democratic Accountability*, Washington D.C.: The Brookings Institution.

Bell, S., and Hindmoor, A. (2009), *Rethinking Governance: The Centrality of the State in Modern Society*, Cambridge: Cambridge University Press.

—— Park, A. (2006), "The problematic metagovernance of networks: Water reform in New South Wales," *Journal of Public Policy*, 26(1), pp. 63–83.

Bennett, W., and Entman, R. (2001), *Mediated Politics: Communication in the Future of Democracy*, Cambridge: Cambridge University Press.

Benson, J. K. (1978), "The interorganizational network as a political economy," in L. Karpik (Ed.), *Organization and Environment*, London: Sage, pp. 69–102.

Benz, A., and Papadopoulos, Y. (2006), *Governance and Democracy*, London: Routledge.

—— Scharpf, F. W., and Zintl, R. (1992), *Horisontale Politikverflechtung: Zur Theorien von Verhandlungssystemen*, Frankfurt: Campus.

Bertok, J., Hall, J., Kraan, D.-J., Malinska, J., Manning, N., and Matthews, E. (2006), *OECD Project on Management in Government: Comparative Country Data*, Paris: OECD.

Betsill, M. M., and Bulkeley, H. (2004), "Transnational networks and global environmental governance: The cities for climate protection program," *International Studies Quarterly*, 48(2), pp. 471–93.

Bevir, M., and Rhodes, R. A. W. (2003), *Interpreting British Governance*, London: Routledge.

Bexell, M., and Mörth, U. (2010), *Democracy and Public–Private Partnerships*, Basingstoke: Palgrave Macmillan.

Blau, P. M. (1956), *Bureaucracy in Modern Society*, New York: Random House.

Bodansky, D. (1999), "The legitimacy of international governance: A coming challenge for international environmental law," *American Journal of International Law*, 93(3), pp. 596–624.

241

Bogason, P., and Zølner, M. (Eds) (2007), *Methods in Democratic Network Governance*, Basingstoke: Palgrave Macmillan.

Bogdanor, V. (Ed.) (2005), *Joined-up Government*, Oxford: Oxford University Press.

Bohman, J. (2005), "From demos to demoi: Democracy across borders," *Ratio Juris*, 18(3), pp. 293–314.

Boin, A., and Goodin, R. E. (2007), "Institutionalizing upstarts: The demons of domestication and the benefits of recalcitrance," *Acta Politica*, 42(1), pp. 40–57.

Booher, D., and Innes, J. (2010), *Planning with Complexity*, London: Routledge.

Borrás, S. A. (2007), "Governance networks in the EU: The case of GMO policy," in M. Marcussen and J. Torfing (Eds), *Democratic Network Governance in Europe*, Basingstoke: Palgrave Macmillan, pp. 111–29.

Bouckaert, G., and Peters, B. G. (2002), "Performance measurement and management: The Achilles heel of administrative modernization," *Public Performance and Management Review*, 25(4), pp. 359–62.

Bovens, M. A. H., 't Hart, P., and Peters, B. G. (2001), *Success and Failure in Public Governance*, Cheltenham: Edward Elgar.

Bozeman, B. (2007), *Public Values and Public Interest: Counterbalancing Economic Individualism*, Washington D.C.: Georgetown University Press.

Bratton, M., and Hyden, G. (Eds) (1992), *Governance and Politics in Africa*, Boulder: Lynne Rienner.

British Government (2010), *Working Together—Public Services on Your Side*, Norwich: UK Government.

British Home Office (2010), *Community Policing: Citizen-Focused Policing*, http://police. homeoffice.gov.uk/community-policing/citizen-focused-policing/index.html (accessed March 2010).

Buchanan, J. M., and Tullock, G. (1962), *The Calculus of Consent*, Ann Arbor: University of Michigan Press.

Burns, D. (2000), "Can local democracy survive governance?," *Urban Studies*, 37(5–6), pp. 963–74.

Burns, J. (2010), "Western models and administrative reform in China: Pragmatism and the search for modernity," in J. Pierre and P. W. Ingraham (Eds), *Comparative Administrative Change and Reform: Lessons Learned*, Montreal: McGill-Queen's University Press, pp. 182–206.

Buuren, A., Edelenbos, J., and Klijn, E.-H. (2007), "Interactive governance in the Netherlands: The case of the Scheldt Estuary," in M. Marcussen and J. Torfing (Eds), *Democratic Network Governance in Europe*, Basingstoke: Palgrave Macmillan, pp. 150–73.

Callon, M., Lascoumes, P., and Barthe, Y. (2001), *Agir dans un monde incertain*, Paris: Le Seuil.

Calvert, R. (1995), *The Rational Choice Theory of Institutions: Implications for Design*, Boston: Kluwer.

Camilleri, J. A., and Falk, J. (1992), *The End of Sovereignty*, Cheltenham: Edward Elgar.

Cawson, A. (Ed.) (1985), *Organized Interests and the State: Studies in Meso-Corporatism*, London: Sage.

Christensen, T., and Lægreid, P. (Eds) (2007), *Transcending New Public Management: The Transformation of Public Sector Reforms*, Aldershot: Ashgate.

—— Piatonni, S. (2003), *Informal Governance in the European Union*, Cheltenham: Edward Elgar.

Christiansen, P. M., and Togeby, L. (2006), "Power and democracy in Denmark: Still a viable democracy," *Scandinavian Political Studies*, 29(1), pp. 1–24.

Cohen, J. (1989), "Deliberative democracy and democratic legitimacy," in A. Hamlin and P. Pettit (Eds), *The Good Polity*, Oxford: Blackwell, pp. 17–34.

Colebatch, H. K. (2009), "Governance as a conceptual development in the analysis of policy," *Critical Policy Studies*, 3(1), pp. 58–67.

Considine, M., and Giguère, S. (Eds) (2008), *Theory and Practice of Local Governance and Economic Development*, Basingstoke: Palgrave Macmillan.

—— Lewis, J., and Alexander, D. (2009), *Networks, Innovation and Public Policy*, Basingstoke: Palgrave Macmillan.

Cook, T. (2005), *Governing with the News: The New Media as Political Institutions*, Chicago: University of Chicago Press.

Coser, L. A. (1956), *The Functions of Social Conflict*, New York: The Free Press.

Crouch, C., Le Gales, P., Trigilia, C., and Voelzkow, H. (Eds) (2004), *Changing Governance of Local Economies: Responses of European Local Production Systems*, Oxford: Oxford University Press.

Crozier, M. P. (2007), "Recursive governance: Contemporary political communication and public policy," *Politics of Communication*, 24(1), pp. 1–18.

—— (2010), "Rethinking systems: Configurations of politics and policy in contemporary governance," *Administration and Society*, 42(5), pp. 504–25.

—— Huntington, S. P., and Watanuki, J. (1975), *The Crisis of Democracy*, New York: New York University Press.

Cutler, T., and Waine, B. (1997), "The politics of quasi-markets," *Critical Social Policy*, 17(51), pp. 3–26.

D'Aspremont, J. (2006), "Legitimacy of governments in an age of democracy," *NYU Journal of International Law and Politics*, 38, pp. 877–918.

Dahl, R. A. (1956), *A Preface to Democratic Theory*, Chicago: University of Chicago Press.

—— (1957), "The concept of power," *Behavioral Science*, 2(2), pp. 201–5.

—— (1961), *Who Governs? Democracy and Power in an American City*, New Haven: Yale University Press.

—— (1963), *Modern Political Analysis*, Englewood Cliffs: Prentice Hall.

—— (1989), *Democracy and its Critics*, New Haven: Yale University Press.

Dahlstrom, C., Pierre, J., and Peters, B. G. (Eds) (2011), *Steering from the Centre: Strengthening Political Control in Western Democracies*, Toronto: University of Toronto Press.

Damgaard, B. (2006), "Do policy networks lead to network governing?, *Public Administration*, 84(3), pp. 673–91.

—— Torfing, J. (2010), "Network governance of active employment policy: The Danish experience," *Journal of European Social Policy*, 20(3), pp. 248–62.

Danish Ministry of Finance (2005), *Public Governance: Kodeks for god offentlig topledelse i Danmark*, Copenhagen: Forum for Offentlig Topledelse.

References

Dannestam, T. (2008), "Rethinking local politics: Towards a cultural political economy of entrepreneurial cities," *Space and Polity*, 12(3), pp. 353–72.

De Grassi, A. (2008), "Neopatrimonialism and agricultural development in Africa: Contributions and limitations of a contested concept," *African Studies Review*, 51(3), pp. 107–33.

Dean, M. (1999), *Governmentality: Power and Rule in Modern Societies*, London: Sage.

DeHoog, R. H. (1990), "Competition, negotiation or cooperation: Three models for service contracting," *Administration & Society*, 22(3), pp. 317–40.

Demirag, I. S. (1998), *Corporate Governance: Accountability and Pressures to Perform*, Stanford: JAI Press.

Dente, B., Bobbio, L., and Spada, A. (2005), "Government or governance in urban innovation? A tale of two cities," *DISP*, 162(3), pp. 41–52.

Deutsch, K. W. (1963), *The Nerves of Government: Models of Political Communication and Control*, New York: The Free Press.

Dewey, J. (1927), *The Public and its Problems*, New York: Holt.

DiMaggio, P. J., and Powell, W. W. (1991), *The New Institutionalism in Organizational Analysis*, Chicago: University of Chicago Press.

Djelic, M.-L., and Sahlin-Andersson, K. (Eds) (2006), *Transnational Governance: Institutional Dynamics of Regulation*, Cambridge: Cambridge University Press.

Doner, R. F. (1992), "Limits of state strength: Toward an institutionalist view of economic development," *World Politics*, 44(3), pp. 398–431.

Downs, G. W., and Larkey, P. D. (1986), *The Search for Government Efficiency: From Hubris to Helplessness*, Philadelphia: Temple University Press.

Doyle, T., and McEachern, D. (1998), *Environment and Politics*, London: Routledge.

Dror, Y. (1986), *Policymaking Under Adversity*, New Brunswick: Transaction Books.

Dryzek, J. S. (2000), *Deliberative Democracy and Beyond*, Oxford: Oxford University Press.

—— (2007), "Networks and democratic ideals: Equality, freedom and communication," in E. Sørensen and J. Torfing (Eds), *Theories of Democratic Network Governance*, Basingstoke: Palgrave Macmillan, pp. 262–73.

Du Gay, P. (2000), *In Praise of Bureaucracy*, London: Sage.

Dunleavy, P. (1991), *Democracy, Bureaucracy and Public Choice*, London: Harvester Wheatsheaf.

Dyrberg, T. (1997), *The Circular Structure of Power*, London: Verso.

Easton, D. (1965a), *A Systems Analysis of Political Life*, New York: Wiley.

—— (1965b), *A Framework for Political Analysis*, Englewood Cliffs: Prentice Hall.

Edelenbos, J., and Eshuis, J. (2009), "Dealing with complexity through trust and control," in G. R. Teisman, A. van Buuren, and L. Gerrits (Eds), *Managing Complex Governance Systems*, London: Routledge, pp. 193–212.

—— Klijn, E.-H. (2006), "Managing stakeholder involvement in decision making: A comparative analysis of six interactive processes in the Netherlands," *Journal of Public Administration Research and Theory*, 16(3), pp. 417–46.

Edquist, C., and Hommen, L. (1999), "Systems of innovation: Theory and policy for the demand side," *Technology in Society*, 21(1), pp. 63–79.

Eggers, B., and Singh, S. (2009), *The Public Innovators Playbook*, Washington D.C.: Harvard Kennedy School of Government.

Elmore, R. F. (1978), "Organizational models of social program implementation," *Public Policy*, 26(2), pp. 185–228.

—— (1985), "Forward and backward mapping: Reversible logic in the analysis of public policy," in K. Hanf and T. A. Toonen (Eds), *Policy Implementation in Federal and Unitary Systems*, Boston: Nato ASIS Series, pp. 33–70.

Esmark, A. (2007*a*), "Network management in the EU: The European Commission as network manager," in M. Marcussen and J. Torfing (Eds), *Democratic Network Governance in Europe*, Basingstoke: Palgrave Macmillan, pp. 252–72.

—— (2007*b*), "Democratic accountability and network governance: Problems and potentials," in E. Sørensen and J. Torfing (Eds), *Theories of Democratic Network Governance*, Basingstoke: Palgrave Macmillan, pp. 247–61.

—— (2009), "The functional differentiation of governance: Public governance beyond hierarchy, market and networks," *Public Administration*, 87(2), pp. 351–71.

Esping-Andersen, G. (1990), *The Three Worlds of Welfare Capitalism*, Cambridge: Polity Press.

Etzioni, A. (1964), *Modern Organizations*, Englewood Cliffs: Prentice Hall.

Etzioni-Halevy, E. (1993), *The Elite Connection: Problems and Potential of Western Democracy*, Cambridge: Polity Press.

—— (2003), "Network governance as a challenge to democratic elite theory," *Centre for Democratic Network Governance Working Paper Series*, no. 2, Roskilde: Roskilde University.

Eulau, H. (1961), *Class and Power in the Eisenhower Years*, New York: The Free Press.

Evans, P. B. (1995), *Embedded Autonomy: States and Industrial Transformation*, Princeton: Princeton University Press.

—— Rueschemeyer, D., and Skocpol, T. (1985), *Bringing the State Back In*, Cambridge: Cambridge University Press.

Ferlie, E. (1992), "The creation and evolution of quasi-markets in the public sector: A problem for strategic management," *Strategic Management Journal*, 13(1), pp. 79–97.

Fisher, F., and Forester, J. (Eds) (1993), *The Argumentative Turn in Policy Analysis and Planning*, Durham: Duke University Press.

Foucault, M. (1986*a*), "Nietzsche, genealogy, history," in P. Rabinow (Ed.), *The Foucault Reader*, Harmondsworth: Penguin, pp. 76–100.

—— (1986*b*), "The subject and power," in H. L. Dreyfus and P. Rabinow (Eds), *Michel Foucault: Beyond Structuralism and Hermeneutics*, Brighton: Harvester, pp. 208–26.

—— (1990), *The History of Sexuality*, vol. 1, Harmondsworth: Penguin.

—— (1991), "Governmentality," in G. Burchell, C. Gordon, and P. Miller (Eds), *The Foucault Effect*, Hertfordshire: Harvester Wheatsheaf, pp. 87–104.

Fox, C. J., and Miller, H. T. (1995), *Postmodern Public Administration: Toward Discourse*, Thousand Oaks: Sage.

Freeman, G. P. (1985), "National styles and policy sectors: Explaining structured variation," *Journal of Public Policy*, 5(4), pp. 467–96.

Freeman, J. (1999), "Collaborative governance in the administrative state," *UCLA Law Review*, 45(1), pp. 1–98.

Fung, A. (2004), *Empowered Participation: Reinventing Urban Democracy*, New York: Princeton University Press.

—— Wright, E. O. (Eds) (2003), *Deepening Democracy: Institutional Innovations in Empowered Participatory Governance*, London: Verso.

References

Fung, A., Graham, M., and Weil, D. F. (2007), *Full Disclosure: The Perils and Promise of Transparency*, Cambridge: Cambridge University Press.

Geissel, B. (2008), "Do critical citizens foster better governance? A comparative study," *West European Politics*, 31(5), pp. 855–73.

George, A. L., and Bennett, A. (2005), *Case Studies and Theory Development in the Social Sciences*, Cambridge: MIT Press.

Giddens, A. (1994), *Beyond Left and Right: The Future of Radical Politics*, Stanford: Stanford University Press.

Gintis, H. (2000), *Game Theory Evolving*, Princeton: Princeton University Press.

Goertz, G. (2004), *Social Science Concepts: A User's Guide*, Princeton: Princeton University Press.

Goetz, K. H. (2008), "Governance as a path to government," *West European Politics*, 31(2), pp. 258–79.

Goldsmith, S., and Eggers, B. (2004), *Governing by Network: The New Shape of the Public Sector*, Washington D.C.: Brookings Institution Press.

Greve, C. (2007), *Contracting for Public Services*, London: Routledge.

Grindle, M. S. (2004), "Good enough governance: Poverty reduction and reform in developing countries," *Governance*, 17(4), pp. 525–48.

Grote, J. R., and Gbikpi, B. (Eds) (2002), *Participatory Governance: Political and Societal Implications*, Opladen: Leske and Budrich.

Gurr, T. R., and King, D. S. (1987), *The State and the City*, Basingstoke: Macmillan.

Gustafsson, G. (1987), *Decentralisering av politisk makt*, Stockholm: Carlsson.

Haas, P. M. (1992), "Epistemic communities and international policy coordination," *International Organization*, 46(1), pp. 1–35.

Haber, S. (1964), *Efficiency and Uplift*, Chicago: University of Chicago Press.

Habermas, J. (1996), *The Theory of Communicative Action*, Cambridge: Polity Press.

Haggard, S. (1998), "Business, politics and polity in East and Southeast Asia," in H. S. Rowen (Ed.), *Behind East Asian Growth: The Political and Social Foundation of Prosperity*, London: Routledge, pp. 78–104.

—— (2004), "Institutions and growth in East Asia," *Studies in Comparative International Development*, 38(4), pp. 53–81.

Hajer, M. (1993), "Discourse coalitions and the institutionalization of practice: The case of acid rain in Britain," in F. Fisher and J. Forester (Eds), *The Argumentative Turn in Policy Analysis and Planning*, Durham: Duke University Press, pp. 43–76.

—— (1995), *The Politics of Environmental Discourse: Ecological Modernization and the Policy Process*, Oxford: Clarendon Press.

—— (2003), "Policy without polity? Policy analysis and the institutional void," *Policy Sciences*, 36(2), pp. 175–95.

—— (2009), *Authoritative Governance*, Oxford: Oxford University Press.

—— Wagenaar, H. (Eds) (2003), *Deliberative Policy Analysis: Understanding in the Network Society*, Cambridge: Cambridge University Press.

Hansen, A. D. (2007), "Governance networks and participation," in E. Sørensen and J. Torfing (Eds), *Theories of Democratic Network Governance*, Basingstoke: Palgrave Macmillan, pp. 247–61.

't Hart, P. (1994), *Groupthink in Government: A Study of Small Groups and Policy Failure*, Baltimore: Johns Hopkins University Press.

Hartley, J. (2005), "Innovation in governance and public service: Past and present," *Public Money and Management*, 25(1), pp. 27–34.

Hasnain-Wynia, R., Sofaer, S., Bazzoli, G., Alexander, J., Shortell, S., Chan, B., and Sweney, J. (2003), "Members' perception of community care network partnerships' effectiveness," *Medical Care and Research and Review*, 60(4), pp. 40–62.

Healey, P. (1997), *Collaborative Planning*, Basingstoke: Macmillan.

—— (2007), *Urban Complexity and Spatial Strategies: Towards a Relational Planning for Our Time*, London: Routledge.

Hebson, G., Grimshaw, D., and Marchington, M. (2003), "PPPs and the changing public sector ethos: Case-study evidence from the health and local authority sectors," *Work, Employment and Society*, 17(3), pp. 481–501.

Heclo, H. (1978), "Issue networks and the executive establishment," in A. King (Ed.), *The New American Political System*, Washington D.C.: American Enterprise Institute, pp. 87–124.

—— Wildavsky, A. (1974), *The Private Government of Public Money*, Berkeley: University of California Press.

Hedmo, T., and Sahlin-Andersson, K. (2007), "The evolution of a European governance network of management education," in M. Marcussen and J. Torfing (Eds), *Democratic Network Governance in Europe*, Basingstoke: Palgrave Macmillan, pp. 195–213.

Heffen, O. V., Kickert, W. J. M., and Thomassen, J. A. (Eds) (2000), *Governance in Modern Society: Effects, Change and Formation of Government Institutions*, Dordrecht: Kluwer Academic Publishers.

Hegel, G. W. F. (1967 [1821]), *Philosophy of Right*, Oxford: Clarendon Press.

van der Heiden, N. (2010), *Urban Foreign Policy and Domestic Dilemmas*, Colchester: ECPR Press.

Heinrich, C. L., Lynn, L. E., and Milward, H. B. (2009), "A State of agents? Sharpening the debate and evidence over the extent and impact of the transformation of governance," *Journal of Public Administration Research and Theory*, 20(suppl. 1), pp. 3–19.

Held, D. (2006), *Models of Democracy*, Cambridge: Polity Press.

—— McGrew, A. G. (2002), *Governing Globalization: Power, Authority and Global Governance*, London: Polity Press.

Helmke, G., and Levitsky, D. S. (2004), "Informal institutions and comparative politics: A research agenda," *Perspectives on Politics*, 2(4), pp. 725–40.

Héritier, A., and Lehmkuhl, D. (2008), "The shadow of hierarchy and new modes of governance," *Journal of Public Policy*, 28(1), pp. 1–17.

—— Knill, C., and Minges, S. (1996), *Ringing the Changes in Europe*, Berlin: Walter de Gruyter.

Hirschman, A. O. (1970), *Exit, Voice, and Loyalty: Responses to Decline in Firms, Organizations, and States*, Cambridge, MA: Harvard University Press.

Hirst, P. (1994), *Associative Democracy*, Cambridge: Polity Press.

—— (2000), "Democracy and governance," in J. Pierre (Ed.), *Debating Governance*, Oxford: Oxford University Press, pp. 13–35.

References

Hix, S. (1994), "The study of the European Community: The challenge to comparative politics," *West European Politics*, 17(1), pp. 1–30.

Hjern, B., and Hull, C. (1984), "Going interorganizational: Weber meets Durkheim," *Scandinavian Political Studies*, 7(3), pp. 197–212.

—— Porter, D. O. (1981), "Implementations structures: A new unit of administrative analysis," *Organization Studies*, 2(3), pp. 211–27.

Hobbs, H. H. (1994), *City Hall Goes Abroad: The Foreign Policy of Local Politics*, London: Sage.

Hodge, G., and Greve, C. (2005), *The Challenge of Public–Private Partnerships*, Cheltenham: Edward Elgar.

Hogwood, B. W., and Peters, B. G. (1982), *Policy Dynamics*, Brighton: Wheatsheaf.

Hood, C. (1986), *The Tools of Government*, Chatham: Chatham House.

—— (1991), "A public management for all seasons?," *Public Administration*, 69(1), pp. 3–19.

—— (2006a), "Transparency in historical perspective," in C. Hood and D. Heald (Eds), *Transparency: The Key to Better Governance?*, Oxford: Oxford University Press, pp. 3–24.

—— (2006b), "Beyond exchanging first principles? Some closing comments," in C. Hood and D. Heald (Eds), *Transparency: The Key to Better Governance?*, Oxford: Oxford University Press, pp. 211–25.

—— D. Heald (Eds) (2006), *Transparency: The Key to Better Governance?*, Oxford: Oxford University Press.

Hooghe, L., and Marks, G. (2003), "Unraveling the state, but how? Types of multilevel governance," *American Political Science Review*, 97(2), pp. 232–43.

Hovik, S., and Vabo, S. I. (2005), "Norwegian local councils as democratic metagovernors?," *Scandinavian Political Studies*, 28(3), pp. 257–75.

Howlett, M. (2000), "Managing the 'Hollow State': Procedural policy instruments and modern governance," *Canadian Public Administration*, 43(4), pp. 412–31.

Huber, J. D., and McCarty, N. (2004), "Bureaucratic capacity, delegation and political reform," *American Political Science Review*, 98(3), pp. 481–94.

Huntington, S. P. (1968), *Political Order in Changing Societies*, New Haven: Yale University Press.

Hutter, B. M., and Jones, C. J. (2007), "From government to governance: External influences on business risk management," *Regulation and Governance*, 1(1), pp. 27–45.

Hyden, G., Court, J., and Mease, K. (2004), *Making Sense of Governance: Empirical Evidence from 16 Developing Countries*, Boulder: Lynne Rienner.

IMF (2005), *The IMF's Approach to Promoting Good Governance and Combating Corruption: A Guide*, http://www.imf.org/external/np/gov/guide/eng/index.htm (accessed March 2010).

Innes, J. E., and Booher, D. E. (2010), *Planning with Complexity*, London: Routledge.

Jacobsson, K. (2004), "Soft regulation and the subtle transformation of states: The case of EU employment policy," *Journal of European Social Policy*, 14(4), pp. 355–70.

Jemison, D. B. (2007), "The importance of boundary spanning roles in strategic decision-making," *Journal of Management Studies*, 21(2), pp. 131–52.

Jensen, L., and Kähler, H. (2007), "The Danish Ministry of Finance as a metagovernor: The case of public sector digitalization," in M. Marcussen and J. Torfing (Eds), *Democratic Network Governance in Europe*, Basingstoke: Palgrave Macmillan, pp. 174–91.

Jessop, B. (1990), *State Theory: Putting Capitalist States in their Place*, Cambridge: Polity Press.

—— (1998), "The rise of governance and the risks of failure: The case of economic development," *International Social Science Journal*, 50(155), pp. 29–45.

—— (2002), *The Future of the Capitalist State*, Cambridge: Polity Press.

—— (2004), "Multi-level governance and multi-level metagovernance," in I. Bache and M. Flinders (Eds), *Multi-level Governance*, Oxford: Oxford University Press, pp. 49–74.

Jones, C. O. (1984), *An Introduction to the Study of Public Policy*, Monterey: Brooks/Cole.

Kahler, M. (Ed.) (2009), *Networked Politics: Agency, Power and Governance*, Ithaca: Cornell University Press.

Kang, D. C. (2002), "Bad loans to good friends: Money politics and the developmental state in South Korea," *International Organization*, 56(1), pp. 177–207.

Katz, R. S., and Mair, P. (1995), "Changing models of party organization and party democracy," *Party Politics*, 1(1), pp. 5–28.

Katzenstein, P. J. (1984), *Corporatism and Change*, London: Cornell University Press.

Kaufman, D. (1999), *Governance Matters*, Washington D.C.: The World Bank.

Keane, J. (2009), *The Life and Death of Democracy*, London: Simon and Schuster.

Kelly, J. (2006), "Central regulation of English local authorities: An example of meta-governance," *Public Administration*, 84(3), pp. 603–21.

Kenis, P. N., and Provan, K. G. (2009), "Towards an exogenous theory of public network performance," *Public Administration*, 87(3), pp. 440–56.

Keohane, R. O., and Nye, J. S. (1977), *Power and Interdependence: World Politics in Transition*, Boston: Little, Brown and Company.

van Kersbergen, K., and van Waarden, F. (2004), "'Governance' as a bridge between disciplines: Cross-disciplinary inspiration regarding shifts in governance and problems of governability, accountability and legitimacy," *European Journal of Political Research*, 43(2), pp. 143–71.

Kesselman, M. (1970), "Overinstitutionalization and political constraint," *Comparative Politics*, 3(1), pp. 21–44.

Kettl, D. F. (2002), *The Transformation of Governance: Public Administration for Twenty-first Century America*, Baltimore: Johns Hopkins University Press.

Khalil, E. L. (1995), "Organizations versus institutions," *Journal of Institutional and Theoretical Economics*, 151(3), pp. 445–66.

Khan, M. H. (Ed.) (2004), *State-Formation in Palestine*, London: Routledge.

Kickert, W. J. M., Klijn, E.-H., and Koppenjan, J. F. M. (Eds) (1997), *Managing Complex Networks: Strategies for the Public Sector*, London: Sage.

Kiser, L. L., and Ostrom, E. (1982), "The three worlds of action: A meta-theoretical synthesis of institutional approaches," in E. Ostrom (Ed.), *Strategies of Political Enquiry*, London: Sage, pp. 179–222.

Kjær, A. M. (2011a), "The debate on African governance," forthcoming.

—— (2011b), "Governance in Africa," *Politics & Society*, forthcoming.

References

Klijn, E.-H. (2008), "Governance and governance networks in Europe," *Public Management Review*, 10(4), pp. 505–25.

—— Koppenjan, J. F. M. (2000*a*), "Public management and policy networks: Foundations of a network approach to governance," *Public Management*, 2(2), pp. 135–58.

——— (2000*b*), "Interactive decision making and representative democracy: Institutional collisions and solutions," in O. V. Heffen, W. J. M. Kickert, and J. A. Thomassen (Eds), *Governance in Modern Society: Effects, Change and Formation of Government Institutions*, Dordrecht: Kluwer Academic Publishers, pp. 114–24.

—— Skelcher, C. (2007), "Democracy and governance networks: Compatible or not?," *Public Administration*, 85(3), pp. 587–608.

—— Snellen, I. (2009), "Complexity theory and public administration: A critical appraisal," in G. R. Teisman, A. van Buuren, and L. Gerrits (Eds), *Managing Complex Governance Systems*, London: Routledge, pp. 17–36.

—— Teisman, G. R. (2000), "Managing public–private partnerships: Influencing processes and institutional context of public–private partnerships," in O. V. Heffen, W. J. M. Kickert, and J. A. Thomassen (Eds), *Governance in Modern Society*, Dordrecht: Kluwer Academic Publishers, pp. 329–48.

Knack, S., Kugler, M., and Manning, N. (2003), "Second-generation governance indicators," *International Review of Administrative Sciences*, 69(3), pp. 345–64.

Kohler-Koch, B., and Eising, R. (Eds) (1999), *The Transformation of Governance in the European Union*, London: Routledge.

—— Larat, F. (2009), *European Multi-level Governance*, Cheltenham: Edward Elgar.

—— Rittberger, B. (2006), "The governance turn in EU studies," *Journal of Common Market Studies*, 44(1), pp. 27–49.

——— (2009), "A futile quest for coherence: The many frames of EU governance," in B. Kohler-Koch and F. Larat (Eds), *European Multi-level Governance*, Cheltenham: Edward Elgar, pp. 3–18.

Kolstad, I., and Wiig, A. (2009), "Is transparency the key to reduce corruption in resource-rich countries?," *World Development*, 37(3), pp. 521–32.

Kooiman, J. (Ed.) (1993*a*), *Modern Governance: New Government–Society Interactions*, London: Sage.

—— (1993*b*), "Governance and governability: Using complexity, dynamics and diversity," in J. Kooiman (Ed.), *Modern Governance*, London: Sage, pp. 35–50.

—— (2003), *Governing as Governance*, London: Sage.

Koonings, K. (2004), "Strengthening citizenship in Brazil's democracy: Local participatory governance in Porto Alegre," *Bulletin of Latin American Research*, 23(1), pp. 79–99.

Koppenjan, J. F. M. (2005), "The formation of public–private partnerships: Lessons from nine transport infrastructure projects in the Netherlands," *Public Administration*, 83(1), pp. 135–57.

—— Klijn, E.-H. (2004), *Managing Uncertainties in Networks: A Network Approach to Problem Solving and Decision Making*, London: Routledge.

Krasner, S. D. (1983), *International Regimes*, Ithaca: Cornell University Press.

Kriesi, H. P., Adam, S., and Jochum, M. (2006), "Comparative analysis of policy networks in Western Europe," *Journal of European Public Policy*, 13(3), pp. 341–61.

Laclau, E., and Mouffe, C. (1985), *Hegemony and Socialist Strategy*, London: Verso.

Laegreid, P., and Verhoest, K. (Eds) (2010), *Governance of Public Sector Organizations: Proliferation, Autonomy and Performance*, Basingstoke: Palgrave Macmillan.

Lake, D. A., and Wong, W. H. (2009), "The politics of networks: Interest, power and human rights norms," in M. Kahler (Ed.), *Networked Politics: Agency, Power and Governance*, Ithaca: Cornell University Press, pp. 127–50.

Lane, J.-E. (1983), "The concept of implementation," *Statsvetenskaplig Tidskrift*, 86(1), pp. 17–40.

—— (1995), *The Public Sector: Concepts, Models and Approaches*, London: Sage.

Laumann, E. O., and Knoke, D. (1987), *The Organizational State: Social Choice in National Policy Domains*, Madison: University of Wisconsin Press.

Lauridsen, L. (2004), "Foreign investment, linkage formation and supplier development in Thailand during the 1990s: The role of State governance," *The European Journal of Development Research*, 16(3), pp. 561–86.

Lax, D., and Sebenius, J. (1992), "The negotiator's dilemma: Creating and claiming value," in S. Goldberg, F. Sander, and N. Rogers (Eds), *Dispute Resolution*, Boston: Little, Brown, and Company, pp. 49–62.

Leach, R., and Percy-Smith, J. (2001), *Local Governance in Britain*, Basingstoke: Macmillan.

Lee, J. N. (2001), "The impact of knowledge sharing, organizational capability and partnership quality on IS outsourcing success," *Information and Management*, 38(5), pp. 323–35.

Lehmbruch, G. (1984), "Concertation and the structure of corporatist networks," in J. H. Goldthorpe (Ed.), *Order and Conflict in Contemporary Capitalism*, Oxford: Oxford University Press, pp. 60–80.

Lewis, J. (2005), "New Labour's approach to the voluntary sector: Independence and the meaning of partnership," *Social Policy and Society*, 4(2), pp. 121–31.

Lichbach, M. (2003), *Is Rational Choice All of Social Science?*, Ann Arbor: University of Michigan Press.

Liguori, M., Sicilia, M., and Steccolini, I. (2010), "Politicians and administrators: Two characters in search of a role," Paper presented at the IRSPM Conference, Berne, April 7–9.

Lijphart, A. (1999), *Patterns of Democracy: Government Forms and Performance in Thirty-six Countries*, New Haven: Yale University Press.

Lindblom, C. E. (1959), "The science of 'muddling through'," *Public Administration Review*, 19(2), pp. 79–88.

—— (1977), *Politics and Markets*, New York: Basic Books.

Lindstedt, C., and Naurin, D. (2006), "Transparency against corruption: A cross-country study," Paper presented at the IPSA 20th World Congress, Fuhuoka, Japan, July 9–13.

Linton, R. (1936), *The Study of Man*, New York: Appleton Century.

Lipsky, M. (1980), *Street-level Bureaucracy: Dilemmas of the Individual in Public Services*, New York: Russell Sage Foundation.

Lopez-Santana, M. (2006), "The domestic implications of European soft law: Framing and transmitting change in employment policy," *Journal of European Public Policy*, 13(4), pp. 481–99.

References

Luhmann, N. (1984), *Soziale Systeme: Grundriss einer Allgemeinen Theorie*, Frankfurt: Suhrkamp.

Lukes, S. (1974), *Power: A Radical View*, Basingstoke: Macmillan.

Lund, C. (Ed.) (2007), *Twilight Institutions*, London: Blackwell.

—— (2008), *Local Politics and the Dynamics of Property in Africa*, Cambridge: Cambridge University Press.

Lundvall, B.-Å. (Ed.) (1992), *National Systems of Innovation: Towards a Theory of Innovation and Interactive Learning*, London: Pinter Publishers.

Management Greenhouse (2008), *Kodeks for god ledelse – i kommuner og regioner*, Copenhagen: The Management Greenhouse.

Mandell, M. P., and Keast, R. (2009), "A new look at leadership in collaborative networks: Process catalysts," in J. A. Raffel, P. Leisink, and A. E. Middlesbrooks (Eds), *Public Sector Leadership: International Challenges and Perspectives*, Cheltenham: Edward Elgar, pp. 163–78.

Mann, M. (1997), "Has globalization ended the rise and rise of the nation-state?," *Review of International Political Economy*, 4(3), pp. 472–96.

March, J. G. (1995), "Should higher education be more efficient?," *Stanford Educator*, Stanford: School of Education News, pp. 3–12.

—— Olsen, J. P. (1984), "The new institutionalism: Organizational factors in political life," *American Political Science Review*, 78, pp. 738–49.

—— —— (1989), *Rediscovering Institutions: The Organizational Basis of Politics*, New York: The Free Press.

—— —— (1995), *Democratic Governance*, New York: The Free Press.

Marchington, M., Grimshaw, D., Rubery, J., and Willmott, H. (Eds) (2005), *Fragmenting Work: Blurring Organizational Boundaries and Disordered Hierarchies*, Oxford: Oxford University Press.

Marcussen, M. (2007), "The Basel Committee as a transnational governance network," in M. Marcussen and J. Torfing (Eds), *Democratic Network Governance in Europe*, Basingstoke: Palgrave Macmillan, pp. 214–31.

Marin, B. and Mayntz, R. (Eds) (1991), *Policy Networks: Empirical Evidence and Theoretical Considerations*, Frankfurt am Main: Campus Verlag.

Marinetto, M. (2003), "Governing beyond the centre: A critique of the Anglo-Governance School," *Political Studies*, 51(4), pp. 592–608.

Marks, G., and Hooghe, L. (2004), "Contrasting visions of multi-level governance," in I. Bache and M. Flinders (Eds), *Multi-Level Governance*, Oxford: Oxford University Press, pp. 15–30.

Marsh, D. (Ed.) (1998), *Comparing Policy Networks*, Buckingham: Open University Press.

—— Rhodes, R. A. W. (Eds) (1992), *Policy Networks in British Government*, Oxford: Oxford University Press.

Marshall, G. S., and Buske, E. (2007), "Framing network style interactions in local governance: Three narratives," in G. Gjelstrup and E. Sørensen (Eds), *Public Administration in Transition*, Copenhagen: DJØF Publishers, pp. 233–47.

—— Ozawa, C. P. (2004), "Mediated negotiation, a deliberative approach to democratic governance," in P. Bogason, S. Kensen, and H. Miller (Eds), *Tampering with Tradition*, Lanham: Lexington Books, pp. 131–48.

252

Martin, J. (2002), *Organizational Culture: Mapping the Terrain*, Thousand Oaks: Sage.

Mayntz, R. (1993*a*), "Modernization and the logic of interorganizational networks," in J. Child, M. Crozier, and R. Mayntz (Eds), *Societal Change between Markets and Organization*, Aldershot: Avebury, pp. 3–18.

—— (1993*b*), "Governing failure and the problem of governability: Some comments on a theoretical paradigm," in J. Kooiman (Ed.), *Modern Governance*, London: Sage, pp. 9–20.

Meier, K. J., and O'Toole, L. J. (2003), "Public management and educational performance: The impact of managerial networking," *Public Administration Review*, 63(6), pp. 675–85.

—— —— (2006), *Bureaucracy in a Democratic State*, Baltimore: Johns Hopkins University Press.

Menkhaus, K. (2002), "Governance without government in Somalia," *International Security*, 31(3), pp. 74–106.

Meuleman, L. (2008), *Public Management and the Metagovernance of Hierarchies, Networks and Markets*, Heidelberg: Physica Verlag.

Meyer, M. K., and Vorsanger, S. (2003), "Street level bureaucracy," in B. G. Peters and J. Pierre (Eds), *Handbook of Public Administration*, London: Sage, pp. 245–56.

Michels, R. (1915), *Political Parties: A Sociological Study of the Oligarchical Tendencies of Modern Democracy*, New York: The Free Press.

Migdal, J. (1988), *Strong Societies and Weak States: State–Society Relationships and State Capabilities in the Third World*, Princeton: Princeton University Press.

Miliband, R. (1983), *Class Power and State Power*, London: Verso.

Mill, J. S. (1820), *Essays on Government, Jurisprudence, Liberty of the Press, and Law of Nations*, New York: Augustus M. Kelly Publishers.

—— (1991), *Considerations on Representative Democracy*, New York: Prometheus Books.

Miller, J. H., and Page, S. E. (2007), *Complex Adaptive Systems: An Introduction to Computational Models in the Social Sciences*, Princeton: Princeton University Press.

Milliken, J., and Krause, K. (2002), "State failure, state collapse, and state reconstruction: Concepts, lessons and strategies," *Development and Change*, 33(5), pp. 753–74.

Milward, H. B., and Provan, K. G. (2000), "Governing the hollow state," *Journal of Public Administration Research and Theory*, 10(2), pp. 359–79.

—— —— (2006), *A Manager's Guide to Choosing and Using Collaborative Networks*, Washington D.C.: IBM Endowment for The Business of Government.

Mintzberg, H. (1979), *The Structuring of Organizations*, Englewood Cliffs: Prentice Hall.

Mollenkopf, J. H. (1983), *The Contested City*, Princeton: Princeton University Press.

Montin, S. (1990), "Den kommunala multiorganisationen: Om nya normer och institutioner i kommunerna under 1980-talet," *Statsvetenskaplig Tidskrift*, 93(1), pp. 247–60.

Moran, M. (2002), "Review article: Understanding the regulatory state," *British Journal of Political Science*, 32(2), pp. 391–413.

Moravcsik, A. (1998), *The Choice for Europe*, Ithaca: Cornell University Press.

Morgan, G. (1986), *Images of Organizations*, London: Sage.

Morgenthau, H. (1954), *Politics among Nations*, New York: McGraw-Hill.

Mörth, U. (2004), *Soft Law in the European Union*, Cheltenham: Edward Elgar.

Mouffe, C. (1993), *The Return of the Political*, London: Verso.

—— (2005), *On the Political*, London: Routledge.

Moulaert, F., and Cabaret, K. (2006), "Planning, networks and power relations: Is democratic planning under capitalism possible?," *Planning Theory*, 5(1), pp. 51–70.

Muelemann, L. (2008), *Public Management and the Metagovernance of Hierarchies, Networks and Markets*, Leipzig: Physica.

Musso, J. A., Weare, C., Oztas, N., and Loges, W. E. (2006), "Neighbourhood governance reform and networks of community power in Los Angeles," *The American Review of Public Administration*, 36(1), pp. 79–97.

Mwenda, A. M., and Tangri, R. (2005), "Patronage politics, donor reforms and regime consolidation in Uganda," *African Affairs*, 104(416), pp. 449–67.

Nambisan, S. (2008), *Transforming Government through Collaborative Innovation*, Washington D.C.: Harvard Kennedy School of Government.

Naurin, D. (2007), *Deliberation Behind Closed Doors: Transparency and Lobbying in the European Union*, Colchester: ECPR Press.

Nedergaard, P. (2005), "The Open Method of Coordination and the analysis of mutual learning processes of the European Employment Strategy," *International Center for Business and Politics Working Paper Series*, no. 4, Copenhagen: Copenhagen Business School.

Newman, J. (2005), *Remaking Governance: Peoples, Politics and the Public Sphere*, London: Policy Press.

—— Clarke, J. (2009), *Publics, Politics and Power*, London: Sage.

Newman, P. (2000), "Changing patterns of regional governance in the EU," *Urban Studies*, 37(5–6), pp. 895–908.

Ney, S. (2007), *Resolving Messy Policy Problems*, London: Earthscan.

Norris, P., and Newton, K. (2000), "Confidence in public institutions," in S. Pharr and R. S. Putnam (Eds), *Disaffected Democracies*, Princeton: Princeton University Press, pp. 52–73.

North, D. C. (1990), *Institutions, Institutional Change, and Economic Performance*, Cambridge: Cambridge University Press.

O'Brien, R., Goetz, A. M., and Scholte, J. A. (2000), *Contesting Global Governance*, Cambridge: Cambridge University Press.

OECD (2007), *Performance Budgeting in OECD Countries*, Paris: OECD.

Offe, C. (2008), "Governance: 'Empty Signifier' oder sozialwissenschaftliches Forschungsprogramm?," in G. F. Schuppert and M. Zurn (Eds), *Governance in einer sich wandelnden Welt*, Wiesbaden: Verlag für Sozialwissenschaften, pp. 61–76.

—— Preuss, U. K. (2006), "The problem of legitimacy in the European polity: Is democratization the answer?," *Constitutionalism Web-Papers*, 6, Belfast: Queen's University Belfast.

Okimoto, D. (1989), *Between MITI and the Market: Japanese Industrial Policy for High Technology*, Stanford: Stanford University Press.

Olsen, J. P. (2002), "Maybe it is the time to rediscover bureaucracy?," *Journal of Public Administration Research and Theory*, 16(1), pp. 1–24.

O'Neill, O. (2006), "Transparency and the ethics of communication," in C. Hood and D. Heald (Eds), *Transparency: The Key to Better Governance?*, Oxford: Oxford University Press, pp. 75–90.

Osborne, D., and Gaebler, T. (1992), *Reinventing Government: How the Entrepreneurial Spirit is Transforming the Public Sector*, Reading: Addison Wesley.

Ostrom, E. (1990), *Governing the Commons: The Evolution of Institutions of Collective Action*, Cambridge: Cambridge University Press.

—— Walker, J., and Gardner, R. (1992), "Covenants with and without a sword: Self-governance is possible," *American Political Science Review*, 86(2), pp. 404–17.

O'Toole, L. J. (2007), "Governing outputs and outcomes of governance networks," in E. Sørensen and J. Torfing (Eds), *Theories of Democratic Network Governance*, Basingstoke: Palgrave Macmillan, pp. 215–30.

—— Meier, K. J. (2004), "Public management in intergovernmental networks: Matching structural networks and managerial networking," *Journal of Public Administration Research and Theory*, 14(4), pp. 469–95.

Page, E. C., and Jenkins, B. (2004), *Policy Bureaucracy*, Oxford: Oxford University Press.

Painter, M., and Pierre, J. (2006), *Challenges to Policy Capacity*, London: Routledge.

Papadopoulos, Y. (2003), "Cooperative forms of governance: Problems of democratic accountability in complex environments," *European Journal of Political Research*, 42(4), pp. 473–501.

—— (2007), "Problems of democratic accountability in network and multilevel governance," *European Law Journal*, 13(4), pp. 469–86.

Parker, G. (2007), "EU globalisation fund questioned," *Financial Times*, May 27.

Parsons, T. (1951), *The Social System*, New York: The Free Press.

Peters, B. G. (1978), *The Politics of Bureaucracy: A Comparative Perspective*, London: Longman.

—— (1987), "Politicians and bureaucrats in the politics of policy-making," in J. E. Lane (Ed.), *Bureaucracy and Public Choice*, London: Sage, pp. 256–82.

—— (1998), "With a little help from our friends: Public–private partnerships as institutions and instruments," in J. Pierre (Ed.), *Partnerships in Urban Governance: European and American Experience*, London: Macmillan, pp. 11–34.

—— (1999), *Institutional Theory in Political Science*, London: Continuum.

—— (2001), *The Future of Governing*, Lawrence: University Press of Kansas.

—— (2007a), "Virtuous and vicious circles in democratic network governance," in E. Sørenson and J. Torfing (Eds), *Theories of Democratic Network Governance*, Basingstoke: Palgrave Macmillan, pp. 61–77.

—— (2007b), "The meta-governance of policy networks: Steering at a distance, but still steering," *Department of Political Science and International Relations Working Papers Online Series*, no. 78, Madrid: Ciudad Universitaria de Cantoblanco.

—— (2008), "The two futures of public administration," *Public Money and Management*, 28(4), pp. 195–6.

—— (2010), "Governing in the shadows," *European Governance Program Working Paper Series*, Berlin: Free University of Berlin.

—— Pierre, J. (2001), "Developments in intergovernmental relationships: Towards multilevel governance," *Policy and Politics*, 29(2), pp. 131–5.

—— —— (2003), "Introduction," in B. G. Peters and J. Pierre (Eds), *Handbook of Public Administration*, London: Sage, pp. 1–11.

References

Peters, B. G., and Pierre, J. (2004), "Multi-level governance and democracy: A Faustian bargain?," in I. Bache and M. Flinders (Eds), *Multi-Level Governance*, Oxford: Oxford University Press, pp. 75–92.

—— —— (2005), "Swings and roundabouts? Multilevel governance as a source of and constraint on policy capacity," in M. Painter and J. Pierre (Eds), *Challenges to State Policy Capacity: Global Trends and Comparative Perspectives*, Basingstoke: Palgrave Macmillan, pp. 38–51.

Pettai, V., and Illing, E. (2004), "Governance and good governance," *Trames*, 8(4), pp. 347–51.

Piattoni, S. (Ed.) (2001a), *Clientelism, Interests and Democratic Representation*, Cambridge: Cambridge University Press.

—— (2001b), "Clientelism in historical and comparative perspective," in S. Piattoni (Ed.), *Clientelism, Interests and Democratic Representation*, Cambridge: Cambridge University Press, pp. 1–31.

Pierre, J. (1986), *Partikongresser och regeringspolitik*, Lund: Kommunfakta Förlag.

—— (1994), *Den lokala staten*, Stockholm: Almqvist & Wiksell.

—— (2000), *Debating Governance*, Oxford: Oxford University Press.

—— (2011), "Stealth economy? Economic theory and the politics of administrative reform," *Administration & Society*, forthcoming.

—— Peters, B. G. (1998), "Governance without government? Rethinking public administration," *Journal of Public Administration Research and Theory*, 8(2), pp. 223–43.

—— —— (2000), *Governance, Politics and the State*, Basingstoke: Palgrave Macmillan.

—— —— (2005), *Governing Complex Societies: Trajectories and Scenarios*, Basingstoke: Palgrave Macmillan.

—— —— (2009), "From a club to a bureaucracy," *Journal of European Public Policy*, 16(3), pp. 378–94.

Pierson, P. (1995), *Dismantling the Welfare State? Reagan, Thatcher and the Politics of Retrenchment*, Cambridge: Cambridge University Press.

—— (2000a), "The three worlds of welfare state research," *Comparative Political Studies*, 33(6–7), pp. 791–821.

—— (2000b), "Increasing returns, path dependence, and the study of politics," *American Political Science Review*, 94(2), pp. 251–67.

Pitkin, H. F. (1967), *The Concept of Representation*, Berkeley: University of California Press.

—— (2004), "Representation and democracy: Uneasy alliance," *Scandinavian Political Studies*, 27(3), pp. 335–42.

Plato (1991), *The Republic*, New York: Vintage Books.

Pollitt, C. (2010), "Simply the best? The international benchmarking of reform and good governance," in J. Pierre and P. W. Ingraham (Eds), *Comparative Administrative Change and Reform*, Montreal: McGill-Queen's University Press, pp. 91–113.

—— Bouckaert, G. (2004), *Public Management Reform: A Comparative Analysis*, Oxford: Oxford University Press.

—— Talbot, C. (Eds) (2003), *Unbundled Government: A Critical Analysis of the Global Trend to Agencies, Quangos and Contractualisation*, London: Routledge.

Poulantzas, N. (1978), *Political Power and Social Classes*, London: Verso.

Powell, W. W., and DiMaggio, P. (1983), "The iron cage revisited: Institutional isomorphism and collective rationality in organisational fields," *American Sociological Review*, 48(2), pp. 147–60.

—— —— (1991), *The New Institutionalism in Organizational Analysis*, Chicago: University of Chicago Press.

Power, M. (1997), *The Audit Society*, Oxford: Oxford University Press.

Pressman, J. L., and Wildawsky, A. (1973), *Implementation: How Great Expectations in Washington are Dashed in Oakland*, Berkeley: University of California Press.

Provan, K. G., and Kenis, P. N. (2008), "Modes of network governance: Structure, management, and effectiveness," *Journal of Public Administration Research and Theory*, 18(2), pp. 229–52.

—— Milward, H. B. (1991), "Institutional-level norms and organizational involvement in a service-implementation network," *Journal of Public Administration Research and Theory*, 1(4), pp. 319–417.

—— —— (1995), "A preliminary theory of interorganizational network effectiveness: A comparative study of four community mental health systems," *Administrative Science Quarterly*, 40(1), pp. 1–33.

—— —— (2000), "Governing the hollow state," *Journal of Public Administration Research and Theory*, 10(2), pp. 359–80.

—— —— (2001), "Do networks really work? A framework for evaluating public-sector organizational networks," *Public Administration Review*, 61(4), pp. 414–23.

—— Sebastian, J. G. (1998), "Networks within networks: Service link overlap, organizational cliques and network effectiveness," *Academy of Management Journal*, 41(4), pp. 453–63.

—— Isett, K. R., and Milward, H. B. (2004), "Cooperation and compromise: A network response to conflicting institutional pressures," *Nonprofit and Voluntary Sector Quarterly*, 33(3), pp. 489–514.

Qian, Y. (2003), "How reform worked in China," in D. Rodrik (Ed.), *In Search of Prosperity: Analytical Narratives of Economic Growth*, Princeton: Princeton University Press, pp. 297–333.

van Raaij, D., and Kenis, P. N. (2005), "How do network actors assess networks: An exploration of norms used in networks," Paper presented at the 8th Public Management Research Conference, Los Angeles, September 29–October 1.

Radin, B. A. (2006), *Challenging the Performance Movement: Accountability, Complexity and Democratic Values*, Washington D.C.: Georgetown University Press.

Ragsdale, L., and Theis, J. T. (1997), "The institutionalization of the American presidency, 1924–92," *American Journal of Political Science*, 41(4), pp. 1280–318.

Rhodes, R. A. W. (1986), *The National World of Local Government*, London: Allen & Unwin.

—— (1995), "The institutional approach," in D. Marsh and G. Stoker (Eds), *Theory and Methods in Political Science*, Basingstoke: Palgrave Macmillan, pp. 42–57.

—— (1996), "The new governance: Governing without government," *Political Studies*, 44(4), pp. 651–67.

—— (1997a), *Understanding Governance*, Buckingham: Open University Press.

References

Rhodes, R. A. W. (1997*b*), "Foreword," in W. J. M. Kickert, E.-H. Klijn, and J. F. M. Koppenjan (Eds), *Managing Complex Networks: Strategies for the Public Sector*, London: Sage, pp. xi–xvi.

—— (1999), "Traditions and public sector reform: Comparing Britain and Denmark," *Scandinavian Political Studies*, 22(4), pp. 341–70.

—— (2000*a*), "The governance narrative: Key findings and lessons from the ESRC's Whitehall Programme," *Public Administration*, 78(2), pp. 345–64.

—— (2000*b*), "Governance and public administration," in J. Pierre (Ed.), *Debating Governance. Authority, Steering, and Democracy*, Oxford: Oxford University Press, pp. 54–90.

Riccio, J., Bloom, H. S., and Hill, C. J. (2000), "Management, organizational characteristics and performance: The case of welfare-to-work programs," in C. J. Heinrich and L. E. Lynn (Eds), *Governance and Performance: New Perspectives*, Washington D.C.: George Washington University Press, pp. 167–97.

Rihoux, B., and Ragin, C. C. (2008), *Configurational Comparative Methods*, London: Sage.

Riker, W. (1980), "Implications from the disequilibrium of majority rule for the study of institutions," *American Political Science Review*, 74(2), pp. 432–46.

Risse, T., and Lehmkuhl, U. (2010), *Governance in Areas of Limited Statehood*, New York: New York University Press.

Ritchie, B. K. (2005), "Progress through setback or mired in mediocrity? Crisis and institutional change in South-East Asia," *Journal of East Asian Studies*, 5(2), pp. 273–313.

Rittberger, B., and Mayer, P. (1995), *Regime Theory and International Relations*, Oxford: Oxford University Press.

Rittel, H. J. W., and Webber, M. M. (1973), "Dilemmas in the general theory of planning," *Policy Science*, 4(2), pp. 155–69.

Roberts, N. (2000), "Organizational configurations: Four approaches to public sector managements," in J. L. Brudney, L. J. O'Toole, and H. G. Rainey (Eds), *Advancing Public Management*, Washington D.C.: George Washington University Press, pp. 217–34.

Rock, M. T., and Bonnett, H. (2004), "The comparative politics of corruption: Accounting for the East Asian paradox in empirical studies of corruption, growth and investment," *World Development*, 32(6), pp. 999–1017.

Rockman, B. A., and Weaver, R. K. (Eds) (1993), *Do Institutions Matter? Government Capabilities in the United States and Abroad*, Washington D.C.: The Brookings Institution.

Roniger, L. (2004), "Political clientelism, democracy and the market economy," *Comparative Politics*, 36(3), pp. 353–74.

Ronit, C., and Schneider, V. (2004), "Global governance through private organizations," *Governance*, 12(3), pp. 243–66.

Rose, N. (1999), *Powers of Freedom: Reframing Political Thought*, Cambridge: Cambridge University Press.

—— Miller, P. (1992), "Political power beyond the State: Problematics of government," *British Journal of Sociology*, 43(2), pp. 173–205.

Rose, R. (1974), *The Problem of Party Government*, London: Macmillan.

Rosenau, J. N., and Czempiel, E.-O. (1992), *Governance without Government: Order and Change in World Politics*, Cambridge: Cambridge University Press.

Rosenau, P. V. (Ed.) (2000), *Public–Private Policy Partnerships*, Cambridge: MIT Press.

Rosenbloom, D. H. (1998), *Understanding Management, Politics and Law in the Public Sector*, New York: McGraw-Hill.

Ross, F. A. (1997), "Cutting public expenditures in advanced industrial democracies: The importance of avoiding blame," *Governance*, 10(2), pp. 175–200.

Rotberg, R. I. (2004), *When States Fail: Causes and Consequences*, Princeton: Princeton University Press.

Sabatier, P. (1986), "Top-down and bottom-up approaches to implementation research," *Journal of Public Policy*, 6(1), pp. 21–48.

—— (1988), "An advocacy coalition framework of policy change and the role of policy-oriented learning therein," *Policy Sciences*, 21(2–3), pp. 129–68.

—— Jenkins-Smith, H. C. (1993), *Policy Change and Learning: An Advocacy Coalition Approach*, Boulder: Westview Press.

—— Weible, C. M. (2007), "The advocacy coalition framework: Innovations and clarifications," in P. Sabatier (Ed.), *Theories of the Policy Process*, Boulder: Westview, pp. 189–220.

Salamon, L. M. (Ed.) (1989), *Beyond Privatization*, Boston: MIT Press.

—— (2001), "Introduction," in L. M. Salamon (Ed.), *The Handbook of Policy Instruments*, New York: Oxford University Press, pp. 3–43.

—— (2002), "The new governance and the tools of public action," in L. M. Salamon (Ed.), *The Tools of Government: A Guide to the New Governance*, New York: Oxford University Press, pp. 1–47.

Sartori, G. (1970), "Concept misformation in comparative politics," *American Political Science Review*, 64(4), pp. 1033–53.

Saward, M. (2006), "The representative claim," *Contemporary Political Theory*, 5(3), pp. 297–318.

—— (2008), "Representation and democracy: Revisions and possibilities," *Sociology Compass*, 2(3), pp. 1000–13.

Schaap, L. (2007), "Closure and governance," in E. Sørensen and J. Torfing (Eds), *Theories of Democratic Network Governance*, Basingstoke: Palgrave Macmillan, pp. 111–32.

Scharpf, F. W. (1988), "The joint decision trap: Lessons from German federalism and European integration," *Public Administration*, 66(3), pp. 239–78.

—— (1993), "Coordination in hierarchies and networks," in Scharpf (Ed.), *Games in Hierarchies and Networks: Analytical and Empirical Approaches to the Study of Government Institutions*, Frankfurt: Campus Verlag, pp. 125–66.

—— (1994), "Games real actors could play: Positive and negative coordination in embedded negotiations," *Journal of Theoretical Politics*, 6(1), pp. 27–53.

—— (1997), *Games Real Actors Play: Actor-Centred Institutionalism in Policy Research*, Boulder: Westview.

—— (1999), *Governing in Europe: Effective and Democratic?*, Oxford: Oxford University Press.

—— (2001), "Notes toward a theory of multi-level governing in Europe," *Scandinavian Political Studies*, 24(1), pp. 1–26.

References

Schattschneider, E. E. (1960), *The Semi-Sovereign People: A Realist's View of Democracy in America*, New York: Holt, Rhinehart and Winston.

Schmidt, V. A. (2010), "Taking ideas and discourse seriously: Explaining change through the discursive institutionalism," *European Political Science Review*, 2(1), pp. 1–25.

Schmitter, P. C. (1974), "Still the century of corporatism," *Review of Politics*, 36(1), pp. 85–131.

Schoenbrod, D. (1993), *Power without Responsibility: How Congress Abuses the People through Delegation*, New Haven: Yale University Press.

Scholte, J. A. (2002), "Civil society and democracy in global governance," *Global Governance*, 8(3), pp. 281–304.

Schumpeter, J. A. (1946), *Economic Theory and Entrepreneurial History: Change and the Entrepreneur*, Cambridge, MA: Harvard University Press.

—— (1976), *Capitalism, Socialism and Democracy*, London: Allen & Unwin.

Scott, J., and Trubek, D. M. (2002), "Mind the gap: Law and new approaches to governance in the European Union," *European Law Review*, 8(1), pp. 1–18.

Scott, W. R. (1995), *Institutions and Organizations: Ideas and Interests*, Thousand Oaks: Sage.

Selznick, P. (1948), "Foundations of the theory of organization," *American Sociological Review*, 13(1), pp. 25–35.

—— (1984), *Leadership in Administration: A Sociological Interpretation*, Berkeley: University of California Press.

Shamir, J., and Shamir, M. (1997), "Pluralistic ignorance across issues and over time: Information cues and biases," *Public Opinion Quarterly*, 61(2), pp. 227–60.

Shepsle, K. A., and Weingast, B. (1981), "Structure induced equilibrium and legislative choice," *Public Choice*, 37(3), pp. 503–19.

Simon, H. (1997), *Administrative Behaviour*, New York: The Free Press.

Skelcher, C., and Torfing, J. (2010), "Improving democratic governance through institutional design: Civic participation and democratic ownership in Europe," *Regulation and Governance*, 4(1), pp. 71–91.

—— Mathur, N., and Smith, M. (2005), "The public governance of collaborative spaces: Discourse design and democracy," *Public Administration*, 83(2), pp. 573–96.

Smith, B. C. (1985), *Decentralization: The Territorial Dimension of the State*, London: Allen & Unwin.

Smith, G. (2005), *Power Beyond the Ballot: 57 Democratic Innovations from Around the World*, London: The Power Inquiry.

—— (2009), *Democratic Innovations: Designing Institutions for Citizen Participation*, Cambridge: Cambridge University Press.

Smullen, A. (2010), *Translating Agency Reform: Rhetoric and Culture in Comparative Perspective*, Basingstoke: Palgrave Macmillan.

Sørensen, E. (2004), "Democratic governance and the role of public administrators," in P. Bogason, S. Kensen, and H. Miller (Eds), *Tampering with Tradition*, Lanham: Lexington Books, pp. 107–30.

—— (2006), "Metagovernance: The changing role of politicians in processes of democratic governance," *The American Review of Public Administration*, 36(1), pp. 98–114.

—— (2007a), "Democratic theory as a frame for decision making: The challenges of discourse theory and governance theory," in G. Morcöl (Ed.), *Handbook of Decision Making*, London: Taylor and Francis, pp. 151–67.

—— (2007b), "Local politicians and administrators as metagovernors," in M. Marcussen and J. Torfing (Eds), *Democratic Network Governance in Europe*, Basingstoke: Palgrave Macmillan, pp. 89–108.

—— Torfing, J. (2001), "Scandinavian studies of power and democracy," *Public Administration*, 79(1), pp. 223–33.

—— —— (2003), "Network politics, political capital, and democracy," *International Journal of Public Administration*, 26(6), pp. 609–34.

—— —— (2005a), "Network governance and post-liberal democracy," *Administrative Theory and Praxis*, 27(2), pp. 197–237.

—— —— (2005b), "The democratic anchorage of governance networks," *Scandinavian Political Studies*, 28(3), pp. 195–218.

—— —— (Eds) (2007), *Theories of Democratic Network Governance*, Basingstoke: Palgrave Macmillan.

—— —— (2009), "Making governance networks effective and democratic through metagovernance," *Public Administration*, 87(2), pp. 234–58.

—— Triantafillou, P. (2009), *The Politics of Self-Governance*, London: Ashgate.

Sørensen, G. (2006), *The Transformation of the State: Beyond the Myth of Retreat*, Basingstoke: Palgrave Macmillan.

SOU (1983), *Politisk styrning, administrativ självständighet*, Stockholm: Liber/Allmänna förlag.

Stinchcombe, A. L. (1965), "Social structures and organizations," in J. G. March (Ed.), *Handbook of Organizations*, Chicago: Rand-McNally, pp. 142–93.

Stoker, G. (1998), "Governance as theory: Five propositions," *International Social Science Journal*, 50(155), pp. 17–28.

Stone, C. N. (1989), *Regime Politics: Governing Atlanta 1946–1988*, Lawrence: University Press of Kansas.

Strange, S. (1996), *The Retreat of the State*, Cambridge: Cambridge University Press.

Strathern, M. (2000), "The tyranny of transparency," *British Educational Research Journal*, 26(3), pp. 309–21.

Straus, D. (2002), *How to Make Collaboration Work*, San Francisco: Berrett-Koehler Publishers.

Struyven, L., and Steurs, G. (2005), "Design and redesign of quasi-market for the reintegration of jobseekers: Empirical evidence from Australia and the Netherlands," *Journal of European Social Policy*, 15(3), pp. 211–29.

Suleiman, E. (2003), *Dismantling Democratic States*, Princeton: Princeton University Press.

Svara, J. H. (1999a), "The shifting boundary between elective officials and city managers in large council-manager cities," *Public Administration Review*, 59(1), pp. 44–53.

—— (1999b), "Complementarity of politics and administration as a legitimate alternative to the dichotomy model," *Administration & Society*, 30(6), pp. 676–705.

von Sydow, B. (1978), *Kan vi lita på politikerna? Offentlig och intern politik i socialdemokratins ledning 1955–60*, Stockholm: Tiden.

References

Tao, J., Cheung, A. B. L., Painter, M, and Chenyang, L. (Eds) (2010), *Governance for Harmony in Asia and Beyond*, London: Routledge.

Tavits, M. (2005), "The development of stable party support: Electoral dynamics in post-communist Europe," *American Journal of Political Science*, 49(2), pp. 383–98.

Teisman, G. R. (1992), *Complex Decision-making: A Pluricentric View*, The Hague: Vuga.

Termeer, C. J. A. M., and Koppenjan, J. F. M. (1997), "Managing perceptions in networks," in W. J. M. Kickert, E.-H. Klijn, and J. F. M. Koppenjan (Eds), *Managing Complex Networks: Strategies for the Public Sector*, London: Sage, pp. 79–97.

Teubner, G. C. M. (1983), "Substantive and reflexive elements of modern law," *Law and Society Review*, 17(2), pp. 239–54.

—— (Ed.) (1986), *Dilemmas of Law in the Welfare State*, New York: Walter de Gruyter.

—— (1989), *Recht als autopoietisches System*, Frankfurt am Main: Suhrkamp.

Thatcher, M. (1998), "The development of policy network analyses: From modest origins to overarching frameworks," *Journal of Theoretical Politics*, 10(4), pp. 389–416.

The EU Commission (2001), "European governance," *EU Commission White Paper*, COM 2001, 428 final, Brussels: European Foundation Centre.

Thelen, K. (2003), "How institutions evolve: Insights from comparative historical analysis," in J. Mahoney and D. Rueschemeyer (Eds), *Comparative Historical Analysis in the Social Sciences*, Cambridge: Cambridge University Press, pp. 208–40.

—— Steinmo, S. (1992), "Historical institutionalism in comparative politics," in S. Steinmo, K. Thelen, and F. Longstreth (Eds), *Structuring Politics: Historical Institutionalism in Comparative Analysis*, Cambridge: Cambridge University Press, pp. 1–32.

The World Bank (1989), *Sub-Saharan Africa: From Crisis to Sustainable Growth*, Washington D.C.: The World Bank.

—— (2000), *Can Africa Claim the 21st Century?*, Washington D.C.: The World Bank.

—— (2007), *A Decade for Measuring the Quality of Governance*, Washington D.C.: The World Bank.

Tilly, C. (2001), "Mechanisms in political processes," *Annual Review of Political Science*, 4(1), pp. 21–41.

Torfing, J. (1999), *New Theories of Discourse: Laclau, Mouffe and Žižek*, Oxford: Blackwell.

—— (2007a), "Discursive governance networks in Danish activation policies," in M. Marcussen and J. Torfing (Eds), *Democratic Network Governance in Europe*, Basingstoke: Palgrave Macmillan, pp. 111–29.

—— (2007b), "Empirical findings: Seven network stories," in P. Bogason and M. Zølner (Eds), *Methods in Democratic Network Governance*, Basingstoke: Palgrave Macmillan, pp. 41–73.

—— (2009), "Power and discourse: Towards an anti-foundationalist concept of power," in S. R. Clegg and M. Haugaard (Eds), *Handbook of Power*, London: Sage, pp. 108–24.

Treib, O., Bähr, H., and Falkner, G. (2005), "Modes of governance: A note towards conceptual clarification," *European Governance Papers*, N-05-02.

Triantafillou, P. (2007), "Governing the formation and mobilization of governance networks," in E. Sørensen and J. Torfing (Eds), *Theories of Democratic Network Governance*, Basingstoke: Palgrave Macmillan, pp. 183–98.

—— (2008), "Normalizing active employment policies in the European Union: The Danish case," *European Societies*, 10(5), pp. 689–710.

262

Truman, D. B. (1951), *The Governmental Process: Political Interests and Public Opinion*, New York: Knopf.

Tsoukas, H. (1997), "The tyranny of light: The temptations and the paradoxes of the information society," *Futures*, 29(9), pp. 827–43.

UNESCAP (2009), *What is Good Governance?*, http://www.unescap.org/pdd/prs/ProjectActivities/Ongoing/gg/governance.asp (accessed March 2010).

't Veld, R. J., Termeer, C. J. A. M., Schaap, L., and van Twist, M. J. W. (Eds) (1991), *Autopoesis and Configuration Theory*, Dordrecht: Kluwer.

Vickers, G. (1965), *The Art of Judgment*, New York: Basic Books.

Vogel, S. K. (1996), *Freer Markets More Rules*, Ithaca: Cornell University Press.

Waldo, D. (1948), *The Administrative State: The Study of the Political Theory of American Public Administration*, New York: Ronald Press.

Walker, C., and Smith, A. J. (1995), *Privatised Infrastructure: The Build Operate Approach*, London: Thomas Telford.

Walters, W. (2004), "Some critical notes on 'governance'," *Studies in Political Economy*, 73(3), pp. 27–45.

Waltz, K. N. (1979), *Theory of International Politics*, New York: McGraw-Hill.

Warren, M. E. (2002), "What can democratic participation mean today?," *Political Theory*, 30(5), pp. 677–701.

——(2009), "Governance-driven democratization," *Critical Policy Studies*, 3(1), pp. 3–13.

Wasserman, S., and Faust, K. (1994), *Social Network Analysis: Methods and Applications*, Cambridge: Cambridge University Press.

Weber, M. (1978), *Economy and Society*, vol. 1, Berkeley: University of California Press.

Weiss, L. (1998), *The Myth of the Powerless State*, Cambridge: Cambridge University Press.

Wendt, A. (1992), "Anarchy is what states make of it: The social construction of power politics," *International Organization*, 46(2), pp. 391–426.

Whettenhall, R. (2003), "The rhetoric and reality of public–private partnerships," *Public Organisation Review*, 3(1), pp. 77–107.

Whitehead, M. (2003), "In the shadow of hierarchy: Meta-governance, policy reform and urban regeneration in the West Midlands," *Area*, 5(1), pp. 6–14.

Wiig, K. M. (1997), "Knowledge management in public administration," *Journal of Knowledge Management*, 6(3), pp. 224–39.

Wildavsky, A. (1968), *The Politics of the Budgetary Process*, Boston: Little, Brown, and Company.

Williams, P. (2002), "The competent boundary spanner," *Public Administration*, 80(1), pp. 103–24.

Williamson, O. (1985), *The Economic Institutions of Capitalism: Firms, Markets, Relational Contracting*, New York: The Free Press.

Wilson, W. (1887), "The study of administration," *Political Science Quarterly*, 2(2), pp. 197–222.

Winter, S. (2003), "The implementation perspective," in B. G. Peters and J. Pierre (Eds), *Handbook of Public Administration*, London: Sage, pp. 205–11.

References

Wright, W., and Ørberg, J. W. (2009), "Paradoxes of the self: Self-owning universities in a society of control," in E. Sørensen and P. Triantafillou (Eds), *The Politics of Self-Governance*, London: Ashgate, pp. 117–36.

Yanacopulos, H. (2009), "Cutting the diamond: Networking economic justice," in M. Kahler (Ed.), *Networked Politics: Agency, Power and Governance*, Ithaca: Cornell University Press, pp. 67–78.

Young, I. M. (2000), *Inclusion and Democracy*, Oxford: Oxford University Press.

Zurbriggen, C. (2011), "Beyond governance theories: A Latin American perspective," forthcoming.

Index

265

Index

Lightning Source UK Ltd.
Milton Keynes UK
UKOW04n0926290813

216181UK00001B/19/P

9 780199 596751